THE SPEAKER ANTHOLOGY

VOL. 1

Blooming Twig Books / New York, NY

THE SPEAKER ANTHOLOGY, VOL. 1

ISBN 978-1-933918-62-4
FIRST EDITION

THE SPEAKER ANTHOLOGY

VOL. 1

Edited by

DR. KENT GUSTAVSON

&

SALLY SHIELDS

BLOOMING TWIG BOOKS / NEW YORK, NY

TABLE OF CONTENTS

FOREWORD

By Joseph Sherren

fancy ← nag-wash!

✳

A few years back, on my way from Canada to an engagement in the United States, I had all of the appropriate paperwork completed and in order. However, when the immigration officer attempted to look up "professional speaking" in his guide, it did not exist.

In fact, professional speaking is not only an existing profession; it is one of the oldest professions. The industry of professional speaking has been around for more than a millennium and its roots run even deeper. Long before the Bible was written, information about events, history and people were told orally, from one town to the next, by professional storytellers. These orators were revered in their villages for their vast knowledge and ability to teach through the use of analogies and metaphors. Some would say even the Disciples were early professional speakers.

We speakers, however, had our beginnings even further back than that. Although African history was first written in Arabic and European languages in the most recent millennia, societies in the Sahel and Savanna regions of West Africa have long kept their own history, in the form of oral epics. The men in charge of remembering these long histories were called *griots,* masters of words and music.

Griots would be paid through personal gifts, such as large, hand-woven blankets, and they inspired villagers in times of fear and hopelessness, before a battle, or after a tragedy. They were mentors for the young. Professional speakers today, like the griots, provide inspiration, entertainment, motivation, history, education, mentorship, and hope for a better life.

✳

In the ancient city-state of Athens, Greece, public speaking was a central part of everyday life. Athenians placed great importance on the art of public speaking, specifically persuasive rhetorical speech, which was used to sway public opinion and implement political reform.

Orators who excelled at the craft of speaking were known as Sophists. The Greek words *sophos* or *sophia* had the meaning of "wise" or "wisdom" and originally connoted anyone with expertise in a specific domain of knowledge or craft. During that time, the term *sophistes* was also a synonym for "poet," and at the time, poets were considered the official teachers of society. Therefore, the name became associated with a person who teaches, in particular through the performance of prose works or speeches that impart practical knowledge.

Sophists were essentially traveling public speaking teachers. They would trek from city to city offering their paid services in public performance and speech writing as well as instruction in argumentation and style. They were positive thinkers, and for the most part, they believed that anyone, regardless of natural ability, could benefit from speech instruction.

✳

Professional speaking became popular in the Middle East and Europe about 1000 years ago. One especially well-known group of entertainers called gypsies, were often short, dark, and well proportioned with jet black hair and eyes. Some of the men were very handsome, and the women, beautiful. They traveled on carts drawn by donkeys and horses, and they told a romantic tale of a flight from Egypt to escape the Saracens.

One old expression in the entertainment industry is, "Have you earned your nut this month?" This actually comes from these wandering entertainers, who often liked to ride silently away during the night without paying for the food and housing they had received on credit from the local innkeeper. The innkeepers, enraged that the gypsies would depart without paying their room and board, refused to house them, much to the chagrin of the townspeople, who loved the wares and performances the gypsies brought with them. The innkeepers came up with ingenious solution: they would remove the main axle nut from each of the gypsy wagons to prevent them from leaving without paying. Then, when the performers had made enough money to pay the innkeeper, they would pay him in order to get their axle nut back. So, when speakers today have earned enough money to cover their monthly expenses, we often refer to that as "earning our nut."

✳

Of course we cannot ignore another group of early professional speaking enthusiasts who existed in North America in the 18th century. It was those charismatic speakers who travelled from town to town with wonderful stories of greater health, more hair, a happier disposition and a promise of longer life. I am referring to, of course, the Great American snake oil salesmen.

Snake oil was a product brought originally from China that didn't really do what it was advertised to do, but in the 1800s when it was sold across the country alongside other elixirs and potions of all kinds, promised as a cure-all for every ail.

In order to enhance sales, the speaker would usually hire an accomplice in the crowd (a shill) who would often attest to the value of the product in an effort to provoke buying enthusiasm. But then, the doctor would often prudently leave town before his customers realized they had not received the magical cure for which they had hoped. These professionals were charming, knew how to move a crowd to action and then sell their products at the back of the room (whoops, I mean wagon!). The practice of selling dubious remedies for real (or imagined) ailments still occurs today, albeit with some updated Internet-style marketing techniques.

Looking back at the history of speaking, the gypsies and snake oil salesmen didn't build a great reputation of honesty, but their charisma and drive were nevertheless a huge part of the past of professional speaking.

✳

On the pages of The Speaker Anthology are the stories of 101 of our modern-day griots and Sophists, the teachers and trainers of the present.

From surviving 9/11 in New York City to surviving the loss of a parent, and from learning to communicate in business to dropping everything and starting all over again, these are the stories of our lives and the stories of our varied cultures.

Sit back and enjoy the songs and stories.

JOSEPH SHERREN

CERTIFIED SPEAKING PROFESSIONAL,
INDUCTED MEMBER OF CANADIAN SPEAKING HALL OF FAME,
PRESIDENT, CANADIAN ASSOCIATION OF PROFESSIONAL SPEAKERS *(2005-2006)*
PRESIDENT, GLOBAL SPEAKERS FEDERATION *(2007-2008)*

PART I

∽

INSPIRING STORIES

"THERE ARE DIFFERENT WELLS WITHIN YOUR HEART.
SOME FILL WITH EACH GOOD RAIN,
OTHERS ARE FAR TOO DEEP FOR THAT."

— *Hafiz*

"YOU'RE ONLY GIVEN A LITTLE SPARK OF MADNESS.
YOU MUSTN'T LOSE IT."

— *Robin Williams*

[t s gentle tremble shoh

"IN A GENTLE WAY
YOU CAN SHAKE THE WORLD."

— *Mahatma Gandhi*

CHAPTER ONE:

Inspiration

"NOTHING IS MORE INTENSE THAN ACHIEVING A GREATNESS
YOU NEVER KNEW YOU HAD INSIDE YOU."

You have an amazing ability to make a difference, no matter the cause, no matter the challenge. Rest on the confidence that you have been given in order to make *today* the day that you overcome adversity and fear, replacing them with appreciation and resolve. Find the hero within yourself.

— Dan Holdridge,
survivor of the 9/11 attack on the U.S. Pentagon,
and author of "Purpose Conduit."

‒ THE PURPOSE CONDUIT™ ‒

by Dan Holdridge, Survivor of the 9/11 Attack on the Pentagon

ONE NANOSECOND OF IMPACT CHANGED MY LIFE FOREVER.

184 people died right next to me, and I think about them every day and every night. But those of us who lived also died that day to our former lives, and we were reborn into a new life filled with appreciation.

I would never take back that day, as horrible as it was. I would never want to go back to the life I used to live, because I was missing out in so much of my life and I didn't even know it.

9/11 forced me to look at my life as I had never had the ability to do before. I could never have conceptualized hitting a stop button in my life and saying out loud to myself, "Am I doing everything that I really should be doing with my life? Am I appreciating everything that I have? Is there something missing in my life?"

I had been living the life in Washington, D.C., working at the Pentagon on their first big renovation project in forty years. I mean, I was living in a beautiful apartment overlooking the city; I was the kind of person who you could describe to other people as being successful, and my company wanted to throw me right up the corporate ladder, not have me climb it.

Despite my success, I was living my life for everybody else. And in that way, 9/11 was a gift to me. Awful things happened on that day, but I can honestly never look at that day and say it was the worst day of my life. Sure, I still have pain from my injuries, and I still have a few aftereffects from the blast, but I was blessed to have fewer injuries than many others. And of course I live with the sorrow that so many of my friends and colleagues tragically lost their lives. But the real gift I received on that day was the gift of appreciation. I now have the ability to be thankful for everything that I have. And I never forget that.

If you want to appreciate life, volunteer at an oncology ward. Go see people fighting for their lives. Volunteer at a soup kitchen and watch people appreciate every bite of food. That's what life is. Life is about appreciating what we have. And if you need a reminder of how valuable life is, then go see somebody who doesn't have what you have.

Some people now look at me and say, "That guy is nuts. Look how happy he is."

You know what? They're darn right I am. And there's nothing wrong with that. And you know what else? Yeah, I have bad things happen in my life. We all have our 9/11. But it's how we decide how it's going to affect us that shows whether we're going to rise above it or fall beneath it. And we rise above it when we don't let it tear us down.

✳

After 9/11, I searched for the answer as to why I was given a second chance at life. I searched for the energy to let go of my hatred of and anger at the attackers, and to find forgiveness and resolution to that day. I found an answer where I least expected it. I now describe it as the Purpose Conduit™.

Since 9/11, I have been able to find purpose by giving of my positive energy from within, channeling it, and doing my best to provide light to those who need it most.

I grew up around my father's electrical engineering business, and in the same way that some people talk about baseball (I fit that category too, as a die-hard Red Sox fan), I can talk about electricity. A concept that has always intrigued me is the "conduit," the tube that carries all of the electrical wires between one place and another, channeling energy towards darkness and eventually providing light. Although it's one of the most basic terms in the field of electrical engineering, it always resonated with me. When I began speaking after 9/11, I immediately turned to the metaphor of the conduit for inspiration.

The Purpose Conduit™ can be applied to any person, at any age, and at any time. If you want to find your true purpose in life, search for the energy from within, and connect with a passion that will enable you to give of yourself to those who need you.

Consider the conduit effect that Robert F. Kennedy spoke of in June of 1966: "Each time a man stands for an ideal, or acts to improve the lot of others, or strikes out against injustice, he sends a tiny ripple of hope, and crossing each other from a million different centers of energy and daring, those ripples build a current which can sweep down the mightiest walls of oppression and resistance."

Now imagine that you can start that conduit today, by finding your true purpose in life, and you will see that you will not only "light up" those to whom you connect, but they will in turn spread that light to those with whom they in turn connect.

Go out and spread the light.

— BROKEN STEM BEAUTY —

by Cynthia Blomquist Gustavson

❦

POETS HESITATE TO CALL THEMSELVES POETS. They are waiters or businesspeople or nurses. They are labels that might afford a steadier paycheck because poets don't get real paychecks. A great reward for a poet might be two copies of a journal, or a certificate printed on cotton-bond paper.

In looking back, I surely was a poet from the time I first lovingly spoke the words of Yeats or Frost, but I never trusted myself to call myself poet. After college, I called myself teacher, and after graduate school, I called myself social worker but never poet.

Shortly after my 40th birthday in 1987, my first book of poetry, *Scents of Place*, was released, and I finally was able to call myself poet. It was an empowering and exciting moment in my life, but after nearly two decades of marriage, it was also a relief to my husband, a pediatrician and rational thinker. I overheard him conversing with another doctor about his wife, the poet. He explained how for years he had not understood the workings of her irrational mind, had been confused by the stream of unconsciousness she substituted for logic, and how he could now finally categorize her.

✳

In 1996, a woman from the J.B. Harville Alternative School in Shreveport, Lousiana called me and asked if I would talk to her class of 14- and 15-year-old pregnant girls and mothers. I only said, "Yes" because I had just had a new book published, a workbook using poetry as therapy.

The social worker in me recognized that these young women were at a vulnerable time in their lives, and maybe I could help them get in touch with their feelings.

The poet in me wanted to read Lucille Clifton: "listen, woman, you not a no-place anonymous girl."

The girls filed in, slowly, found places around a long, round table and looked at me with that long-faced, "you really think we're going to listen to poetry?" look.

But they did listen. Lucille Clifton's words mesmerized them, along with poetry by Langston Hughes and Maya Angelou. They all listened intently, except for one girl who looked even younger than the rest. She was slouched over the table with her eyes closed, as if she were asleep. She never commented, smiled; never opened her eyes.

I asked the students to participate in a poetry therapy exercise. They were to think of an object in nature, or make of car, that symbolized who they used to be, and then change that symbol according to who they had become.

One girl wrote, "I used to be a rusty Chevy with a honkety-honk horn, but now I'm pure Cadillac and I don't need to make no noise."

The girls giggled and patted her back, amused and amazed by her accomplishment. Each subsequent student shared her vision of herself via poetry, until we came around to the young one who still seemed asleep at the table.

The teacher had noticed her writing something on her tablet. She looked over the girl's shoulder and silently read the words on the page.

"Please, LaShandra read your poem. Everyone wants to hear it," she said.

Silence.

"LaShandra, it's your turn. Please read your poem," urged the teacher.

LaShandra barely lifted her head and whispered, "I used to be a beautiful flower"... She swallowed, took a breath and continued..."but now I am a stem, because I am broken."

Before any of us could tell her how wonderful her words were, we all had to swallow the lump in our own throats, and catch hold of feelings we didn't want to feel.

The other girls praised her, knowing immediately she had written a bit of their truth as well as her own.

LaShandra sat up in her chair. "Can I take this home and show it to Mama?" she asked, simply.

"Of course," I replied, and asked her to see me after class was over; I told her how proud I was of her.

At the end of our brief conversation, I told her, "I don't want you to stay where this poem is. In the next couple of weeks, I want you to write, 'I am a broken stem, but I will be...'"

I hoped that LaShandra and her classmates had fallen in love with Lucille Clifton or Maya Angelou that day, but I knew that these 14- and 15-year-old girls would soon be mothers, and poetry might be the furthest thing from their minds.

Instead, I found that these young girls profoundly changed me that day. I will never again look at a teenaged mother without seeing the image of a broken flower, at the same time knowing that hiding within that stem lays a poet.

— An Unexpected Surprise —

by John Meluso

IN THE SUMMER OF 1996, THE ANNUAL CONVENTION FOR THE NATIONAL SPEAKERS ASSOCIATION WAS TO BE HELD IN ORLANDO, FLORIDA. WHAT MAGIC! For five wonderful days, I would have the opportunity to listen to teachers like Zig Ziglar, Brian Tracy, Bill Gove, Jim Rohn, and Og Mandino, all of whom I had admired for many years.

After the convention ended, I decided to linger in the lobby for a few hours, allowing myself to process all of the information I had gathered that weekend. There was a beautiful fountain nearby and the soothing sound of splashing water in the background. I closed my eyes and let my thoughts drift.

When I opened my eyes, I saw someone at the front desk, another guest who had also taken his time checking out. I stared in disbelief. There was Og Mandino. And he was all by himself.

Og Mandino had been my hero for over 25 years, and to me, he always seemed to be larger than life. Until this moment, my awe and commitment to be respectful had prevented me from approaching him. At the conference, he had been continually surrounded by dozens of fans. Even if I had been able to gather enough courage and conviction to approach him, I would have had to be like Moses parting the Red Sea to get anywhere near him. But here was my chance. I mustered up my courage and walked over to introduce myself. I told him how much his books had meant to me.

In the brief conversation that ensued, I told the world-famous speaker about my own speaking career, and how I was about to embark on a cross-country tour for my first book, The Next Step for Positive Living. Then Og and I said goodbye, and he was off for home.

✳

After the conference, though I set out on my book tour full of enthusiasm, unexpected challenges sapped my energy and frustrated my plans.

In Oregon, downpours caused local rivers to overflow, flooding the hotel where my talk had been scheduled.

In the Texas panhandle, lightning and the strongest winds I've ever felt rocked my car. I later found out that I had been in the middle of a tornado.

In Florida, my neck and shoulder went into muscular spasm and cut off the circulation in my right arm. The excruciating pain made even the simplest tasks difficult. A few short weeks before, I had regularly run 40 miles a week to stay physically fit. Now, I was fortunate to have 40 breaths without pain. It took all my strength to continue.

In North Carolina, I ended up right in the path of Hurricane Fran. The morning after my talk, I opened the door to my hotel room to see cars with tree limbs crashing through their roofs. I had slept through all of it without hearing anything! Worst of all, my books and tapes were under three feet of water and six inches of mud.

After my last stop in Houston, on my return trip home, my car's engine blew.

Needless to say, by the time I returned to Portland, I felt miserable, unlucky and more than a little depressed. The sky seemed even a darker shade of gray, and I found it hard to concentrate on anything.

✳

Only two days after this cataclysmically awful tour, I picked up the day's mail, finding nothing special. The usual junk: magazines, bills, a couple of checks, a postcard from a friend and a very large manila envelope. I set the oversize manila envelope aside thinking that it was probably the replacement for a software manual I had requested.

Finally, at 4 a.m., when sleep just wouldn't come, I got up and decided to open the manila envelope, expecting to find the instruction manual for how to install some new computer program.

I glanced at the postmark on the envelope: New Hampshire.

New Hampshire seemed like an odd place for a computer company to set up business. It was equally strange that the envelope had no return address. But I brushed those fleeting thoughts away, and, expecting a software manual, I was surprised to see a folded piece of paper fall to the floor. I picked it up and saw that my name was handwritten on the top.

I took another look at the envelope. Sure enough it was addressed to me, John Meluso. I was trying to figure out who might have sent me this mysterious package. I only knew one person in the world who lived in New Hampshire and that was my role model, Og Mandino. But I thought to myself, "It can't be him," remembering that he had sadly passed away at his home several weeks before. Besides, why would I get a personal message from him anyway? I had only met him by chance that one time in Florida before the worst book tour ever.

My hand shook as I opened the letter. "Wait a minute," I thought to myself, thinking that there had to be some mistake. The letter was addressed to me. In my amazement, I continued to read:

Dear Mr. Meluso:

Several months ago, I was on my way to deliver the enclosed documents to the author Og Mandino. Then sadly, I learned of Og's passing.

So instead, I am turning to you. Although we have never met, I know of your reputation as an outstanding communicator and speaker. That is why I am turning to you for help. I believe that you are the perfect person for this important mission.

Please accept this precious gift, a treasure that I call, "The Greatest Translation in the World." I know that you will take the necessary steps to share these documents and their profound message with the world.

Your humble servant,

Joseph Goldenbaum

I sat down in shock. How could this be? Why would Joseph Goldenbaum choose me? How could he think that I compared in stature to Og Mandino and his powerful book, The Greatest Salesman in the World?

After what seemed like an eternity, I looked inside the manila envelope. Within was a thick typewritten manuscript. I pulled it out and began to read:

Dear Mr. Mandino,

I am a scholar in ancient languages and have been most fortunate to be blessed with the honor of translating several ancient Sacred Scrolls that dramatically changed my life. Why am I telling you this? During my work, I uncovered many wonderful secrets. Yet the biggest surprise of all was this: the scrolls I have been translating were the same ones you mentioned in your book, The Greatest Salesman in the World.

The Ten Sacred Scrolls for a Successful Life are real! Of course, as often happens, their actual meaning had been lost in translation as the scrolls were transcribed from Aramaic and Sanskrit to Latin, Greek and, much later, English.

In fact, there were 12 scrolls, not just the 10 you discuss in your book. In addition, there were even more surprises that I will tell you about later.

This was indeed a remarkable gift.

— PROBLEMS AND PURPOSE —

by Dr. Steven Steinberg

BECAUSE OF MY PARKINSON'S DISEASE, I WAS FORCED TO RETIRE FROM THE JOB I LOVED AS A DENTIST. Every day, I had the opportunity to take someone who was in pain, and to bring them comfort and healing. I could help turn someone who could not chew anything at all into someone who could go to a restaurant and have a grand old time. I could take someone who refused to smile because her teeth embarrassed her, and with my hands, I could restore that smile. I would wake up each morning and look forward to another day filled with meaning, purpose, joy, and inner peace. But then I had to stop.

Immediately, I asked, "Why me?"

I allowed the question to percolate in my mind from dawn until dusk. The question plagued me for weeks and months, until Albert Einstein helped me to figure things out. He once said, "The significant problems we face today cannot be solved at the same level of thinking we were at when we created them." In other words, the biggest problems facing us do not come from the problems themselves; rather from the way we think about those problems.

The way I see it, there are two ways to think about problems:

A. The ordinary response is to answer the question "Why me?" with an answer that starts out, "Because of *this* or *that*." We often try to blame our problems on something or someone else. Blaming helps us to feel better, allowing us as victims, to say that the problems weren't our fault and that we aren't responsible. In other words, we believe that we are entitled to a life without suffering or unanswered questions. But this kind of thinking cannot solve our problems.

B. An *extra*-ordinary response requires that we shift the focus of our thinking from, "What caused my problem?" to "How can I solve my problem?" We must shift our focus from feelings to values, and from rights to responsibilities. We must move the focus of our thinking away from, "Why do I suffer?" and towards, "Why do I exist?"

Here are some tools for shifting focus:

1. When facing problems of any kind, try to see them as opportunities to learn and grow.

2. Most of the time, we think about life in terms of winning and losing. Instead, focus on *learning*, and you will always win.

3. Problems are little messengers trying to tell you, "It's time to change. It's time to find or renew your sense of purpose." Use the opportunity, and start searching.

4. Find your personal purpose. It should be something that serves others where you can find joy, meaning, success, connection with higher values, and timeless truths. And it should give others value, helping to solve a problem they have or create an opportunity for them.

5. Create a statement of purpose for both your home and business life.

6. In everything you do at home or at work, allow the power of purpose to override the pain of problems.

When I was diagnosed with Parkinson's disease, I first asked, "Why me?" After asking the question over and over again with no forthcoming answers to my question, I began to simply shift my focus and see the way forward. I found opportunity where I had only seen pitfalls and excitement where I had felt fear.

If I had never been diagnosed with this disease, I would still be busy in my dental office, comfortably thinking about retirement to the sound of my dental drill. You may not like that sound, but it was music to my ears! But had I remained a dentist, I would have never had the opportunities I have now to speak and write and reach audiences I never expected to reach.

Without Parkinson's, I never would have realized *this* dream of healing people through words. As a doctor of dentistry, I was simply helping to heal patients. Now, through my speaking and writing career, I am helping to heal people's souls. I could not think of a more wonderful transition, and in many ways, I am grateful for this disease.

As a result of every experience, good or bad, paths open up before us. If we spend our time looking back, we may never see the opportunities that lie ahead, even in the face of sickness and struggle.

No matter what your circumstances are, no matter how painful and difficult, you possess the great freedom to choose your response to these conditions. I challenge you to choose a response that is extraordinary. I implore you to choose to live *on purpose*.

In this life, our job is to transform the world around us. We have the ability to change a world filled with suffering, pain, and problems into an extra-ordinary world filled with success, joy, and inner peace. If we all focus on purpose instead of problems, there will be no limit to the problems we can solve, to the healing we can bring, or to the extraordinary harmony that we can create.

— A Failed Business Plan —

by Barry Maher

A few years ago, a management and sales expert came up with what he considered a first-rate idea. With so many unhappy and lonely people in the world, he figured he could provide them with a little comfort and make money at the same time by offering them personalized, written advice on their problems.

Since so many people have problems that are similar, he figured he could train his employees to write a quick paragraph or two of personalization, and then fill up the rest of the letter with appropriate boilerplate.

He placed trial ads in all the leading tabloids. The problems and the checks came pouring in.

He read four letters and immediately killed the project.

"I realized I was dealing with living, breathing people," he said, "not a marketing opportunity. I realized the answers I'd provide would have an effect on their lives. They all had such heavy burdens compared to anything I'd ever gone through. Their problems went far beyond the scope of any boilerplate, quick answers. And I was completely unqualified to tamper in their lives. I ended up returning their money and absorbing the price of the ads."

But he did a little more than that. With each refund, he sent along a personal, handwritten response. This is one of those letters.

Dear Lorie,

Thanks for writing. Sorry to hear of your situation. Sometimes we simply have to endure until we finally get the life we deserve. And you've endured. I'm returning your $9.95 because I want you to have the money. From your letter, it sounds like you need it more than I do and I want the best for you. I also want you to want the best for you.

I know you feel small. I know you feel alone. But you're not alone. You're a human being, which means that you're related to all of us—a relative—a part of us all.

Biologically—in your genes—all your ancestors going back to the beginning of time are a part of you. They struggled and slaved so that you, their descendant, would someday walk this planet. It's taken billions of years to create the universe of possibilities that's within you.

If you undervalue yourself—if you sell yourself short—you're undervaluing all of us, and all of those who came before you.

And even beyond that, Lorie, you are, as an individual human, a miraculous being, more alike than unlike the greatest men and women who ever lived. More alike than unlike Jesus and Einstein and Lincoln and Mozart and Mother Teresa and Vincent Van Gogh—with many of their greatest qualities lying somewhere inside you. With thoughts and feelings and desires.

And—most miraculous of all—the divinity within you which we call free will, which gives you the ability to control those feelings and desires, and therefore to control your own destiny, to actually control what you are today and what you will be tomorrow.

Your responsibility, as I see it, is to use that free will to make the most of every instant of the life which so many, including yourself, have participated in creating.

Always the best,

Barry Maher

— THE ABRACADABRA PRINCIPLE —

by Alicia Dunams

❧

"WHATEVER YOU CAN DO OR DREAM YOU CAN, BEGIN IT.
FOR BOLDNESS HAS GENIUS, POWER AND MAGIC IN IT."

— Johann Wolfgang von Goethe

WHEN WE'RE CHILDREN, MAGIC IS A LIVING, BREATHING THING. It lives in the North Pole, under our pillows when we've lost a tooth, and in our yards where brightly-colored Easter eggs lay hidden and waiting for us to discover them. Magic makes campgrounds out of living rooms, sailor's hats out of folded newspapers, and best friends out of ratty old dolls who've long since lost their hair. Nothing short of a blizzard—or chocolate chip cookies—

can stop our belief in magic. If we want to be cowboys or cowgirls then, by golly, that's what we'll be: now, ten years from now, and a thousand years from now.

Over time, however, this *living magic* gets drummed out of us. Some *friend* or another out the Tooth Fairy, Santa Claus and the Easter Bunny and, newsflash after newsflash, our belief in magic slowly turns to disbelief.

I used to not believe in my own magic or, for that matter, anyone else's, until one night several years ago when I went with a date to the *Magic Castle*, a members-only supper club and magic theatre in Los Angeles. I asked my date what *abracadabra* meant. He said, "I create, as I speak." The rest of the evening was nothing short of, well, magical—but I couldn't get those five little words out of my head: "I create, as I speak."

I didn't realize what a powerful statement that would become, and what kind of impact those few words would have in my life.

✳

The thought that I could create something—a moment, a thing, an actual event—merely from speaking a hope or dream aloud resonated throughout my very being. What a unique concept. Or was it?

Wasn't this what I had been doing throughout my childhood? Hadn't I been creating my own reality when I spoke the words, "I want to grow up to be a fairy princess?" What had happened to my belief in magic? And how quickly could I get it back?

I soon realized that the timeline for getting my belief in magic back was entirely up to me. I began to create something out of my dreams, *willing* my most precious thoughts into actions and, eventually, realities.

From that day on, I practiced the Abracadabra Principle. Everything I desired in life, I spoke aloud with confidence and absolute faith.

You, too, can take advantage of the Abracadabra Principle. Magic happens every day. Some of it is accidental: the timely phone call from a long lost friend in your time of need, or the random act of kindness by a total stranger that lifts your spirits and reinforces your belief in humanity.

The words I use now are, in and of themselves, magical. Why? Because they're born of passion, dreams and hope. I create as I speak, and I'm proud to say that I speak my truth.

✳

Do not underestimate the power of the spoken word. Words don't have the same meaning to us that they used to. We use them too lightly and say them too easily—like "love." How many things do we love? We love our new hardwood floors, our new car, our new kitten, or our new blouse. What word can we then use to describe our feelings for the *people* we love?

At the same time, words have more meaning than ever, particularly the negative ones we ascribe to ourselves. Don't believe me? Just perk your ears up and listen. I'm continually amazed at how my friends run themselves down.

"I'm so fat."

"I knew I'd never get that job."

"This looks horrible on me."

"Why do I always choose the wrong man?"

The comments go on and on. I'm not judging. I'm just as guilty—or, at least, I used to be.

Today, I know that our words become self-fulfilling prophecies. Our spoken words activate our thoughts, and vice versa. So be careful with your words. They're not just letters strung together, but living, breathing things that have real meaning in your life. Since the beginning of time, words have always become reality when spoken with passion, conviction and authority. They're the most powerful tools we've been given.

So you miss out on that new promotion. What is your response? A negative one might be, "I'm not good enough to be promoted."

A positive response might be, "This frees me up to reassess my performance and make calculated improvements in advance of my next opportunity."

So you didn't qualify for the loan on that new investment property. How will you respond? You can choose to go the negative route and say, "This is a sign that investing in properties isn't right for me."

On the other hand, you can think positively and say, "The loan officer explained the specific flaws in my credit rating that held up the loan. Now I can work on those for next time and be better prepared."

The negative choices you made yesterday? Forget them. Today is yours to control. The power of the Abracadabra Principle is yours. Stop backing yourself into a corner with negative thinking and paint your way out positive thinking and powerful words.

Think positively. Speak positively. *Act* positively.

Success will surely follow.

— ALLOW YOUR MIND TO EVOLVE: —
HOW CREATIVE QUESTIONS™ CAN AND WILL CHANGE YOUR WAY OF THINKING FOREVER!

by Dr. Monica Garaycoechea

AS YOU KNOW, THERE ARE NO ACCIDENTS IN LIFE. In 2001, Arne Rantzen, the founder of Creative Questions, and my beloved life partner came to me and told me about his realization of how questions can stimulate our creativity in a way affirmations cannot.

At that point in time, I was tired of the mind thing. I wanted to focus more on getting rid of the mind, and I wanted to simply wake up spiritually. It took several years of my inability to not "get" what questions are really all about. A crucial change occurred one day while discussing a certain point with Arne. He was asking for my opinion and feelings about something, and I realized that I needed to listen on a much deeper level. I discovered that questions are the expression of our curiosity, and that curiosity is a quality of our True Nature that is always evolving and always creative.

I realized that as children, we constantly ask questions! Do you remember that? I remember my son, Alejandro, and how innocently curious he was, always asking questions about everything! And when one response was offered that he did not grasp, he would continue asking until he was satisfied! He questioned everything to the point where I recall telling him not to ask any more questions. How ignorant I was then! The truth is that perhaps I myself did not know the correct response to offer him, which no doubt left me feeling stupid or challenged. At that time I didn't know how to ask the Universe to help me, and I did not know how to support him to receive his responses from beyond our limiting minds.

At that point in my son's life, I was stuck within my own *linear thinking* patterns. This type of thinking is based on statements and affirmations or declarations. It affirms that which already is, period! There is no aliveness, emotion or embodiment in it, and no creativity. It is full of flat, demanding, forceful energy. I soon came to realize that instead of linear thinking, we could ask Creative Questions instead, and activate our Creative Power! With Creative Questions, we can experience and understand how our left (linear-thinking) and right (intuitive/feeling) sides of your brain are able to work together.

Let me explain a little more about our brains. The left hemisphere is sometimes referred to as the masculine side, which employs linear and factual thinking patterns. The right hemisphere is sometimes referred to as the feminine side, which is relational, intuitive, fresh, and creative.

If I were to ask you a question, you can answer from your masculine, linear side, and look for logical answers, or you can wait for your feminine side, which shows up when you wait, listen and, with an open heart, feel the empty space that opens up just after a Creative Question is asked. That space *is divine intelligence!* That space is fresh, new and free of attachment; so you can gently receive your response and then let it go again, expressing your curiosity, as Alejandro had done as a child.

When you ask a Creative Question like, "Why can I trust?" you can come up with reasons that you have learned in the past, or already know in some form. This would be your masculine side speaking. Or you could *wait* and feel, using the feminine side to your brain.

A Creative Question is a conscious and empowering question that directs our Creative Power towards what we are seeking. What that means is that unconsciously and through habit we often ask questions that do not support our success, such as, "What is wrong with me?" But if we desire to change and support our evolution and success, we need to make another choice! The beauty of Creative Questions is that they are the bridge to the *unlimited potential of free consciousness.*

Creative Questions will open the bridge for you to make peace with your mind, to master your Creative Power and to feel confident in your capacity to re-educate your mind away from fearful, scarcity-driven, powerless, separation programming towards your true, free, loving, abundant, safe, powerful, successful, and real Eternal Program.

For example, using the Creative Question "Why am I successful?" can only give you the responses that support you being successful, something that is in total alignment with the Truth of your Being.

Let me test a Creative Question on myself. I ask, "Why can I trust?" Hmmm... let's see...

The first response that came to my awareness after waiting in the silence was, "Because I am connected with the Source."

Now if I can feel the response, enjoy it, and then let it go. I can then ask the question again and this way I will not stop the Unlimited Potential Source that is and that I have at my disposal.

So I ask again, "Why can I trust?" Hmmm..."Because I choose to." And from here, I can keep going on and on, building up the reasons my limited mind needs to believe in trust.

After having opened the door to conceive this idea of Trust, I am ready to go to the Creative Question that will ask, "How do I feel when I trust?"

Hmmm... Let's see... Ahhh..."Open, relaxed, safe." You notice by my response that I am immediately in the frequency of trusting! What that means is that I am manifesting this frequency of Trust right here and right now. And I receive not only immediate manifestation, but also immediate connection with Source!

I like to say that Creative Questions are the Thought Prayers of our days. This is truly a way of thinking that connects us with our Presence and Oneness, promotes freedom, and allows us to experience Love and Beauty right here and now.

Are you ready to explore and use Creative Questions in your life? Then the first thing you can do is to get familiar with this new Creative Questions language. It is new to all of us and is what I call the next step in our conscious evolution on how to use our minds at this point in time in connection with the Universe. Evolving from linear thinking to organic thinking is like the change necessary to evolve from crawling and only seeing what is in front of you to walking upright with your head held high, able to see for miles and miles.

I honor and celebrate your evolving aliveness!

— IT WILL BE OKAY: —
SAVING STORIES IN THE SERVICE OF LOVE

by Alli Joseph

TWO YEARS AGO, I UNDERWENT A SEA CHANGE. I lost someone most precious to me, and in what only in hindsight seems to have been a divine gift, gained a greater understanding of what it means to be of service—to believe in the service of love.

When I was two months pregnant with my daughter, I found out that my mother had cancer. She was our family historian, and lived her life in the service of love. She wasn't rich, but she had abundant gifts of wisdom and the kind of love she taught me to pass on. She liked good wine, but never spent money on other material things. She gave her nights, her weekends, and her holidays to her students and perfect strangers alike, counseling them on unwanted pregnancies, abuse, and much else of difficulty. Mother, in the truest sense, always paid it forward.

Throughout my mother's seven-month illness in 2007, which began with her late-stage diagnosis of carcinosarcoma during a hysterectomy in April, I observed an incredible strength with which she fought the very idea that she might have a fatal disease. Even until the week of her passing, Mom was still fighting for answers, for ideas, and for possibility. She also held strongly to her dignity until the last days, when powerful opiate drugs did little for the pain but highlighted her declining ability to speak, to have a political argument, to hold a cup—things so vital to her independence. She took the loss of the use of her legs with consummate, angry grace, vowing to walk again, to use the commode brought by hospice care, to travel with me to the Bahamas—where I'd promised her that we could swim with dolphins.

My mother always loved to work; it brought her great happiness. And when she was working, she did her best to fit in the other thing that brought her joy: time with me. While writing her dissertation on the study of human need—a topic she considered crucial to the field of social work—Mom had me. She laughed at her own naiveté when she remembered how she thought she'd take "a couple of weeks off," instead bringing me along to her classes, nursing me during breaks in social theory.

Using American Sign Language as a guideline, Mom taught me sounds and signs as one would a hearing-impaired child, so that I would speak early, and I did. She placed my hands around cups with different temperatures of water in them next to the kitchen stove's burner to teach me what "hot" meant. I learned fast. She re-wrote all of my children's books, coloring characters with magic marker to look like our multi-ethnic family, and replacing words and themes she found harmful using White-Out—a quirk I now understand to have been central to her child-rearing philosophy.

In the '80s, Mom came home after 14-hour days as a Hofstra University program director; falling asleep as she tried to read me *National Velvet* (this fostered my great distaste for snoring). Then, she got up at six o'clock the next morning in order to make my lunch and see me off to school.

Throughout my childhood, my mother always told me things would "be okay." Her use of the phrase came from a children's book she bought and inscribed to me in 1979 called *Will It Be OK?* The book explored themes that frighten children, told through the eyes of a mother and daughter.

The Thursday before Mom died, I found the worn cover of the familiar old book in my old bookshelf, and I took it down and read it to her.

In the book, the daughter says to her mother, "But what if you die?" The mother replies, "My loving doesn't die. It stays with you, as warm as two pairs of mittens on top of each other. When you remember you and me, you say: 'What can I do with so much love? I will have to give it away.'"

I'm not sure if Mom could feel me sitting by the bed, reading to her as she had done for me so many years earlier, but I hope she could. In any case, just as she carried me along with her to class as a child, she'll always be with me: through my actions, my words and in my daughter, to whom I will give away Mom's love—as she gave hers to me and so many others.

❋

When I learned of my mother's illness, I wondered when she would be paid back in love for all of the love she had always so readily expended. She turned her helping heart and mind to me countless times throughout our time together. When I became a journalist and producer in my twenties, my mother, in love, longed to tell me her family's stories. Sadly, I did not listen; like some others in their twenties, I was disinterested and focused on other things.

When my mother was diagnosed with cancer, the news hit me like a Mack truck: I spent much of that year desperately trying to capture her thoughts, voice and face on different media before she died just six short months later. In the end, I felt that I had failed, and that will always be one of my greatest regrets.

✳

One wintry day, confounded by my loss, exhausted as a new mother, confused about what next to do with my life, I got an answer in the subtlest of ways.

Walking down a frozen street, a friend shared a memory; she told me of being sent to boarding school in Switzerland, away from an abusive and troubled family. I had never heard this story; I wondered if her three children had either, and then it hit me. Mom had given me a shove towards the service of love. I knew what I should do.

Soon after, infant in arms, I founded my story-saving company to help others benefit from my mistake. And now, I am living the Native American conservation philosophy, "Seventh Generation," which says we should act in a way that will positively affect seven generations living after us.

I now believe in the service of love as my mother did. I teach people how to do the work of saving stories themselves. I evangelize to audiences, imploring them to care now, not later. Today, more people are honoring their elders in a way that I learned the need for the hard way. This is my way of paying it forward, and hopefully, paying Mom back. At least, I like to think so.

LET INSPIRATION POWER THE SWITCH OF MOTIVATION

by Laurenzo Thomas

"PEOPLE OFTEN SAY MOTIVATION DOESN'T LAST.
WELL, NEITHER DOES BATHING—THAT'S WHY WE NEED IT DAILY."

- Zig Ziglar

JUST AS POWERFUL MOTORS, MACHINES, OR COMPUTERS ARE OF NO USE WITHOUT A POWER SOURCE TO MAKE THEM WORK, AS HUMANS WE NEED A POWER SOURCE, AND THAT SOURCE IS INSPIRATION. That inspiration then allows us to utilize the switch of motivation, turn it on, and see positive results.

We must appreciate, especially with negativity around us and inherent in us that can sap our energy, our power, and our drive to succeed, that there is a need for a daily infusion of this inspiration in order to continue moving forward.

Some may feel that the world is glutted with motivational speakers, tapes, books and seminars, perhaps over-saturated. And it is true that all of these things would be of no value if a person weren't self-motivated or inspired to put them to use. But there is no question as to the importance of motivation in helping us achieve success in school, business, sports, and most importantly, in life.

So what's the big difference between inspiration and motivation? These two concepts are closely related, but there are a few very important differences. Whereas inspiration can have a tremendous impact coming from any source, motivation can only really be effective if it starts from within an individual. Inspiration, wherever it comes from, rouses the spirit, and if the spirit isn't roused, if one's faculties aren't stimulated to a high level of feeling, one will not be motivated or moved.

Inspiration *begets* motivation.

A light switch will not work if there is no power flowing into its wires. Likewise, motivation will not work without the power of inspiration behind it.

As mentioned, inspiration can realistically come from anywhere. So ask yourself, "What's my inspiration?" What can I use to motivate myself, to flip that switch?

For me the positive experiences that come from having a loving, beautiful family, from learning a trade I wasn't necessarily geared for, from being a minister who helps others, from developing strong friendships and from teaching others are definitely inspirational. But inspiration also means being close to eviction, not being able to buy my wife a decent anniversary gift, having my bank accounts closed, not having the money to buy my kids socks, feeling guilty because I spent 89 cents for something to eat instead of buying gas for the car, not being able to help out my parents when they are in need, and feeling powerless, sleeping in my car in a hotel parking lot to attend a seminar I couldn't afford… All of these are inspiration, whether positive or negative.

Inspiration can also come from the powerful words of another.

David Viscott: "Your ultimate goal in life is to become your best self. Your immediate goal is to get on the path that will lead you there."

Jesus Christ: "There is more happiness in giving than in receiving."

Mike Laughlin: "The greatest enemy to human potential is your comfort zone."

Dr. Rob Gilbert: "It's all right to have butterflies in your stomach. Just get them to fly in formation."

And my favorite quote of all time from an anonymous source: "You'll never know where you're going if you're always looking back."

Inspiration can also come from a slogan or saying that you create for yourself. Years ago, in my early teens, I created the *Four Ds of Success*. They have helped me immensely in times when I felt discouraged. They are Desire, Discipline, Dedication, and Determination. The four Ds have been my inspiration.

Inspiration can come from examining the lives of others. The importance of having a mentor cannot be over-emphasized. Whether it's a parent, a teacher, an athlete, a historical figure or someone established in the field in which we work, we would do well to study and examine their life course. Follow their steps closely. For me, the greatest man who ever lived was Jesus Christ, who exemplified the qualities of love, humility, wisdom and strength: a truly inspirational figure. Even if you already have a mentor or if you don't, it's always beneficial to examine the lives of other successful individuals. Why? Inspiration.

There will be any number of obstacles or circumstances—physical, emotional, financial—that will impede us from feeling motivated. At times, everything might even feel completely out of our control. But no matter what our situation is, if we plug into our power source of inspiration, and then turn on the switch of our motivation, we will see the light.

As a licensed electrician, one of the greatest joys, as simple as it may sound, is turning on a switch and watching the lights come on, knowing that the whole system has come together. As frail and imperfect human beings, we need inspiration to push that motivation switch in our lives so that we can shine our light out into the world.

CHAPTER TWO:

⚜

Making It

"PRINCIPLES DON'T CHANGE.
ONLY TECHNIQUE AND APPLICATION DO."

Those who desire to make it must discover the principles used by others that lead towards success, and make those principles work within their own life story. Knowing the principle is simply not enough; understanding is not the secret; owning it, mentally, is not sufficient. In order to make it, we must *act*, and we must *do* the things that lead towards success.

Making it requires knowing exactly what we want to achieve, why we want to achieve it, and designing a path that will lead us towards our desired outcome.

I charge you to discover the principles you need to succeed; understand how you can make them work for you; then internalize them and act on them daily.

— *Gary O'Sullivan,*
author of "Dream, Work, Believe"

⌁ IDEAPHORIA ⌁

by Paul Lee Marr

❧

MUSIC HAS ALWAYS BEEN MY PASSION. One of my earliest memories is rocking back and forth in a chair in my parents' house, singing songs I'd made up. As early as third grade, I was forming bands with neighborhood kids. Since we were clueless about how to play real songs, we made up our own. Singing accompanied by beating on cans and boxes is not quite fit for Carnegie Hall. But it was my roots.

Thankfully, I had developed and honed my craft by the time I got out of college. I wanted to write and play music for a living, but I couldn't imagine how to make a living doing it. So I put my music on the back burner and moved from job to job, never really inspired by what I was doing.

In my late twenties, frustrated with my lack of direction, I undertook to really figure out my gifts, my skills and my calling. I read several books, talked to lots of people, wrote volumes, made lists.

I read about a place in Chicago that assessed a person's aptitudes using a plethora of tests, and then sent them away with clear direction for their future. There were testimonials from a cop who discovered she should be a professional singer; a lawyer who learned he should be a doctor; a dog groomer who realized party planning was her calling.

I decided to go so that I could ace the musical tests, and prove to myself and the world that a musician is what I was destined to be. I sent the company a bunch of money and headed for the Windy City.

✳

Two intensive days of testing confirmed many paths I shouldn't take. There was the spatial visualization test. The tester disassembled a wooden structure in front of me. With a mess of pieces strewn on the table, he told me to reassemble the structure. He might as well have said, "Build a skyscraper." Had I not seen him take the structure apart, I would have sworn it was impossible for those pieces to fit together. I asked him how long I had. He said it didn't matter.

That's good, because it would have taken me a millennium to put that thing back together. In fact, a millennium may not have been long enough. You see, I can't visualize spatial relationships. I'm mystified, frustrated and downright angry at puzzles. Why would anyone put him or herself through the agony of putting a puzzle together? Why not just find pleasure in looking at the completed picture on the box.

So, as the minutes ticked by, the sun went down, the sun came up again. Frustrated beyond his wildest dreams, the tester finally screamed "Uncle!" I scored in the first percentile in spatial visualization. The hundredth percentile is the best you can do. You do the math.

✱

Comforted to know that bridge-building wasn't my calling, yet feeling completely humiliated and assuming I was aptitude-less, I moved on to the other tests. Most of them aren't all that memorable to me except *Ideaphoria*. I know, I also asked, "Idea-*whatieya*?" The goal is to write as much as you can in a set amount of time. I was happy there was a time limit for this one given that the tester had grown a lengthy beard in the time it took me to complete the spatial visualization test. Let me clarify, I never actually finished that test. The pieces were still intact where the tester had originally placed them. Oh, I touched each piece and moved them all around; I just didn't have a clue what to do with them.

On to Ideaphoria. I was poised to begin. The buzzer went off and I wrote like a madman. I wrote so fast I had no clue what I was writing. In fact, I wasn't writing coherently. They told me to write as much as I could in the given timeframe. They didn't tell me it had to mean anything. And it didn't.

Turns out I scored off the charts in Ideaphoria. Hooray! Did that mean my calling was to be an Ideaphorist? It was by far my best test score of the two days. But what I'm still troubled by all these years later is that what I wrote made absolutely no sense. Yes, I can write fast, but they didn't read what I wrote, and I didn't let on that it was 100-percent gibberish. So, did I score as high as one could score because I was a fast writer or because I was able to generate lots of wonderful ideas quickly? If it's the latter, I flunked.

With the newfound knowledge that I could be an Ideaphorist, I imagined what that could mean and how I could change the world. I imagined getting paid for writing as fast as I could even though no one would be able to read it or make sense of it.

✱

Once all the testing was done, they sat me down in a room and analyzed my results. It reminded me of a tarot card or palm reading. They recommended I venture into advertising, sales, or teaching. Thank the Lord, they didn't get my results mixed up with someone who aced the spatial visualization test, or I would now be in an insane asylum somewhere in Montana after failing miserably in an architecture career.

However, I walked away disappointed and mystified. What happened to justifying my lifelong desire to be a musician? Turns out, although I scored above average in the musical tests, I didn't ace them. Music never came up in my analysis. I kept thinking they were saving it for last. When they got done telling me I'd be an advertising enthusiast, I wanted to say, "And what else? Come on, you can tell me now."

How come that cop got to be a musician? I got the impression she never sang a note in her life. Yet after taking some aptitude tests, she wrote her last ticket for 10-over in a 25-mile-per-hour-zone and hopped onto the world stage. What's up with that? How can you not know you're a musician until aptitude tests tell you so? I was a musician and the aptitude tests told me, "Not so fast slick, you should sell appliances." Hey, I wonder how that cop, 'er, I mean world-famous opera star, did on Ideaphoria?

✳

Sales and advertising don't appeal to me, but teaching turned out to be my passion. I love facilitating learning, whether through speaking, writing, or music. I love seeing people's eyes light up as they discover they can master the task or skill at hand. I love motivating people to want to go to the next level or discover and use their gifts. Maybe it's because I struggled forever to figure out what I was here for.

I guess it just takes some of us longer than others to figure out our place on this planet. I'm just happy I was still vertical when it hit me.

— DISCOVERING MY AUTHENTIC VOICE —

by Linda Shields

❧

WHEN I WAS FOUR YEARS OLD, MY FATHER SUDDENLY DIED, AND I STOPPED SPEAKING. For one solid year, I never uttered a single word to anyone. If I couldn't talk to him, I didn't want to talk to anybody.

It was only through the loving attention of grade school and junior high teachers that I began to speak more than just a few words without crying and being bullied by other children. Then, through the coaching of many mentors over the years, and with a lot of soul searching on my part, I stumbled into my life's calling as a professional speaker.

✳

After earning my masters degree in speech pathology, I began to practice in a little farming community near Ann Arbor, Michigan. I saw children with speech and voice problems, ranging from mild lisps to incomprehensible stutters. Others, at age eight or nine, already had nodes on their vocal cords because they had misused their voices from the time they started speaking.

After a while, I shifted gears and taught drama in Ohio, Pennsylvania, North Carolina and overseas in Germany, at a military high school. It was great fun, and I learned even more about the power of vocal image as I helped many students eliminate Southern drawls or cultivate a British accent for school plays.

I took various other jobs having to do with communication and speech, including a directorship at the Cleveland Hearing and Speech Center in Ohio. Not bad for a formerly pathetically shy, speech-challenged, only child from Detroit, Michigan.

I also had a regular speech-communications spot on WJKW-TV8's live noontime show. Life was good. I was at the top of my profession as a speech and drama personality, dating the anchorman for the Evening News and auditioning for a show called "PM Magazine." I enjoyed the television spotlight and was not ashamed of having been bitten by the showbiz bug.

I worked on what I thought was the perfect three-minute piece on autograph-collecting for the "PM Magazine" spot. Every word was carefully crafted and memorized. I even contacted a cosmetologist, hired a professional image consultant and bought the perfect television-worthy attire. I was determined to look good, feel good and sound good in that audition. As a seasoned professional, I was confident that all my preparation would pay off.

Family and colleagues said I had been groomed for this spot. "It's a slam dunk," they said. "You're a natural. The job was made for you."

You're probably thinking at this point that I aced the audition.

Believe it or not, I bombed. I was crushed.

"It was a speaking part," I reminded myself. "I'm a speech communications professional. It's what I do for a living. How could I have failed to impress them with my consummate communications skills?"

I allowed myself a good cry first, but I soon made another appointment with the show's producer and director. Have you ever heard the expression, "If you don't want to know, don't ask?" Well, I asked, and the answer I received changed my life forever.

✳

The director replayed the tape of my presentation. Then he said, "Linda, if you had auditioned for Romper Room, you would have every agent in America wanting to represent you."

I cracked a suspicious smile. And then I said, "Thanks, but I hear a 'but' tucked away in that compliment."

He nodded. Then he said something I've never forgotten: "Linda, you've got the most pedagogic voice I have ever heard. If you want to make it in this business, you're going to have to get a new voice!"

I remember my lower jaw dropping into my lap. Before I could regain my composure, he continued: "You're a bright, beautiful, articulate woman, but you sound like an insecure kindergarten teacher."

I was stunned! I still don't remember how I made it back to the speech center where I worked, but I remember how shaken I was by his comments. And I remember the confused look on my solemn twin's face in the car mirror. I remember my embarrassment and shame. But I also remember a new woman was born that day. I resolved that very afternoon to find the perfect voice—my perfect voice—so I'd never have to apologize for the way I sound again.

I have since come to realize that my audition wasn't for "PM Magazine." I was auditioning for a career as a voice coach.

With a lot of hard work and study, my "kindergarten teacher" voice became rich, resonant and melodic. It became a voice that people listened to… and a voice I learned to love. So I began a speaking and coaching business to help others develop their vocal and verbal skills, and overcome the fear of public speaking. Just as I had received loving attention from my teachers in grade school, and learned to speak with confidence again, I work with others to find their confidence and courage on stage.

I have finally found my perfectly authentic voice. It is the voice that reminds me each day with every encounter the powerful truth of who I was authentically created to be.

— TOUCHING HEARTS —

by Lynda Young

༥

"THANK YOU FOR YOUR TALK TODAY—IT WAS JUST FOR ME," the tear-streaked woman said. She grabbed my hand and leaned close to my ear. "I've desperately needed someone to give me hope. My son committed suicide last year," she whispered.

Speaking opportunities open doors to others hearts. After I speak, I stand at the door as the audience leaves, and I am privileged to meet those hurting hearts—one by one.

"Oh, I'm so sorry about your son," I said, and as we hugged, she sobbed into my shoulder. For a moment, it seemed we were the only ones in the room.

Speaking opportunities also carry responsibilities, but bring such rewards. My topics deal with coming alongside those in need—especially families coping with a chronically or critically ill child. I know I've touched the hearts of listeners when a knowing light sparks in their eyes, and the nodding heads assure me that the words are hitting the holes in their hearts.

Pain is pain is pain, and you can't live on planet Earth long before you experience pain of some kind. Many never share those pains with others sitting around them, even family members, but you, as the speaker, will come and leave. You're a safe person with whom to share a broken heart, and a hug.

✳

I love the story of the tremendously tall trees in the redwood forest. The forest ranger told us interesting facts about these gigantic trees: they grow in families and have shallow roots which grow horizontally toward each other, intertwining and root wrapping. When strong storms blow in from the Pacific Ocean, the huge trees sway and bend—but they don't break.

We as humans do the same. Some people are acquaintances, some friends, but when severe storms hit our lives, we reach out to one another; we "root wrap" and hold on.

✳

We moved from California to Georgia in 2002 so that my husband could continue his cancer research at Emory University. I learned of a schoolroom in the children's hospital on campus; my retired teacher gene kicked in, and I began volunteering.

One day, the small schoolroom was packed with children in wheelchairs and their intravenous poles—all crowded around the tables. You could tell the ones from the oncology floor because of their precious bald heads.

"Do you have time to do a bedside tutoring," one of the teachers asked me. "There's a seven-year-old girl in room 357 in isolation—in for a bone marrow transplant."

I went down to the third floor, hit the entry button to the isolation wing and washed my hands in the metal sink. Then I knocked softly on the door.

"Come in," a muffled voice said.

I slowly opened the door and peeked in, "I'm Lynda Young from the school room, here to help Danielle with her school work."

"Come on in," said her mom. "I'm Hedy and I just have to brush my teeth when I get a chance."

I looked at Danielle propped up in bed, her face framed by a blue scarf. "Do you feel like doing some schoolwork, Danielle?" I asked.

She shook her head wanly, leaned back on her pillow and closed her eyes as the intravenous meds dripped into her arm.

"Do you have time to sit and talk?" her mom asked.

"Sure." And as she shoved her books to one side of her combination bed and sofa, I saw her well-worn Bible lying open on her chair.

Hedy told me their story. How Danielle met the protocol (procedures to help with her cancer) in Atlanta—and their move from Miami, Florida—and all the challenges they'd met. When they arrived in Atlanta, the job her husband was promised fell through, as did the house they were to rent.

"The place storing our furniture is charging four times the amount quoted, so they're basically holding our furniture hostage," she said with a laugh.

She continued telling me about their two baby girls, ages one and two, and then added, "Oh, and our car was rear-ended—but we're all okay." She told just how everything was without complaining. And now, life is in isolation 24/7.

That day when I left, we hugged, prayed together and root wrapped. Her precious Danielle survived two bone marrow transplants, horrendous suffering, but passed away a few years later. From that day in 2002 to this in 2010, our families have been root wrapping. That's what you do in and out of crisis-mode.

When I speak, I look from person to person in the audience and say, "Don't miss an opportunity to root wrap with someone in need. You will bless them, but you'll be blessed as well."

I notice some in the audience giving knowing glances to those sitting next to them such as patting a hand and giving a smile. I know they've root wrapped in the past.

✳

That day, standing back at the door after speaking, I continued to shake hands as people left. As they came, their stories began. Each story was poignant, unique, and needing to be shared.

"My mother had breast cancer," Martha whispered, then took a breath. "But she didn't make it."

"I can't believe you talked about the redwood forest," Lisa in Georgia said. "That was the last thing my sister in San Francisco whispered to her husband as we leaned over her hospital bed. 'Take her to see the big trees.' She also died of cancer."

And then came that mascara-smeared lady who had lost her only son. She wasn't the last one in line, but the line froze as she sobbed and we hugged. Like the gigantic redwood trees, we have a great need to root wrap with one another. And with our roots entwined, we may sway and bend, but we will not break.

~ LIGHT, AIR AND WATER ~

by Merilyn Davis

"WHAT DO YOU WANT TO BE WHEN YOU GROW UP?"

Each week, my reply would change. It seemed foolish to the inquiring minds as I told them what I wanted to be: a writer one day, a fashion model the next; a teacher one day, a married lady the next; an artist one day, a journalist the next; a person of importance one day, and the next day somebody who helps people. Through the trials, tribulations and treasures of life, somehow, some way, those wishes and desires—the night dreams and daydreams—eventually, imminently, have come true, one by one by one.

At times, those dreams seemed far away, on paths I wasn't even on, or they simply seemed impossible to attain. There were times I could sense them, see them, feel them—practically, taste them, but where people, places or things showed up to hinder, prevent or deter me. But life's lessons, the attainment of wisdom, ultimately kept me on track, leading me to, and through, many stations and seasons of my life.

That brings me to tell the story of a seven-year-old child who taught me an important life lesson. While I was taking care of him, I asked him to make his bed. After he had finished, he excitedly brought me to his room. To my surprise, his bedding was disheveled, and in total disarray!

Not knowing of my disappointment, the boy looked up at me with pride and exclaimed, "Look! I did it, I made my bed up!"

Out of my frustration with him over his imperfect bed, words of wisdom quietly came to me: "Think, before you speak." I wanted to be careful not to break his spirit. I thought to myself, "He is who he is. Don't cut off his light, his air, and his water! Give him space and time, and let him make the best of who he is."

Instead of being upset with the boy, I smiled at him, and said, "And you did such a great job!" I continued, "And tomorrow, if you just pull that… and shift this… it'll be a bit straighter. Okay? I can see you worked really hard on it today. Wait until your parents see it! Come on! You've earned ice cream!"

"Okaaay!!" He says. "You dish it right up, and I'll be right down."

I went downstairs and scooped the ice cream into our two bowls, and I expected to hear his feet on the stairs. I waited until the ice cream had melted to cold soup, and I began to think he had crawled into bed and started sleeping or something when I heard him call my name from upstairs.

When I reached his doorway, he exclaimed, "Ta-da!"

His bed was in front of me, perfectly made, and the boy stood there next to it, beaming with pride.

✳

We had a fresh bowl of ice cream, the child and I. He spoke continuously about making his bed, and his eyes never stopped dancing. He even said, "Wait! I'm gonna go see if my bed is still made up!"

He then hurriedly left the table and dashed up the stairs. When he returned to the table, into his chair, he said breathlessly, "Yessss! My bed is still made up. I had to smooth a little wrinkle out though. I'll go check on it again, later!"

✳

We have to allow people to make mistakes, and to use those experiences as building blocks of esteem and confidence, and not as wrecking balls that tear holes into the soul that can poison and paralyze us for a lifetime.

My hope is that this young boy will realize his dreams one by one as I have throughout my life. And that, as a result of positive encouragement, will say, "A test at school is no longer difficult for me, because I am smarter, than the test!" Or perhaps he will say, "I don't get sick anymore, because I am stronger than any illness!" As he charts his course in life, I hope he will be the captain of his ship.

As the captain of my own ship, it is incredibly important to be reminded of the light, air and water of youth, and to realize that I have become what I always wanted to be when I grew up.

— MIND OVER ILLUSION —

by Anakhanda Shaka Mushaba

I WAS A YOUNG MAN WHO DIDN'T FINISH HIGH SCHOOL. I grew up in the North End of Hartford, Connecticut, an area plagued by gangs, drugs, police brutality and little opportunity. Out of that environment, I searched for and found my calling early in life. At 14, I began to teach martial arts in the basement of my home.

Because I was such a young man, it was difficult for me to get people to trust that I had the knowledge and talent to run a school for the martial arts in the basement of my home, so I decided to hold a free public exhibition to showcase my skills. The event went tremendously well and I began to get students almost immediately. Everyone was amazed not only at my skill level but at how I was able to speak with such seasoned wisdom. For over 30 years, that school has remained open.

As I grew older, I began to form youth groups, even creating the first youth police commission in my city, holding public forums where youth of all races and economic backgrounds could speak together in open dialogue, expressing thoughts and ideas with one another. These groups were featured on our local ABC Television channel and in several local newspapers. I was a successful and involved young man.

✳

Everything changed for me when I let my older brother borrow my car. The police later came to my school with a search warrant for this car, which they say had been used in a bank robbery. They were looking for the money that had been stolen. I, of course, was stunned! The police never found anything that day, and they eventually also let my brother go. I didn't believe he had done this thing anyhow. Only later would I find out how much more he was involved in the streets than I knew.

A couple of weeks later, I saw my brother walking along with two of his friends. He flagged me down and asked if I would drop them off at their friend's apartment. As I was driving them to their destination, the police pulled us over. They again searched the car, and this time they found drugs stuffed into my back seat.

Everyone was taken in and questioned. I was told that my brother said the drugs were mine, so I would be going to jail for a long time. Of course, I knew that this was one of the tactics police would sometimes use in order to get people to talk. They said that if I told them about the money from the robbery they would let me go. I insisted that I knew nothing about drugs, money, or the robbery, but they insisted that I did. They said to me, "We will do anything we have to do to get your brother, even if it means taking an innocent person down with him."

I didn't know what to do. I knew nothing and they sent me to the lock-up. I went to court, and my oldest brother and my father talked to the prosecutor. He understood what was happening and knew that I was not like my brother. He made a financial deal and the charges were dropped against me. However, I had an arrest record and that worked against me being a black American man.

I got very discouraged after this entire experience, and felt that I would have little chance to become successful and someday get myself out of the North End. Everywhere I went and everything I tried led back to my arrest record coming up. I started having many doubts and fears, and felt that my life was over and that I would never be able to get beyond eking out a meager living just to survive.

✳

One day, I ran across a book in the library called *The Science of Mind.* That led me to reading others of like subject matter. I started to understand that regardless of the odds, I could overcome them all using the power of my own mind. I started to incorporate aspects of what I had learned into my life. The trick was to disallow myself from being fooled by my so-called "reality" and instead using my mind to live a new reality in my thinking and imagination. It was a challenge for sure, but after time, I was able to accomplish my goal. My mind had freed me from the fear that I had no way to a better life. I eventually began teaching what I had learned, writing and speaking about the mind and how every individual has the ability to change his/her own life.

One of the tools that I use is called "giving your ego a new job description." This allows your ego to work with you and not against you. It clears up that negative mental chatter which comes from your ego. The mind is awesome if used as it was intended.

People get pulled into what they perceive as the reality of life, which for many isn't pretty. We have to move beyond this.

Our thinking will either free us or enslave us.

Our thoughts are what transform us into our beliefs.

You are a walking physical manifestation of your beliefs.

— WEST TEXAS GIRL —

by Patti Beckham

筇

"NATURAL ABILITY WITHOUT EDUCATION HAS MORE OFTEN RAISED A MAN TO GLORY AND VIRTUE THAN EDUCATION WITHOUT NATURAL ABILITY."

— Cicero

I AM A WEST TEXAS GIRL WHO GREW UP IN THE SMALL TOWN OF ORLA, TEXAS. Orla is nothing more than an ultra-rural crossroads, but in my life, this town played a huge part in my early learning. Orla taught me the lessons of everyday life.

There was a post office of only 100 boxes, and at that time, I'm not even sure they were all taken. My mother was the "Post Mistress." Dad was a welder, tying in gas wells in the West

Texas oilfields. My brother worked at the only gas station at the time. Later, one other was opened for competition. And, of course, I was the waitress at the Orla Café. My little sister was too young to work, so I spent all my money on her each payday.

Our little white stucco church was Baptist on one Sunday and Methodist on the other. We were quite ecumenical.

From little Orla, I rode the school bus fifty miles one way just to get an education. That was a long ride! Graduating in 1969, I was glad not to have to ride the bus any more.

It was always nice when we had our substitute bus driver, "Mr. Workman." He enjoyed us Orla kids and picked me as his favorite. I had a front-row seat on the steps for direct communication for at least an hour of drive-time. He spent a tremendous amount of time explaining what I should be doing and learning. I spent a lot of time telling him what I was not going to do and the reasons why not. Right then and there, people started to see that I was going places.

Much to my surprise, my career has moved me throughout the state of Texas on highways and in traffic, making a living traveling much more than what I had to do back then on that yellow school bus.

✳

I hold a BA in Black Automobile University. You see, my company furnishes this vehicle for me and I am planted in the driver's seat most of the weekdays and weekends. My classes (on the road) consist of Zig Ziglar, Stephen Covey and Mark Sanborn. Believe it or not, I hold a 4.0 average, and have met numerous people across the great state of Texas. The automobiles during my two careers have brought about opportunities I never would have believed I'd encounter.

Well, this wasn't quite enough for me, so I went on to earn my MBA: the "Mop Bucket Attitude." This degree meant you do what is asked of you in your career.

Most bosses, I have found, will not ask you to work on an assignment that they haven't already been in the trenches doing themselves. Earning your way to the top takes work. You can have all the sheep skin degrees with all the pretty writing but if you are not willing to put that foot out each day, it won't happen, folks!

So you see, education is rolling up your sleeves and getting with the program. It's not about being a big shot. Education is about doing what is necessary to become successful.

⌐ Getting Up When Life Turns You Upside Down ⌐ (Unbreakable Faith)

by Versie L. Walker

It was during the summer of '93 when my world turned upside down, literally.

My old friend Ken had always had drive and ambition, ever since we were kids. When he was ten years old, it was said that he didn't like his bicycle looking like other kids' bicycles in his neighborhood. So he went to an auto body shop and convinced the owner to paint his bike a different color. In high school, most of us were chasing girls or hanging out while Ken was piecing together old cars and heading off to pursue his dreams. Ken always had an eye for business, and was determined to succeed—and so was I.

He and I spoke one day and decided to meet to discuss business. After we met, we went to an area where the youth of the day hung out, showing off their cars and motorcycles. It was here where we both decided to become a little wild and race. We were warned only to race in one direction, because the opposite direction had a curve that had proved to be too much for most racers to handle. Initially, we followed this advice. However, we couldn't resist the temptation of racing back in the opposite direction. And at nearly 98 miles an hour, I crashed.

I still remember seeing Ken's brake lights as a blur of red lines swerving around the curve as he spun out of control in front of me. It wasn't until I came to, seeing a swarm of people leaning over me, that I realized something had gone terribly wrong.

After being helped to my feet, reality set in. My knees were split wide open, virtually in half, warm blood pouring down my legs as though from an open water facet. I immediately became hysterical, and began to yell! I vaguely recall Ken yelling at his girlfriend as they rushed me to the hospital, saying, "Keep talking to him, and don't let him fall asleep." I could hear his tires scraping the wheel well of his car as he sped over bump after bump.

I suffered severe head trauma, injury to my left shoulder, ten stitches in my right knee and over 15 staples in my left. Needless to say, I was in bad shape and fortunate to be alive. I recall a nurse in the operating room saying, "Breathe, young man. Breathe. Doctor, he's not breathing. Breathe young man."

My friends and family were praying for me to pull through. Given the extent of my injuries, they were also praying for me to walk again. This was the concern of a young female anesthesiologist as well, who secretly cautioned me to leave the hospital and look for a better surgeon to perform the delicate knee surgery.

✳

In my physical condition, I needed help with virtually everything; yes, everything. A week after surgery, my sister took me for a walk to help strengthen my legs. It was then I realized, perhaps for the first time in life, I'd been running fast but going nowhere. Suddenly, I asked her to stop. She was immediately concerned, thinking I was exhausted or perhaps in pain.

I explained, "No, I'm okay." I asked her to listen to the sound.

She said, "What sound?"

"Those sounds, the sounds of birds," I said. "The smell of fresh cut grass, look at how amazingly blue the sky is." I was now seeing life through new eyes, and I began to cry. My sister believed that I had lost my mind!

It wasn't until after my surgery that I discovered what Ken actually did for a living; he was a debt collector and a very good one at that. And during my recovery, I studied for eight to ten hours a day. I read the various laws and practices of debt collecting.

Because I was immobile and spent an entire month studying, my friend scheduled an interview for me as a debt collector. The same day of the interview was my first doctor's appointment to begin therapy and rehabilitation for my legs. There was no rescheduling either appointment.

The pain of this therapy session was so intense and excruciating that I blacked out once or twice. I yelled at the nurses and therapist, pleading for them to stop! They insisted this had to be done to separate scar tissue and for me to gain full mobility of my legs. Afterwards, still in a great deal of pain and refusing any pain medication, I got dressed and headed to my car. A simple two-minute walk took me ten minutes.

✳

I drove two miles to the expressway's entrance with tears rolling down my face. I wondered what to do next. If I turned right, two exits and less than ten minutes later, I would be home. If I turned left, I would drive for 45 minutes in pain towards a new world, a new beginning to an environment that I knew nothing about. I knew if I went home, I'd find comfort and sympathy. I asked myself, "If I go left, will I be given a chance to change my life, to start performing to my full capabilities and to begin fulfilling my destiny?" In the 60 seconds it took the light to change, every emotion known to man had erupted inside of me. I felt a sense of fear, euphoria, insecurity, doubt, anger and anxiety. As quickly as these feelings and emotions came, they went and were replaced with an overwhelming sense of calmness and peace. Still in pain with tears streaming down my face, I turned left, and in doing so, transformed my life.

After working as a debt collector for nearly three months, I discovered I had made more money during this time than I'd made in an entire year as a train conductor before the accident. I was now in a relaxed office setting and had recently been promoted to a supervisory position. I was confident and comfortable with the processes and demands of the job, and I felt a tremendous sense of accomplishment.

During this time, I began reflecting back on the days and weeks since the accident. Still feeling the effects of that accident, I realized how far I had come. It was at that moment I began to pray.

I prayed to God, thanking Him for letting me see another day and asking Him to allow me to grow stronger and to one day have me inspire others.

✳

It's been nearly 17 years since my accident. Both my personal and professional lives have taken several twists and turns, but at no point did I ever question, "Why me?"

At no point did I ever lose my faith. I have stayed hopefully optimistic about what life has in store for me. I've stayed obedient and have followed my heart's desires.

My journey hasn't been easy. However, it's been rewarding. And my prayers to walk, run, jump and soar through life have all been answered.

— BE PREPARED —

by J. Aday Kennedy

WHO KNEW THAT THE DAY I WOKE UP WITH AN EARACHE MY LIFE, AS I KNEW IT, WOULD END? My illness worsened. Within a week, my sickness grew into spinal meningitis. I stroked at my brainstem, descended into a coma, was diagnosed as brain-dead, and regained consciousness as a ventilator-dependent quadriplegic.

What good was I? I felt like a thing… nothing more than an animated head with a useless body attached.

"Mom, please take off my ventilator and let me die," I begged for the first six months after my stroke.

She replied, "It will get better. Give it time."

I gave it time. For five months I stayed in the rehabilitation hospital with no improvement. I begged, "Please take off the vent. Let me die."

"No. We'll find a way. It's just a matter of time," she said.

I gave it time. For six years, I tried to move, feel and speak. Progress was made. My finger wiggled. I took a breath on my own. I lifted my arm. It wasn't enough. "Mom, please take me off the ventilator. I can't live like this any more."

"No." Her response remained the same. "Just try to move. Try to feel. I know you can do this. You will get better. It's just going to take time."

Time? How much time? I thought. Will she ever let me go? I watched her stretch my arms and legs, but felt nothing. I regained the ability to speak, and to move one arm and hand. Yet, I could not feel the movement. After hours, days and weeks passed, I did not walk or breathe more than a few hours without the ventilator.

Mom was thrilled and encouraged with these milestones. "You've come so far." I yearned for an end to this existence. These "improvements" did little to raise my spirits. My thoughts revolved around what I could not do.

"I hate being this way. What good am I? I want to die! Please help me."

"You know I can't do that."

I longed to stomp my feet, slam a door shut and scream. The independent woman inside me clamored for release. Day in and day out, physical therapy and inklings of incremental improvements in my physical condition could not slake my thirst for a "real life."

✳

My respiratory therapist asked me to participate as a case study at a few continuing education classes for respiratory therapists. I was eager for anything different and new. Physical therapy eight hours a day did not make me feel fulfilled. The therapists were in awe of my lung health and story. My spirits soared.

I became the central spokesperson and presented information about patient advocacy, lung maintenance on a ventilator, and rehabilitation and recovery. I received many standing ovations.

People approached me after my speeches and said wonderful things like, "I've never seen things as clearly from the patient's point of view," or "I'm usually fighting to stay awake at these seminars, but I enjoyed every minute of your speech."

Regardless of the praise I received from audiences, when I watched a playback, I noticed my speech sounded stilted and unnatural. I knew that I would have to time my words in between my ventilator's dispensation of air. I rewrote my speeches and rehearsed. After many videotaped practice sessions, my delivery began improving.

Soon I discovered that my disabilities served to strengthen the impact of my speeches. My audience laughed when I said, "I'm not really paralyzed and vent-dependent. I'm just very lazy. I don't even bother breathing on my own." I was on a roll. I found new speaking opportunities around every corner, and during speeches, I saw faces light up with hope.

But I grew overconfident and strayed from my proven formula. I stopped practicing my speeches out loud. Soon, I fell on my face.

At one event, I launched into my speech, but without practice and carefully timed phrases, my sentences grew stilted. Sweat trickled down my back. My speech's content suffered, too. Instead of uplifting my audience, I pulled their spirits down and depressed them. No laughter and no happy tears. I struggled through, but could tell I was flopping. After every other speech I had given, the physical therapists oozed approval and complimented my content and delivery.

Someone shook my hand afterward and said, "That was… interesting." Another invitation was not forthcoming.

When I called to schedule another event I was told, "We're not interested at this time." My confidence plummeted. I watched the videotape and confirmed what I knew. It was awful. No, that was too kind a description. It was depressing and discouraging. What have I done?

More than just enduring a failed speech, these people lost hope from the example I set. I mentally kicked myself and quit soliciting speaking engagements. The possibility of failing myself and the audience loomed too great. I sank into self-derision.

✳

My brother-in-law's father needed a speaker for his rotary club. I agreed to fill the slot after a bit of cajoling. Plagued by insecurity, I prepared. I ran through my speech dozens of times. I worried over my clothing, jewelry and hair. My wheelchair and medical equipment caused me to be self-conscious and unsure.

Rolling across the stage and looking at the sea of faces, my throat became dry. I clipped my microphone to my shirt and began. I stumbled. The words I had memorized escaped me. My hand shook. I cleared my throat. All eyes were trained on me. I cleared my throat again. People shifted in their seats. A rumble of conversation began.

My speech had barely started, and I was already losing my audience. A silent prayer ran through my mind. I cleared my throat again. I had to do something and fast. Luckily, I remembered my name. I introduced myself.

I glanced down to reference my notes. My eyes refused to focus. I squeezed them shut for a second and the page swam into view. I repeated my name and jumped into my speech. I was a bit rusty, but I perched a smile on my lips and continued.

Laughter, tears and smiling faces swept the room. A man severely debilitated by cerebral palsy approached me afterward, his speech garbled and his body twisted from his affliction. My speech had moved him and he said it would give him courage to speak in front of others. "Thank you."

That young man thanked *me*, but I owe *him* the gratitude. Since that day, each time I speak, I remember that young man. His compliment helped me to realize that I *am* a speaker, devoting my life to teaching, entertaining and inspiring audiences.

~ DREAM, WORK, BELIEVE ~

by Gary O'Sullivan

I WAS FIVE YEARS OLD WHEN MY MOTHER MOVED ME FROM INDIANA TO SOUTH CAROLINA. She had started a new life with her new husband, my new stepfather, as we moved into our new home: a basement. The year was 1958, and I was five years old.

Mr. and Mrs. Day lived right above us. They owned the service station next door in the late '50s, where my stepdad worked.

In the center of our living area there was a set of stairs that led up to the Days' home. The entrance to the stairs was covered by drapes, and that would soon prove to be the curtains in front of an imagined stage for a beaming five-year-old. My mother, Mary, would have me go behind the drapes, and she would introduce me: "Now, ladies and gentlemen, let's give a big Grand Ole Opry round of applause to Gary Dale." Dale is my middle name, only used when Mom was introducing me from backstage like this or when I was in big trouble. My mother loved country music, and she had a beautiful voice. Her dream was to someday be on the stage of the Grand Ole Opry alongside the country stars of the day like Loretta Lynn, Kitty Wells and Johnny Cash.

My mother passed me her dream in our little basement home. She first gave me a vision of becoming something great. Just by introducing me, she took me from the stairs at the Days' house to the stage of the Grand Ole Opry. Little did I know at the time that she was also introducing me to one of the greatest success principles of all: to dream. Today some might call it a vision, a goal or a burning desire. But for Mom and for me, it was simply dreaming of what seemed to be an impossible dream.

My stepfather had many roles at the gas station where he worked—pumping gas, changing oil, and lubricating cars. He seemed to be able to do it all, even some light mechanical work. He never complained about the work, or even having to work. He just worked. Long hours, six days a week; he worked.

We later moved from the Days' basement into rental houses, trailer parks, and the like. With only a sixth-grade education, my stepfather's options were limited. But his talents of working on and building things allowed him to have opportunities in construction, and eventually he found his way into textile mills.

When I was in my teens, my stepdad taught me the next lesson of success: hard work. We never had a sit-down discussion about it. I just watched him, and it was clear to me. I saw him go to work when he would have preferred to do something else. He worked when others took vacation; he worked when he was sick; and he worked… every day.

I remember once I asked him why he was going in to work when he was sick: "Boy, I told that man down at the plant if he would give me a job I would be there every day I was able. I am sick, but I am still able."

✳

During the eleventh grade of high school, a buddy of mine told me they were hiring at the local grocery store. Not only did I get hired to bag groceries, I was even put in charge of my own aisle. I had to stock it and keep it clean. I thought I was on my way. After I graduated from high school in 1971 with no plans for the future, the company had me slated for management training. These plans changed one summer night.

Upon arriving home from work one evening, I found that my parents had had an unexpected visitor—a lady from the local cemetery selling cemetery plots to families on a pre-need basis. Not only did they buy from her, but she informed them they were looking for people who would do what she had been doing in the community. When she asked my parents if they knew of anyone who might be interested, my stepdad made a statement that would alter the course of my life: "We got a boy who talks a lot."

Just a few days later, I met a man who would teach me the next lesson I needed to succeed. On a Wednesday night, after unloading the grocery truck from our local warehouse and stocking my aisle, I had an interview at 9:30 p.m. with Mr. Fred Renner. During our interview, Mr. Renner talked about many things, including success, goals, becoming your best, personal achievement… Unbeknownst to him, he was talking to someone who had never been exposed to such ideas. I knew about dreaming and hard work, but up to that point I had never thought of how I could put them to work for me.

Fred hired me to sell cemetery plots door to door. But what he really did was far more significant in my life. He taught me to believe that I could have a better life, and that my past was in no way a limiting factor in determining my future success. Within weeks, Fred gave me an introduction to all kinds of people who understood the concepts required to believe and achieve your dreams. He introduced me to the works of Napoleon Hill, Earl Nightingale, Dr. Norman Vincent Peale, W. Clement Stone, and Og Mandino.

Along with Fred's direction and the foundation my parents had given me, I learned how to design the future I desire, work towards it every day, and believe that I—yes I, the guy who lived in someone else's basement—could, in fact, play on the stage.

✳

I love the stories of how people like my mother, who dream of making it to the spotlight of fame, make it. However, mine did not.

I get excited when I read the accounts of how people like my stepdad, a person with limited education, become millionaires through work and diligence. However, mine didn't.

What my parents did do for me was teach me to dream, to take personal responsibility and be accountable, and yes, to work.

✳

From 1971 to 2000 I used the principles of dream, work, and believe in the world of direct selling; a world where countless opportunities for personal and professional growth are available. A world where if people can see what their future can be (dream), if they are determined and diligent (work), and if they accept the fact they can be more than they are today (believe), they can have it all.

From selling door to door for years, from becoming a sales manager to senior vice president of a public company, I practiced the principles I learned from my mother, father, and Fred. Then in 2001, I started living a different dream - one of owning my own company. I knew if I worked hard and true, success was sure. But that vision and effort would not have been enough had I not believed; I believed in me, believed in the principles of success, and believed in the American dream.

Today I am performing on the big stage. No, not the Grand Ole Opry; a bigger one—the stage of the American entrepreneur. From being a professional speaker, thought leader, consultant, and personal leadership coach, I am using the principles I learned to dream, work, and believe.

CHAPTER THREE:

❦

Spirituality

"WE ARE NOT HUMAN BEINGS ON A SPIRITUAL JOURNEY.
WE ARE SPIRITUAL BEINGS ON A HUMAN JOURNEY."

—— *Steven R. Covey*

I like to think that the word inspiration contains within it the words *in spirit*. From within our spirits, something stirs us, and sparks us towards achieving or doing something that is greater than we could have ever imagined.

When we quiet our minds and listen, we hear that *still, small voice* from within, and at these moments, our actions, thoughts and words take on a different reality. They become inspired, or *in spirit*.

—— *Christine Schwan,
author of "Secrets of an Empowered Woman"*

~ JOURNEY IN FAITH ~

by Kris Miller

I SPENT TWO DECADES OF MY LIFE WALKING BAREFOOT FROM TOWN TO TOWN, CLAD ONLY IN A WHITE ROBE, UNCONCERNED WITH POSSESSIONS OR WORLDLY THINGS, TRAVELING SOMETIMES ALONE AND SOMETIMES WITH OTHERS IN A JOURNEY OF FAITH.

Six fellow barefooted pilgrims and I were given a car, and we piled in and drove south. We were headed for South America. We were not missionaries in a traditional sense; instead, we were simply travelers of faith, and barefooted pilgrims with open hearts and observant eyes. We started driving from California with only $200 between us. We were truly counting on our faith to keep us alive.

After driving south for many days, we arrived in Guatemala. When asked if we needed a place to stay, we replied, "Yes," whereupon we were apprehended by the police and incarcerated as vagrants. The prison to which we were sent was unlike any picture of a prison that we had seen before. It looked much like a very large house. The women were on one side, and the men on the other.

On the women's side of this dirty, home prison, the prisoners were forced to sew, embroider and such. If the women produced enough, they could earn their food. Otherwise, they would starve.

Our jailers didn't give us any food to eat, and I'm not sure how many days we went without, but we were very grateful when they finally allowed us to eat. Our fellow prisoners had not fed us either; they had no desire to share their already meager rations, especially with us outsiders in our now dirty white robes.

There was only one cot in the dungeon-like place where we could sleep. There were eight women and one girl there, and one of the women was pregnant. It was a nightmare. There was no place to go to the bathroom except in the corner.

After several weeks, we were deported, and we made the long trip north back to Mexico. Despite our fears, we were placed in cells there that were much cleaner and less terrifying, and we were given good food to eat. And most importantly, we were one step closer to home again.

I will never forget that journey we took from Guatemala to Mexico. All along the route, we witnessed peasants peering at us from the sides of the road. Now I realize that those peasants were the true reason we had come on this journey.

Those poor people who lined the streets all the way from Guatemala to Mexico were special people. We had experienced hospitality from them, and we saw in them the true message of hospitality and love. As we had walked barefooted in our white robes along the streets of their dirty crowded cities, we were offered food and shelter by people who scarcely could afford such luxuries themselves.

As we rode north, we watched out the windows as peasants chased our vehicle, and we remembered that these peasants had taken us in, barefooted strangers. They offered us their home, and their last bowl of beans and bread. The poorest among them would offer us food and shelter, and they would give it to us with their whole heart.

Many years have passed since I walked barefoot in my white robe, trusting that God would provide, traveling from town to town. I will never forget the people who opened up their hearths and their hearts to me. Since then, I have worked for many years in the business world, and know countless millionaires who haggle over every dollar. What a contrast.

Let us all live like peasants and care for one another with full hearts, and a simple bowl of beans and bread.

— THANK GOD I FELL APART —

by Adena Sampson

"OUR GREATEST GLORY IS NOT IN NEVER FALLING
BUT IN RISING EVERY TIME WE FALL."

- Confucius

Everyone and every circumstance present an opportunity for growth. The question is: how far are you willing to go? How deep are you willing to go to find your true essence?

When everything fell apart—my health, my finances and my relationship—my world came crashing down and so did I! I had managed to acquire a resistant strain of a staph in my lymph nodes and right breast tissue that had relapsed for the second time leaving me in critical condition. Four nurses tried to stick me with an intravenous seven different times before it finally took. I lay there thinking "God? Is there something you're trying to tell me?" The message rung out loud and clear: how many times do you have to be pricked before you bleed? When was I going to draw the line and let go of this relationship that no longer served me? When was enough, enough? Was I willing to die for it?

They say love is blind, and I would have to concur. My higher self and intuition had been trying to get my attention from the very beginning. I had been walking on eggshells for far too long, and I was sick and tired of not being seen, heard, or understood. I had unconsciously hooked into an unhealthy dysfunctional pattern that was being repeatedly played out. And by sticking around, I kept the cycle alive.

Part of me was in denial, afraid to let go, afraid that if I did I'd be making a big mistake. And that's when it happened. As I lay there heavily drugged, my partner threw another one of his weekly fits and walked out. For me, this was the last straw! At the time, I was numb. It seemed almost impossible to deal with the immense pain in my heart in addition to all the pain I was feeling in my physical body. I felt abandoned and devastated by the very man who claimed he wanted to be my husband. For when it mattered the most—in what seemed to be my weakest moment, my darkest hour—he wasn't there.

※

I was on the floor gut-wrenched; I felt broken, my wings tattered and torn. I felt like I was dying inside, and in a way I was. There were days I couldn't get out of bed. I would wake up many mornings with an empty pit in my stomach feeling like I was going to hurl. I was angry at myself for not trusting myself, my intuition and all the signs. I felt like a fool. I was hurt, left questioning and trying to renegotiate with the universe. Why, God? Why did I feel so close yet so far away from the man I loved with every inch of my being and breadth of my soul. There must be some mistake. I somehow felt conned, like I had been wronged, baited with a beautiful, shiny, red, juicy apple only to find after taking a bite that it was poisoned.

I found myself in a scary place, a place where fear resides. A place where I had somehow, even for just a moment, forgotten what having faith was. I felt tired and overwhelmed, so far removed from myself, and I just couldn't seem to find my way home…

"WHEN YOU HAVE COME TO THE EDGE OF ALL LIGHT THAT YOU KNOW,
AND ARE ABOUT TO DROP OFF INTO THE DARKNESS OF THE UNKNOWN,
FAITH IS KNOWING ONE OF TWO THINGS WILL HAPPEN:
THERE WILL BE SOMETHING SOLID TO STAND ON
OR YOU WILL BE TAUGHT TO FLY."

- Patrick Overton

※

Nature gives us such a great example of how to live. In life there is a natural cycle of death and rebirth. The waves can be a bit bumpy and there can be some major storms. Sometimes we can get caught in a rip tide, tumbled and thrown around. Most of us are looking for some smooth sailing, aren't we? We may float for a while, but it doesn't last for long. Our lives are like the ocean tides, always in motion, ever changing. If we happen to be in the right place at the right time, sometimes we can catch a wave and ride it for a while. And then it's time to catch another wave.

From nothingness comes everything. This is where creation happens. When we wipe the slate clean, we can repaint our canvas. What a great opportunity to rewrite my story.

There is no right or wrong, good or bad, it just is. For when we surrender all our judgments and perceptions, when we let go of our old programming and the old paradigms that no longer serve us, then we open ourselves up to an endless array of possibilities. It's really amazing how as we grow and move forward on our journey, the road map seems to appear, and other aspects align and come into play. As time passes, the curtain unfolds, revealing to us our true essence and purpose in ways we never could have imagined.

— SECRETS OF AN EMPOWERED WOMAN —

by Christine Schwan

*"Believe in yourself; Find the best that is you.
Let your spirit prevail; Steer a course that is true."*

- Bruce B. Wilmer

AS I STOOD THERE LOOKING AT THE BANK TELLER IN DISBELIEF, I SWORE WITH EVERY OUNCE OF MY BEING THAT I WOULD NEVER BE IN THIS POSITION AGAIN. Simply because I was now divorced, the bank I had been using for over ten years was now requiring me to wait nine months before I could have a debit card issued in my name. My ex-husband, however, had no trouble having one issued immediately in his name.

Who would have ever thought that a single mother of two small children, with a degree in one hand and a steady, full-time job in the other, would have such difficulty trying to establish herself financially? The same scenario played itself out at every turn. My resolve grew stronger and my desire to become an empowered woman was born.

✳

The first secret to becoming empowered is to believe in yourself! I am not talking about the "lip service" we give to others when trying to convince them of how good we are or how well we have done. No, I am talking about the deep down knowing that we *are* as good as anyone else. Breathe in that belief and let it course through your body until others can see it and feel it.

In order to do that, you must look at your self-talk and what your beliefs are about yourself. So close your eyes; slowly breathe in through your nose and out through your mouth. Now ask yourself if you like yourself. Would you want to be friends with someone like you? Now think about how you talk to yourself within, where not a living soul knows what you say. Do you say positive and uplifting things to yourself? Or do you denigrate and criticize yourself on a daily basis?

It took me far too long to learn the most important thing about empowerment. You must simply *choose* to believe in yourself. Choose to talk with kindness and love to yourself. Never wait for someone else to come along and fill that void: it is up to you. Become your own best friend and see what starts to happen in your life!

Good. Now that you are choosing to believe in yourself, you can learn the second secret to becoming empowered. Take positive action towards your dream or goal. By taking action towards your goals and dreams, you set in motion the energy necessary to fulfill your desires.

The third secret is to give yourself permission to feel good. Before you roll out of bed each morning, make a conscious *choice* to actually feel good about yourself in every way. No one will give you permission but *you!* So what are you waiting for? Choose to feel good today! Remember that feeling good isn't based on some tasks you have done, or words you have spoken. It is about allowing yourself to open up to the possibility of feeling good, and then choosing it. Smile, laugh and really notice how good you can feel when you invite good feeling into your life. You will never be the same. And that, my friend, is a great thing!

A journey towards empowerment begins with *choosing* to believe in yourself. As you take each secret and implement it, your journey will become easier, more fulfilling, and rewarding in every way.

~ MY SIX-STEP PATH TO ENLIGHTENMENT ~

by Don Lubov

STEP 1. OBSERVE YOURSELF WITHOUT JUDGMENT

STEP 2. FORGIVE YOURSELF AND OTHERS

STEP 3. ACCEPT WHAT YOU OBSERVE

STEP 4. LOVE YOURSELF UNCONDITIONALLY

STEP 5. AWAKEN FROM YOUR DREAM

STEP 6. CELEBRATE LIFE FOREVER

As Siddhartha and many others have made clear for the past 2,500 years, "Life is suffering." Fortunately, he and others offer a way to transcend this suffering. The way is meditation; this is not necessarily formal meditation. The form of meditation I endorse is informal. It is your daily life as it is.

At first, the Six-Step Path may seem simplistic. Actually, it is—we are complex. Socrates was so right when he said, "The unexamined life is not worth living."

My Six-Step Path begins with Observation. This is not just any observation. This most important step is non-judgmental observation. With non-judgmental observation, you witness your own behavior with all its flaws and weaknesses that all humans possess.

For example, when you get angry, observe that anger. Focus your attention on it. Don't judge it as either justified or wrong, or any other qualifier. Simply see it as a behavior of you, a human being. The more intensely and often you focus your attention on your behavior—all your behaviors—without judgment, the more you will see these behaviors begin to wane. The more you see, the less they will be. As you get more familiar with your true, imperfect self, you will become, little by little, more forgiving of your real self.

This brings us to the second step in the Six-Step Path, that of Forgiveness. The degree to which you judge yourself is the degree to which you judge others. As you begin to lighten up and be more forgiving of yourself, including your own flaws and weaknesses, your judgment of others will also become less frequent and less harsh. In time, this forgiveness of yourself and others leads to step three of the Six-Step Path: Acceptance.

Once you can observe without judgment and forgive imperfections, you naturally adopt an attitude of acceptance. To forgive and accept what you observe, in yourself and others, is the beginning of true spirituality—and, ultimately, enlightenment.

Living a non-judgmental life of observation, forgiveness, and acceptance brings you to the fourth step in the Six-Step Path: Love. Unconditional love, love without conditions, both for yourself and others. This is the true, and only, love that comes from our source, through us, to all life. This love IS our source (and us). At this point, you are in sync with your source, no longer trying to control the world, just letting it be. In Zen, this is "life as it is."

Living in this manner, you will surely Awaken from your dream—your dream of separation from your source into a separate, ego-centered identity. Your awakening—also called satori, enlightenment, epiphany, etc.—is two-fold: first you know, down to your bones, that you are part of something greater than yourself. Next, you realize that you ARE that thing greater than yourself. When this happens, you can't help but want to Celebrate every moment of life for the miracle it is. The way to express this understanding is to serve others, for they are you. All life is one. Celebrate life forever.

As you progress (imagined) from being a fear-based, ego-centric part of the universal problem, you become an accepting, loving, part of the solution. Your self in search of itself has found itself in six steps. You are now back where you started, but with the understanding of what it means to be where you are: in the now.

— MY HEALING... YOUR HEALING —

by Sharon Quinn

ONCE UPON A TIME MY LIFE SUCKED! I WAS BROKEN—battling with alcoholism, dealing with intrusive molestation flashbacks, struggling with being victimized by fraud and violence, dealing with physical injuries, angry, exhausted, losing faith in myself, *ad nauseam.*

Now, my life is quite bright—miraculously different. My pain pool, my agony—it's gone! You need to know I'm not talking about pain diversion, sedation, or numbing myself into a no-feeling state. Quite the contrary: I'm more alive, regenerative, peaceful, and energetic than ever.

I no longer drag myself through life so exhausted that my bed and pillow are dearer to me than my next meal or friendship. Nor am I looking into a mirror, disgusted with rolls of flesh, silently, yet callously, screaming, "Ugly! How did you get so overweight?" Nor am I a raw nerve with rage taking over, causing others pain, and unable to help myself. Nor am I dealing with stress, tension, and frustrations eating away my vigor and good nature. Previously, with both being buried under crap faster than I could sort it out, I was unexpectedly explosive. Yikes!

My inability to control my actions scared me. Imagine falling off the cliffs of your being. Terrifying, eh? I was living with that helplessly lost feeling. I'd worry and dread the possibilities: "What will happen if I hit bottom? Can I? Will I lose my sanity?" In the back of my mind, though I discussed it with no one, was Mom's haunting story of how her dad suddenly "cracked" and whisked away in the dark of night to a sanitarium he never left.

When my mom would share this dreaded tale with stark brevity, delivering "just the facts," as if she were reporting to Joe Friday, I'd sense there was something darker lurking in her unspoken words: in solitude, she too was worrying about probabilities of genetic insanity.

It all started when I was a child—or maybe earlier as I was picking up stale, but meaty, leftovers from previous lifetimes, playing out old patterns of unrequited love, betrayal and denial of expressing my being. I was the oldest of seven, displaced prematurely when my sister was born a mere 11 months later.

I don't recall much detail, which is a blessing, but I was a darned cute blonde, shy to my core, longing to be loved. I was a perfect mark for perpe-*traitors* and so I was unfortunately *chosen*, first by drunken family role models too "out of it" to notice or tell.

While amnesia initially protected me, it later became the makings of a perfect storm. During my teens, I dreamed of suicide's sweet relief. As adulthood loomed larger, I gradually relinquished this dream for a Walter Mitty approach of thirsting for adult empowerment. My fantasies met on life's battlefield where scripts of life's harsh realities, written from a "no pain, no gain" perspective, were producing dramas of suffering and hard knocks. These themes clashed cruelly with my desires for an easy, no-hassle life. I just wanted to be happy…

Debts, denied-anger, the roiling pressure of amnesia, robbery, and date rape charged their wounding swords deep into me. They crushed my tenacious, unrelenting will (Dad called it stubbornness), my eternal optimism, my heart and my intelligence, resulting in a bloodbath, draining my verve, and eventuating a nervous breakdown.

✳

Drugging me, the preferred methodology of professionals seeking to "help" me get "better," meant addressing my symptoms rather than their root causes: there's no healing in that.

I needed a reason to live through the pain, and being numb didn't have enough juice in it for me.

My relentless drive for healing led to what I initially thought sounded hokey: energy medicine. But I had nothing to lose; traditional options had no healing power in them.

Energy medicine changed everything—from the dynamics of healing itself, to a spontaneous and gradual enlightening of my mind and heart that was paralleling a growing recognition about what I could do for others IF only I'd accept our Creator's intention!

I had a burning desire, and stumbled into a way that broke through to authentic self and possible spiritual enlightenment. Wow!

I didn't see that coming until it gained momentum. Then, awareness couldn't be denied. A dream I thought far-fetched was being made real. What a staggering reality and discovery! I had a hard time wrapping my head around it, yet evidence was speaking through shifts in my consciousness and healing—physical, mental and emotional!

✳

Knowing yourself is knowing *Who I Am*—that's *your* SELFGnosis™ coming full circle. You break through your cycles of life and death, entering your *Immortal SELF*, while going about the business of being a parent, a friend, and more. Essentially, you can be a better person in all you think, say and do. Not trying and striving to be idealistic, you can naturally function from a superior inner place that'll inspire and please you. Anyone can progress into wellbeing using baby steps.

I broke through my self-imposed prison and emerged bearing gifts I can't wait to give away.

~ THE NEW REFORMATION ~

by Rev. Daniel Sherar

I AM A RETIRED CITIZEN-SOLDIER VETERAN WITH MORE THAN 30 YEARS OF SERVICE, WITH 23 OF THOSE IN THE ARMY CHAPLAIN CORPS. I am mostly grateful for the time I spent in the service with men and women of honor and distinction. It is in love for God and my country that I have come to think more critically about the continuation of the Protestant Reformation in 21st Century North America. I was in Kuwait and Iraq at the start of Operation Iraqi Freedom in 2003. I understood why Thomas Ricks called it a "fiasco" in 2006. I came to see clearly why Sadaam Hussein misled the world into thinking he had chemical weapons in the interest of keeping Iran in check. Above all, I can see an American Church that became too militant.

Do our judgments carry effective moral authority? If Christians are confident to march off to war based largely on judgments articulated through popular media broadcasts, does the foundation of our very nation come into question? This is the concern that Evangelical Church leadership will have to face in the light of fear-based propaganda that has driven much of our population into dubious crusading. I ask fellow evangelical clergy and laity alike if they truly understand the mind of God for today's Protestant world. If we are yet called to "reform" the church, we will see at least some evidence of divine authority behind that call.

TIME magazine called the first decade of the century, the "Decade from Hell." When I first read this, I began to look inwards, towards my own fellowship of evangelical Christians in seeking the truth. Where liberals had been bashing away at apparent flaws in popular American Christianity in the late 1990s (for example, *Why Christianity Must Change or Die*), conservatives were now piping in (for example, *unChristian, Where Have All the Prophets Gone*, and *Why Johnny Can't Preach*), and I became concerned by the self-righteous arrogance and political excesses of certain strongholds within the western church after 9/11.

I believe there is hope in this new century for Christians everywhere to diligently hammer out the errors of a church that has drifted. There is a hunger that has been left unfed by much of our evangelical Christian preaching. But we should be hopeful about this new decade. We have learned important lessons. But we must do better in our dialogue if we are to truly reform society and the church. It is through constructive dialogue that we will experience better health care, a better economy, better security and other answers to injustice and suffering.

For me, personally, this dialogue includes new classes that I have been taking at Eastern Mennonite University. As a retired military veteran, I find myself involved in new discussion with some of the same people who had always condemned my participation in warfare. Yet, as we fellowship together, we craft a new story of our society. My military experience taught me to appreciate people across cultural barriers. And today, I am learning more about the hope for peace that I share with people I had previously not expected to join in partnership.

I have lived most of my life in evangelical Protestant circles where frequent references were made to the value of "prayer, fasting and waiting on the Lord." Where such dialogue is still common, I will say that, instead, we need to pray, fast, and wait before we join the next campaign bandwagon. Indeed, in our prayers, we might even need to ask God if the Reformation is over.

We Americans have often been described as arrogant, abusive, self-righteous, and many other undesirable adjectives, but we always have the freedom to look at ourselves in new ways. We are indeed much more: people who care, people who provide, and people who bring hope. Each day and each year, we must strive, through dialogue, to continue towards this Reformation.

‒ LISTENING TO THE INNER SELF ‒

by Dr. Laurel Clark

WHEN I WAS A YOUNG CHILD, I KNEW THAT THERE WAS SOMETHING IMPORTANT FOR ME TO DO WITH MY LIFE, BUT I DIDN'T KNOW WHAT IT WAS! I've always had a lot of interests, including writing, helping other people, art and design, and music. I went to college to discover what I was here to do, and graduated Phi Beta Kappa with no more idea of my "calling" than when I entered.

I considered going to law school, wanting to save the world and bring about justice. I thought about earning a Ph.D. in English and becoming a college professor to educate bright young minds. I thought about being an architect, to bring beauty to the world. But I was afraid that if I chose any one path I wouldn't be able to fulfill the others. I didn't really know how to make such a big decision about what to do with my life. I waited, hoping that something would "speak" to me.

I longed to hear an inner voice, or somehow know for certain what my purpose in life was and how to fulfill it. Then someone told me about "past life readings" conducted by the School of Metaphysics. At that time, in 1979, no one spoke about past lives. I was curious. I had a reading done, and instantly knew that it was telling me truth about myself. I became a student of metaphysics to learn how to interpret my dreams, how to develop intuition, how to visualize, how to meditate, how to still my outer mind (the busy chatter) to listen to my inner self. The inner listening aided me to become clearer about my purpose, my calling, and my destiny.

Soon after becoming a student of the School of Metaphysics I knew that I wanted to teach others what I was learning. I loved teaching, and soon after becoming a teacher I accepted the opportunity to direct a branch of the school. One thing led to another, and now I am a teacher, counselor, speaker, and interfaith minister. My home base is the College of Metaphysics, an intentional community on 1,500 acres of land in the Ozarks.

When I look back at my childhood dreams to have many avenues of expression, to help people, to live in a community with people of like minds and high ideals, I feel very fortunate that I have learned to listen to my inner voice and have followed the call to do what I am here to do.

✳

Some people look at their lives and identify a "turning point" or "life-changing moment." I don't know that I can identify one significant tipping point in my life, but I do see a recurring theme of loss and resurrection that has guided some of my choices and insights. When I was fifteen years old my father died. He had been sick with cancer for much of my childhood, although it was only in the last two years of his life that he seemed incapacitated by illness. I didn't even know that he had cancer until I was about thirteen. He was a remarkable man: well educated, charismatic and affectionate, with a great sense of humor. He stimulated me in many ways, inspiring me to think idealistically, to believe in myself, and to know that I was loved. When he died, it seemed as though a part of me died too. I didn't know how to express affection without him. I felt a deep sadness that seemed to pervade everything, and which settled into a dull depression in my early adult years.

When I became a student of metaphysics, and particularly when I became a teacher, much of the depression lifted. Giving to other people cured the sadness, although I didn't become a teacher for self-serving ends. I just became aware after awhile that teaching and serving other people brought me great joy.

At the age of 43, my husband died. This experience resonated with my childhood grief. My husband was much like my father: charismatic, affectionate, loving, and inspiring. His death was very difficult, as he was my closest friend and companion. Again, I discovered that focusing on aiding other people helped me to resolve much of the sadness. Writing and speaking about my experience at first, and then, later, aiding others dealing with grief, helped me in my own healing.

I have learned from these and other experiences of loss that love is much stronger than death. Giving brings joy that is stronger than any kind of temporary hurt. It is well worth it to love, to give and to be fully present with the people we are with. We never know how long they will be in our lives, so it is important to appreciate them in the present.

✳

I don't believe that we are here to "put our mark" on the world. I do believe that we each have a destiny to fulfill, and I view life like a big jigsaw puzzle or orchestra. Each person has a piece to fill that makes the puzzle whole; or if you like, each person is an instrument in our Maker's orchestra. By inner listening, we can each discern what our individual part that fulfills the greater plan is.

Personally, I draw upon the teachings of Holy Scriptures, mythology, and metaphorical writing because the images therein convey truth that is universal. I strive to understand what we all have in common as souls or spiritual beings and to live in alignment with universal law. I think that we each have a tremendous ability to understand wholeness and to live our ideals. One of the responsibilities we each have is to listen to what the inner self guides us to do, to listen to the inner urge that comes from our Creator. In other words, to do what we are called to do rather than making up what we think we should do.

I believe that life is not so much about "doing what I want to do;" it is more about "doing what the Creator wants me to do." In my opinion, "living the life of my dreams" concerns that I am being and becoming rather than what I "do" for a living. This is why I think that a daily practice of inner listening, such as meditation or interpreting dreams is an important element for anyone to know who I am so that I can share my real self with other people. I think this is true for all people.

I have found that people, who live a soul-centered existence, fulfilling an ideal that serves a higher good, the community or humanity, are personally fulfilled as they aid other people. They bring their joy into the lives of everyone they meet. This inner joy, expressed outwardly, makes life worth living. When people are inwardly fulfilled, they are kind and compassionate to others.

Living a life of your dreams makes everyone's life better!

— THE EXTRAORDINARY LIFE — OF AN ORDINARY WOMAN

by Barbara Musser

ༀ

FOR MOST OF MY LIFE, I'VE BEEN ON A LONG PATH OF TRANSFORMATION—DISCOVERING WHY I AM HERE. It's been a fantastic journey, and I've made a career of transformation. When I look back on it all, I think, I have lived an extraordinary life. I feel very blessed about that. But, it didn't start out that way.

I was a very sensitive, tuned-in kid. I felt like an alien in my own typical 1950s middle-class family. Our family looked great on the outside, except Dad was an alcoholic and Mom was codependent, and we didn't talk about anything. Growing up as a girl in that era, I was told that I was going to get married and have kids, so I didn't need college or a career. What's more, I suffered under sexual abuse. It felt like I lived in a big trap that I couldn't get out of. I became a handful to manage. I was angry, unhappy, and uncomfortable in my own skin.

I continued to chase what I thought would bring me happiness once I became an adult. I lived in Europe for a time and had some really interesting jobs, working hard within the corporate world to fill a gaping wound inside that I didn't even realize I had because I was so disconnected from my true self. Then, after ignoring many of those life lessons "knocks," I was diagnosed with breast cancer on my 37th birthday.

At the time, I had a big corporate job, was making lots of money, and had a closet full of suits. It was supposedly a good life, but when I asked myself, "If I had only a year to live, would I be doing this?" The answer was no. So I left.

✳

I started doing yoga and working with a wonderful therapist. I gobbled up books and meditated. At first, it was very painful because there were parts of me that I felt like I couldn't find. My therapist helped me to see that if I could just stop resisting myself and life so much, there might be some space for something else to show up. As I started to reconnect with myself, I realized that I needed to work on loving myself.

And so, I believe I loved myself back into health both physically and spiritually. The cancer was a spiritual turning point for me. I allowed myself to be supported because I really couldn't do it alone. Once I made that realization, things started to shift very fast. I began to understand: "Oh, this is how life can actually be!"

✳

Again, chasing happiness, I started a business doing yoga, meditation and visualization for people with cancer and heart disease. I was giving from my heart, from what I had learned and what had helped me. I wasn't giving because of what I expected to get in return; I was giving just for the sake of giving.

I loved my business, but while I was chasing happiness through yoga and teaching, I soon again found myself in another trap. I met my former husband, married him, and, against all advice, had a daughter. After her birth, we started a manufacturing business together, but after a few years, we closed the business and my marriage fell apart all at the same time. My whole world came crashing down. I was broke and alone with a two-year-old. It was another opportunity to reinvent and transform myself.

✳

I'd been involved for many years with an organization that did personal growth transformational workshops. I became inspired to become a facilitator. At the time, I had no idea how this could happen because they didn't need another facilitator, and there was no training program. I just knew that it was supposed to be. I met with the leaders in the organization who said, "We don't need you." But I didn't go away. I just kept knocking on that door, all the while thinking, "Am I nuts?"

Two years later, I began leading workshops, and I've been leading them for nearly 15 years. I also developed a private coaching practice during that time. I loved doing both. I wanted to take these two different things and combine them as my gift to the world in a bigger way. About a year ago, I decided that I was going to just do it without knowing how. I trusted that what I needed would become obvious to me when I needed it. I made that commitment in a really big way. The journey is still underway and I have no idea what the outcome will be.

The farther I go along the spiritual path, the more humbling it is. It's like I know less in some ways than I did before. Taking this leap of faith to bring my work into the world in a bigger way with no evidence has made my mind busier than ever. I sometimes find myself feeling quite worried about what will happen, because I've bet the ranch on this one. But life is about the journey and it's not a path for the faint of heart.

It's important to get comfortable being uncomfortable, because everything is always changing. Quantum physics tells us that we're in an ever-expanding universe, and spiritual law tells us that everything is for the urge of more life, which is expansion. Allowing yourself to expand along with this allows you to get into the flow if it. When you just stop fighting that flow, then life truly is an incredible ride.

⸺ Finding My Way Back Home ⸺ to Myself in Nature

by Daina Puodziunas

❧

When I divorced the father of my children, I was penniless and homeless with two daughters under the age of two. I was irresistibly drawn to a beautiful piece of land in the country that belonged to my mother. I used to spend the summers there with my grandparents while I was growing up. It had a small spring-fed lake, a half-mile muddy driveway (known by the locals as the driveway from hell), and was very far away from any neighbors.

I knew I could find the peace and healing I needed here. It was also a perfect place to raise children—wild, natural, beautiful… just like them! There was only one problem: I didn't have a driver's license. I was 30 years old and I had a driving phobia. It's interesting how a crisis can get us moving and doing things that otherwise we would never do. I learned how to drive!

On the property was a cement building with a tarpaper roof. I moved into the structure with my two daughters. It had no indoor plumbing, no source of heat, and half of it was flooded with water. I put some wooden skids on the floor and threw some used carpet on top of them. I quickly learned how to live in the country and appreciate all the very simple things in life: having a place to sit and bathe, cooking on a wood stove, and understanding why lime is used in outhouses! But most of all, I appreciated the peace, beauty, and solitude of nature.

Quickly, our home extended to the outdoors. We were spending more time outside than inside! This is when I began to experience the presence of God within me and within nature. Home was not just contained to the structure in which we were living anymore. It encompassed the entire outdoors, and it became my church where I learned how to meditate, contemplate and commune with God in a thousand and one ways.

✳

I feel that my strong connection with nature is a natural part of my Lithuanian heritage. Lithuanians are nature people. I remember my mother and grandmothers couldn't get their hands out of the soil as they created beautiful gardens and enchanting places to walk, sit and just be with nature. We all felt so at home in nature. I also remember large groups of people singing folk songs, dancing folk dances and playing accordions around big fires. I remember beautiful ceremonies where decorated wreaths with candles were carried away by the wind on the lake sending blessings to couples that were courting.

Because I feel so at home working with women, I created a business where I could share my passion for ceremony, nature, and the camaraderie that is available when women come together in a focused way. I designed women's retreats and transformational ceremonies of rebirth and renewal for women on a monthly basis for ten years. I also became a *doula* (Greek for "woman servant") who assists women in their care for a few weeks after they give birth. I worked with lay midwives, was a birthing coach who prepared women for natural childbirth, and was also a certified natural childbirth educator.

During that time, I became driven in creating a life that would provide my daughters with the very best I could give them. I created another business and became a supermom, commuting more than 80 miles a day to bring my daughters to private schools and to go to work.

After I accumulated enough money, in order to stay connected to nature, we moved into a temporary tent home for the summer and early fall months of one year. I designed and helped build a passive solar home that included large windows with beautiful panoramic views of the outdoors. This created the feeling that we were living outside even in the winter while being warm, cozy, and dry (no more wet floors). It was my dream come true!

✳

After many years of going at full speed, I suffered severe burnout and was diagnosed with an autoimmune disease at the start of my midlife. After my daughters moved out on their own, my home in the woods became a healing environment for me once again! I took a midlife sabbatical and learned how to discover a sense of home within myself.

I found that I had created many masks to survive a challenging life. Everyone knew me as fiercely independent, competent and confident. During the sabbatical, my insecurities, fears and tenderness which my strong exterior was covering up rose to the surface. I learned how to love and care for myself. I continue to learn how to feel comfortable being myself in the world without selling out. I also learned that we burn out (literally) not by giving away too much, but by trying to give what we ourselves do not yet possess!

During this time I literally read hundreds of books and wrote on extreme self care, getting out of codependent relationships, perfectionism, procrastination, values clarification, overcoming obstacles, moving through fear, universal principles, discovering our life's purpose, and creating a second life where our light can shine. I found that being true to ourselves takes an enormous amount of courage and that it's often only in midlife that we are willing to go through this journey to discover our authentic self.

I had a healing vision of the relationship between my inner grandmother and grandchild, which showed me how to fill myself with unconditional love and deeply care for myself. This is where the inspiration for the Midlife Fairy Godmothers™ came from. I also physically became a grandmother, and my grandchildren have been teaching me how to play at life and stop taking myself so seriously.

Growing up, I was not given the tools—nor encouraged—to discover who I really was, and to design my life around my strengths, talents and what matters most. But now we can! It's entirely up to us to take the first step. Only then will we find the fulfillment that so many of us crave when we find ourselves losing our identity and familiar way of life in midlife.

The spirit of home lies within us, and once we find it, we can carry it with us and feel at home wherever we may roam.

Enchanted blessings.

‒ On Boards and Broken Pieces ‒

by Paige Lanier Chargois

Winds of change and waves of disappointments can usher in unwanted storms in our lives, leaving us to wonder what to do with what's left.

There is a story in the New Testament, Acts 27, about a ship carrying the apostle Paul to prison in Rome. The ship, sailing in the Adriatic Sea, encountered a great storm. After enduring several days on their battered ship, the ship's crew finally spotted land. While attempting to reach safer waters, the ship ran aground on a sandbar and became so mired that the crew was unable to move the ship another inch. The sailors had off-loaded much of their cargo in a desperate attempt to lighten the ship, but they were unable to rescue the vessel. Everyone on board knew that it would not be capable of sailing to their original destination. Cold waves washed over the crew time and time again as they struggled to keep themselves and their cargo intact. Bodies were bruised. Hopes were dashed.

The ship's centurion was their last hope. He didn't want the ship to go down. He told those who could swim to jump overboard and make it to shore because the waters were not extremely deep and he knew that any good swimmer could handle it. However, the greater problem wasn't with those crew members who could swim but with those who could not. There was no lifeboat. The centurion then turned to those who could not swim and encouraged them to jump overboard and grab hold of a part of the ship that had split off or some bit of their cargo that was floating in the waters.

His advice to them was: "You can make it to shore on boards and broken pieces!"

Sometimes we have to dig mighty deep into our emotional reservoir to find a board or broken piece we can grab hold of for survival's sake. But something is always there. For some, that broken piece might be faith; for others it might be emotional resolve or just the mental doggedness and acuity to bulldoze through adverse circumstances.

Marriage failed? Business collapsed? Friends deserted you? Family members misused or abused you? Job downsized? Financial calamity? Boss doesn't like you? Whatever it is or was that ushered a catastrophe into your life doesn't have the final say in your life. You do. Like being a crew member on that ship, the storm does not determine your destiny any more than the ship breaking up or getting stuck in a sandbar determined their destiny.

Grab hold of one of the pieces that is left – something is always left – and continue the journey towards your dreams! Though the ship broke up and lost its seaworthiness, it offered the crew two other options: swim if you can or grab hold of a flotation device and float your way to shore.

Life is not easy. It would not be so beautiful if it were easy. The stretch of the human mind or the depths of our emotional capacity or our normal, human ability to regroup or to heal ourselves in a myriad of ways all speak to the life requirement – indeed the mandate – to make it to shore even if it is on boards and broken pieces.

PART II

❧

LIFE STORIES

"SPREAD LOVE EVERYWHERE YOU GO. LET NO ONE
EVER COME TO YOU WITHOUT LEAVING HAPPIER."

— *Mother Teresa*

"LEARN TO ENJOY EVERY MINUTE OF YOUR LIFE. BE HAPPY NOW.
DON'T WAIT FOR SOMETHING OUTSIDE OF YOURSELF TO MAKE YOU
HAPPY IN THE FUTURE. THINK HOW REALLY PRECIOUS IS THE TIME
YOU HAVE TO SPEND, WHETHER IT'S AT WORK OR WITH YOUR FAMILY.
EVERY MINUTE SHOULD BE ENJOYED AND SAVORED."

— *Earl Nightingale*

"A MAN IS A SUCCESS IF HE GETS UP IN THE MORNING
AND GOES TO BED AT NIGHT, AND IN BETWEEN
HE DOES WHAT HE WANTS TO DO."

— *Bob Dylan*

CHAPTER FOUR:

❦

Life Lessons

In a glade across the river lived a king with a daughter who grew up with grace and sunshine. She would one day be queen, and so the king promised the princess's hand in marriage to the suitor who solved the riddle: *How do people learn?*

Day and night men waited to guess the answer, and soon the line stretched over the hills and through the trees. The hunter said, "We learn from experience." The teacher said, "We learn from others." A cobbler with a wooden leg said, "We learn from loss," and a cook with freckles and four brothers said, "We learn from love."

The king shook his head in disappointment. Only one man with a perfect back and gait remained, and he stepped forward, faced the king and said, "They are all right and they are all wrong. Man can learn from every one of these ways and more as long as he keeps his eyes open and his feet ready to cut a new path." And the king jumped up, joined the man's hand with his daughter's and crowned him as the future prince.

The true stories in this section show us how we can learn life lessons from love, loss, friendship and more–as long as our hearts and minds allow.

— Dr. Leslie Beth Wish,
author of "A Heart Grown Deep Like the Rivers"

~ The Lifeboat ~

by John Graham

I DIDN'T LISTEN TO MY HEART FOR A LONG TIME, UNTIL I ALMOST DIED.

Jammed back against the railing of the SS Prinsendam, en route from Vancouver to Tokyo, I sat next to my thirteen-year-old daughter Malory at four in the morning, crowded onto the stern amid countless anxious passengers. We watched black smoke boil up out of the bowels of the giant ship. They brought out the ship's orchestra and started playing show tunes from the musical Oklahoma. Once or twice an airplane flew overhead and dumped carbon dioxide canisters. Worried looking firemen clamored up and down the stairs.

At 4:30 a.m., we were ordered to lifeboat stations. Malory and I were assigned to lifeboat number two, far up on the port bow. Malory counted over 90 people waiting there, but a sign on the boat said it was made for 48. We were there perhaps ten minutes when a dull explosion rocked the ship, followed by the shattering of glass. The heat had blown out the windows in the dining rooms and salons. The flames gulped the rush of oxygen, and within thirty seconds, the whole middle of the ship was wrapped in flames that leaped into the night sky.

Jammed back against the railings by the flames, some people screamed. Others moaned quietly. A panic would have sent people into the water, but to jump into the Gulf of Alaska at night, in October, meant certain death: even if you could swim, you'd die from hypothermia very quickly.

✳

I worked in the United States Foreign Service for fifteen years. Most of what I did was connected to wars, revolutions, and arms sales. But mixed in with all that hardball stuff was a set of ideals—about peace, about justice in the world, about ending the suffering caused by wars, revolutions, and arms sales. Those ideals were a small, nagging voice from my heart, and I ignored it for many years because of the power and glamour of my job.

Eventually that power and glamour began to sit like a bad meal in the pit of my stomach. Something was missing, and I didn't know what it was.

I left the Foreign Service in 1980, confused and unhappy. My heart was still trying to talk to me. I listened just enough so that I could tell my friends about my ideals for a better world. I liked the way they patted me on the shoulder and said what a fine fellow I was to have those ideals. But I was all talk.

I wanted to make some money, so I tried to set up a business as a consultant and that failed. Then I applied to work in banks, and that failed. So a friend who knew I could speak well suggested I hire myself out to give lectures on cruise ships. I could tell stories from my years in the Foreign Service.

So that's what I did. I got a job as ship's lecturer on the SS Prinsendam, sailing from Vancouver to Tokyo. I got to bring along my daughter, and all I would have to do was give two lectures.

So Malory and I boarded the ship in Vancouver, and three days later were way up in the Gulf of Alaska, heading for Japan.

That night, we had been awakened at around two a.m. by a call over the public address system. A voice told us that there had been a fire in the engine room, but that it had been put out. Passengers were requested to come up to the ship's lounge while fans blew the smoke out of the corridors. Free drinks would be served. Reassured by the captain's message, Malory and I didn't even take our life jackets with us.

The lounge, however, was full of acrid black smoke, so the passengers spilled out onto the deck. It was October in the Gulf of Alaska, and the night air was cold. Some people pulled cloths off the tables or curtains off the windows and used them as blankets. There was no moon, and a dancing green belt of Northern Lights was so bright it hid the stars. Beneath it, a dark, still ocean spread in all directions. But the most interesting sight was behind us: any fool could see that the smoke coming up from below was getting blacker and thicker. That fire couldn't possibly have been out. The public address message was a lie.

✳

More than two hours later, after we had been assigned to lifeboat number two, the flames grew stronger, and many on the ship's deck began to panic. Suddenly the captain appeared on the bridge in full-dress uniform with a microphone in his hand. "I regret to inform you," he said, "but we have lost the battle with the flames. We must now abandon the ship. Please follow the instructions of the crew."

The ship's six lifeboats and four life rafts began to load 550 passengers and crew. The seamen kept fouling the lines—nobody thought this almost-new ship would ever face conditions like this. But by a series of miracles, all the boats hit the water safely.

It was now 5:30 a.m. and still very dark. The sea then was calm, so the little boats floated low but well.

✳

Almost as soon as we hit the water, a stiff breeze began to blow from the west, and dark clouds erased the Northern Lights that had spread across the sky. The lifeboats began to roll gently in a light chop. A serious storm, the tail end of Typhoon Victor, was headed our way. The rescue effort, when it started, was a race against time.

Currents shoved the lifeboats away from each other and from the burning ship. At first light, three helicopters appeared, sent from shore bases 140 miles away. Each began picking people out of the boats one-by-one, using a metal chair at the end of a long cable. When a chopper had a full load of eight or nine people, it took them to the deck of an oil tanker that had answered the SOS and was steaming in our direction. At about noon, I saw Malory go spinning off into space and into a helicopter.

The storm continued to worsen. By five p.m., there were only sixteen of us left in lifeboat number two, but we were now in thirty-foot seas with 60-knot winds and visibility of less than 100 yards. The helicopter came back one last time and took eight more, but it wouldn't be back—it was suicidal to fly in weather this bad. So now the only hope for the eight of us who were left in lifeboat number two was that a Coast Guard cutter, frantically crisscrossing the ocean in this wild storm, would find us.

By 5:30 p.m., visibility was down to fifty yards. We were all deathly seasick. There was no cover. The crest of every tenth wave or so blew off in the gale, sending torrents of seawater into the lifeboat so cold they sucked the breath out of us. We were dying of hypothermia. We couldn't last three or four more hours before we would either die where we sat, or be thrown out of the boat and drowned.

But the key thing was that now there was only a half-hour of daylight left. The odds were small enough that the cutter could find us in the fading light, but they disappeared completely with the dark. We had no flares and no lights. The radio didn't work. I was tapping out an SOS I remembered from Boy Scouts and it was going nowhere. It seemed certain that our fates would be settled by the darkness—in half an hour.

It was only then that it occurred to me that I might actually die. Until that moment, I'd assumed that this crisis, like all the others I had faced in my life, would take me to the brink but not past. And before, when I'd faced odds this bad, I'd never had this much time to think about it. All those other near misses—whether a bullet in Vietnam or a fall while mountain climbing—had been sudden and passed just as swiftly. This time, I had half an hour before my fate was sealed—then three or four more hours before I would lose consciousness.

✳

I never considered myself a particularly religious person, but let me tell you, in circumstances like these, most would feel led to prayer. But what I did wasn't much of a prayer. Instead I got mad. "It's not fair," I said to whoever up there might be listening. "I've left the Foreign Service and I really want to start a new life of making the world a better place. I've got the skills to do that. So how is it now, just as I'm beginning, I'm being wiped out? It doesn't make any sense. It doesn't make one damn bit of sense."

The more I reflected, the madder I got. Looking through the storm into the fading light, realizing that I was going to die, I condensed my anger into just one word, and I turned my head up and soundlessly hurled that word into the slashing rain: "Why?"

I never knew what the other seven people in that lifeboat saw or heard at that moment, but I know what I did. I heard a voice that drowned out the storm.

"Stop kidding yourself," the voices said, "and stop kidding Me. You've been ignoring what your heart has been telling you for years, and you still are. You love talking about your ideals to your friends but you do nothing more than talk. You try to become a consultant and a banker, and that doesn't work. Then you sign up to lecture on this cruise ship, and if you get out of this one alive you'll find something else to waste your life on.

"So now you have a choice. You can keep running away from your ideals, and you'll die out here. Or you can get serious about your life and do what you know you need to do. It's your choice."

I looked at the other seven shapes in that lifeboat. None of them seemed to have heard anything. I was so seasick, I couldn't even dry heave. I could hardly feel my feet and hands. I had no energy, no resources left. No will to resist.

"Okay," I said silently into the storm. "Okay."

What happened next sounds straight out of a grade-B movie but so help me, it's the truth. At that instant—an instant of total surrender—a dark shape burst out of the storm off the port side. It was the Coast Guard cutter Boutwell, heading right at us in such a way that it would have cut us in two had the lookout not seen us.

✳

All of us have a purpose in life, and that the path to that purpose is service. Some of us find that path easily. Others, like me, are so self-centered that it takes a near-death experience before we see the way.

I came back to New York after we were rescued, and I kept my promise. I started developing and delivering the work as a peacebuilder that has now consumed me for three decades.

A Heart Grown Deep Like the Rivers:
A Tale of Love from an Un-Wicked Stepmother

by Dr. Leslie Beth Wish

❧

THEY WARNED ME. "OUTSIDER," THEY SAID. "That's what you'll be. All effort, no return... Nothing comes from raising another man's child."

They were right and they were wrong. No child could grow in me. His little girl would be a bonus, a chance for more than a toe in the river but a swim in the sea—a fuller life. And so, I said yes to him.

She was eight, with braids as dark as the earth and eyes the color of amber, and I knew I could love her for longer than those things would last because I had a gift from my past that they could not understand.

✳

I met Daisy when I was three. She was nineteen, only a girl herself.

Daisy explained to me years later that she had lied to my parents, saying she was twenty-one. She had to get away—there was this boyfriend of her aunt's. She read the ad for a live-in girl, saw a door open, and walked in to my little life. I didn't know the word "rescue" at the time, but Daisy did. And when she put her dark arms around me, we clung to each other in a hug like a raft.

Besides the easiness of love, Daisy taught me how to dance. "Finger-popping," she called it. We practiced in the basement to the beats of songs from what they called "the Negro station." But my heart had already rid me of colors I didn't need to see. Once, when an eye doctor who fixed my lazy eye asked me if anyone in my family wore glasses, I responded, "Daisy." My parents were amused by my response, and thought this made a good story to tell all their friends to make them laugh.

I was almost ten when I understood that no woman with black skin could truly be my blood relative. However, by then, Daisy was the one who greeted my brother and me at the door after school, who baked cookies, made sure there was chocolate—not just plain— milk and put blankets hot out of the dryer on us whenever we were sick.

She plaited my hair, styled it for school dances, and told me that reds were my color. On nights of thunder and lightening, I'd tiptoe downstairs to her bedroom in the cellar and huddle with her as we sang songs in between the flashes. Her voice was full of stories, and I would nestle in her arms that smelled like almonds and fall asleep.

She took me with her to her church where all the ladies wore big hats and everyone danced and swayed to the music, and I felt as bright as the sun. She became my first audience when I had to practice speeches for school, and taught me that God gave girls only so many kisses, and warned me that if I kissed the wrong boys I wouldn't have any kisses left for the right ones. My lips wouldn't be able to pucker and it would be too late.

She stopped my tears when the girls at school were small and mean, and she explained jealousy and the sides of life that everyone should know about to get through it. She was smart and wise, with an education from the bayous, and woods, scrap crops, and yet still kind. And so I didn't understand why my parents were mean to her, robbed her of the simplest things like the importance of picking out her own nightstand or bedspread. They yelled at her, poked her, shook their heads at her sayings and never saw the closeness between us.

And then it happened. I never thought it would because I believed she was my mother and sister forever. Daisy left. She fell in love and found a place of her own. "Oh," my mother said, "she'll still come to clean and cook, so why are you so upset at your age? Fifteen is too old for you to cry about it."

I cried. The house turned dangerous, all love gone, and I wondered if houses could crumble like in horror stories from lack of it.

I would meet Daisy at church, call her at night. She was my living diary. I told her about boys, my dates, how I was saving my kisses, and she told me she was sorry but that she had to leave. She met a man and just had to go through another door in her life. My parents made her cry and made her feel like a butterfly that couldn't fly. She would have left earlier, she said, years earlier when she could have shared a place with the girl, Maddie, from across the street. "We could ride the bus together, save up for an education…" Maddie told her, "go out dancing and on dates." But Daisy said she couldn't leave me, not in that house, not being so young, not in a house where people yelled mean things at each other and held back even meaner thoughts. No, she couldn't leave. I was her girl, she told Maddie.

Daisy was the mother and sister of my heart, the only flower I will ever like, the woman who took me to a world as big as the sky and sea, and grew me into a strong, brave, and caring person.

✳

Daisy was the one who sacrificed for me, the way good parents do. And I have had the chance to do the same that she had, providing love without strings to a wonderful child. I became the fairy stepmother my husband and his girl needed. Today this daughter-of-my-heart is a successful attorney. Raising her was one of the best gifts that I have ever passed on.

Step-parenting is not easy. Family problems are one of the top reasons second marriages fail. To love another's child and to serve as parenting coach to your partner requires maturity bigger than the sky and sea. It means balancing being both an insider and an outsider at the same time. It often means giving more than you receive, not being the first on the list. But it is also an opportunity—as the songs in Daisy's church taught me—to sing to the heavens, to build a home of love for another, and to give and grow a heart deep like the rivers.

— THE SPIRITUAL SIDE OF MOTHERING: —
IS THERE ONE?

by Leta Hamilton

❧

AS A MOTHER OF THREE YOUNG BOYS BETWEEN THE AGES OF TEN MONTHS AND FIVE YEARS OLD, I HAVE TO DEAL WITH MANY ASPECTS OF LIFE THAT MOST WOULD CONSIDER MUNDANE, TEDIOUS AND DOWNRIGHT DEMEANING.

For example, not long ago I found myself in the bathroom of the local skate park hoisting my five-year-old son's backside into the sink for a wash while my three-year-old danced around the room and my baby struggled to escape from the stroller.

I should have known there would be trouble when my son (who shall remain nameless— he may read this someday and I will try to at least spare him some of the embarrassment) had been playing quietly by himself in the rocks adjacent to the skate park.

I was busy chatting with another mom when I looked over to Wi… oops, my son, and the thought registered, "I bet he needs to go to the bathroom." But instead of interrupting my "grown-up" conversation, I just carried on and, boy, did I pay the price.

After washing his backside, I had the unenviable task of washing his underwear in the sink (again, the location shall remain anonymous in case this happens to be a skate park you also frequent). Then I had to put one of my baby's diapers on him because his "accident" had leaked through to his pants. After what seemed an eternity in this public toilet, we went on with our day. I took the vacuum cleaner to the repair shop. I went to the bank. I sent a fax. Oh, the joys of motherhood!

My son took it in stride. He has a much more positive attitude to life than I do. By that point, the dial on my grump-o-meter had reached *Mommy Monster* and I felt the characteristic green skin, tail and pointy ears coming out. The Mommy Monster isn't very much fun for anyone to be around—including myself—but *goshdarnit*, is there anyone in the whole wide world who would be smiling gaily after washing icky-gooey *poo* off his/her oldest son's favorite pair of Spiderman boxer shorts?

Which leads me to my next question… What would Jesus do? I believe in the tenets of love, compassion and forgiveness, but I think it's a fair question to ask. How would a "spiritual" person handle any number of situations in which a typical mother finds herself on any given day? Would the Dalai Lama have handled three kids, poop and a public lavatory with the graceful demeanor displayed in his photographs? I want to know!

✳

I would love to trade places with a monk for just a day. After my blissful sojourn to the silence of a pristine mountaintop hermitage, we would compare notes as to how long he reckoned it would take him back at the monastery to recover from his one day of mothering and how long it would take me to feel the grump-o-meter tilt decidedly in the direction of Mommy Monster. If I had to wager a guess right now, I'd say four weeks for him and 28 seconds for me.

I consider myself a fairly spiritual person. I go to church. I read books a-plenty on the meaning of life and the key to finding balance between mind, body and spirit. Heck, I even wrote a whole book on the spiritual wisdom of the toddler... Mommy Monster and the kind of person I would like to *think I am* do not go together. Why, then, do the pointy ears and tail keep resurfacing?

Let's face it, humans are fallible. Great teachings are a place to seek guidance on how to be the best person one can possibly be, but the true test comes in the day-to-day events of one's life. Sometimes what you read, what you know and what you do are very different things. Anyone who has ever been around a child knows that composure and motherhood are mutually exclusive states of being a lot of the time.

Jesus, Buddha, Krishna and all the great spiritual teachers of history taught us mere mortals how to find true happiness through compassion, service, forgiveness and love. We still have to do the inner work to remove the blocks that keep us from feeling compassionate, selfless, forgiving or loving. For me, being spiritual means that I am striving to get better at being the best possible version of myself I can imagine. It is a commitment to putting into practice characteristics that I know will make me that person. It doesn't mean, however, that I have to be perfect by tomorrow.

It is a given for most of us that there is a spiritual side to life. Humankind throughout the ages has asked the big questions about the meaning of existence, and cultures everywhere from time immemorial have found great solace in the Divine. Humanness and spirituality are intrinsically linked, but is there a spiritual side of mothering?

Does God exist in poopy Spiderman boxer shorts?

✳

The spiritual side of mothering isn't in the events that occur "out there." It's in my reaction to them. Here's what my five-year-old taught me about the spiritual side of mothering after the "incident:"

1   Just because you poop in your pants doesn't mean your whole day is ruined. This, too, shall pass.

2.   No matter what happens, if you are a mother, it is more likely than not you will have something in your bag that will at least "patch" the situation until you get home. We get to be creative in ways that great artists can only dream of.

3. If you are out with three small children and you are the only adult, yes things might get a bit stressful. This is where prayer comes in really handy. There is no pair of Spiderman boxer shorts too poopy for God, the Universe, or whatever one chooses to call a higher power. When all else fails, surrender through prayer.

4. Everything happens for a reason. Unexpectedly bathing my child in a public restroom sink meant that I arrived at the bank much later than I had originally intended. When I finally did get there, an old friend who I had not seen in over a year was arriving to go to the grocery store next door. We reconnected and now have a play date set up for our sons. If not for what had happened back at the skate park, I completely would have missed her. Call it serendipity, coincidence, or Divine Intervention—I am grateful to be back in contact with this amazing woman.

5. Stressful, frustrating, annoying moments come and go, but when all is said and done, I still have three healthy, happy kids who charm the socks off of my husband and me about 96 percent of the time. (Well, let's say 96 percent of the time for my husband and 90 percent of the time for me!) I have a car to drive me to the skate park. I have a house to live in and food to feed my family. I have more than most people in this world. It's easy to take that for granted when you are in the midst of the latest crisis. However, when one truly knows and appreciates the gifts they have been given in this life, it is much easier to tolerate the seemingly intolerable.

✳

I am sure that if I dug even deeper, I would find more valuable spiritual lessons and insights into the spiritual side of mothering. That is the nature of spiritual inquest. All you really have to do is ask the question and you have already found the answer. Is there a spiritual side of mothering? Yes. If there weren't, I would never have thought to ask the question in the first place.

I still would like to know how Jesus would have handled my situation. He never had any kids (unless you believe the *Da Vinci Code* is fact instead of fiction), but he also said that the Kingdom of God belongs to the children. In a way, motherhood is the most spiritual path one can take in this life, for it is the ultimate test of practicing what you preach when you are surrounded by all manner of bodily functions. Children are still learning the ropes of how to fit in and what their place is in the world. As mothers, we are their first guides. How much more spiritual can you get?

We all have those moments when Mommy Monster replaces Zen Mommy. How long Mommy Monster stays in residence is in direct correlation to how quickly I acknowledge the spiritual side of mothering and the spiritual side of "me." The more I look to my children and their antics for spiritual lessons and insights, the more I tame Mommy Monster. Then, after Zen Mommy returns, I ask myself what I want my children to remember about me? Which persona will stand out in their mind? It doesn't have to be all one or the other, but what will the essence of their memory be when I am long gone from this physical life? I don't want them to remember a mother with a grump-o-meter permanently set to maximum.

So I continue to dig deeper into the spiritual side of mothering in the hopes that when my baby turns five and doesn't tell me he has to go to the bathroom when we are out in public, I'll deal with the situation as a perfectly poised Zen Mommy. I'll feel only unconditional love and compassion as I reassess the day's agenda to accommodate my unenviable new task on the to-do list.

It's a good thing I have another four years between now and then to figure out exactly how to do that.

— Who Are You Calling Grandma? —

by Maridel Bowes

❧

When the unexpected news of my impending grandmother-hood arrived after the expiration of my "mid-life" warranty, I wasn't ready! The famed trimesters ahead reverberated with the echo of life lived, but without expectation of a re-run. After all, I'd had my tubes not just tied, but seared shut. Biological trimesters were officially off the roster. Yet here I was, facing nine months of déjà *voo-doo*: my grandchild in the body of another woman. Ready or not, I had entered what I now call *The Grand Triathlon*.

I was puzzled by my feeling of unreadiness, but I was also curious. Why the reticence? Why not "*Wahoo!*" instead, like so many women my age? I had to know. So I turned to the companion that had helped me sort out my feelings for as long as I could remember: my journal. In the early stages of this process, most of my "journaling" didn't take written form, but was logged into my heart through thoughts, feelings and dialogue. Then random notes appeared. And finally, in the seventh month of my grand-pregnancy, the writing gave birth to itself.

✱

My first (and recurring) roadblock to "*Wahoo!*" was predictable enough. Here I was, ambivalent about even being a grandmother and at the same time already obsessed with this query: "Who gets the baby next Christmas?!!" Underneath that dither lay the true source of my conflict. It was insecurity that, in the familial scheme of things, I would be trumped by the maternal grandparents who were still married, lived closer and had means I didn't have. And my remarried ex-husband closely followed suit. I could see the handwriting on the prenatal wall. I would be the "Thanksgiving Grandma," the "No-Grandpa Grandma," the "Not-as-Many-Goodies Grandma."

Yet, with that insight and its accompanying torrent of feelings, something else dawned. Those feelings were based on fear—not some curse cast by The Reality Witch. I started to look around at other Baby Boomer "grandmothers" who dubbed themselves "Nana," "Nonnie," and "Gigi." I realized the question should be, what kind of person did I want my grandchild to know? What would transcend miles, money, and marital status? How could I be grand in my own inimitable way? The *Wahoo!* was starting to shimmer on my inner horizon.

But before I could whoop out loud, the oldest of all heir-related issues came up for air. Miffed that the maternal grandparents were taking such a heavy hand in the naming of the child they assumed would be of their preferred gender, my new focus grew blurry. And I knew the only thing that would restore clarity again was something I preferred not to do: a bit of self-investigation.

Oh, I might be mute on the issue of the baby name, but simmering inside my skull were vibrant views on childbirth, breastfeeding, and daycare. And underneath each of these agendas sat the great-grandmommy of Control. I'd worked on this nemesis considerably, mind you. But I had yet to apply it to this particular phase of my evolution. Would the need for control infect my budding matriarchy, or would I have the courage to pioneer a new level of letting go? Could I deepen my motto of "Trust the Process" when I wasn't a voting member of the board that would make these crucial decisions? Now I was beginning to understand the roots of my resistance.

✳

Early in the journey, I'd wrestled with questions like, "will I recognize my grand-fetus when I open the envelope sent by its sonogram-smitten parents?" But as the time of the birth grew closer, new questions closed in. Having divested myself yet again of the illusions of control, was I willing to scale the heights of "Mount Caring" without that cherished placebo? Was I willing to fling open the doors of my heart knowing that hallelujah or heartbreak were equal opportunities for growth? Was I willing not only to let go, but unwilling to hold back?

On the morning of the birth, I stood huddled in the entourage of waiting family members, our differences cast to the winds of new life moving through our hearts. All of my reservations about becoming a grandmother had been sorted out and sprouted wings. I could no longer remember their names. I was ready.

From my vantage point at the end of the hall, I saw my firstborn emerge from the delivery room with his firstborn in his arms. As he walked toward us, each step christened our new names and brought us one step closer to the pulse of lineage. Justin presented his child like the hero returning with the Holy Grail. And a holy moment it was, all of us wrapped inside it, gazing on the face we already adored.

When we allow any of life's passages to jostle us from our assumptions, to make an exposé of our insecurities and propel us into our own evolution, we make room for magic. Except that in the case of a first grandchild's birth, even "magic" isn't a word-vessel large enough to hold this one-of-a-kind elixir. For unlike anything that has come before, it offers us our very best shot at unconditional love. And that is the deepest, most cell-reverberating *Wahoo!* on the planet!

— THE POWER OF MAKING A PROMISE — ESPECIALLY TO YOUR MOTHER!

by Matthew Cossolotto

SEVERAL YEARS AGO, WHEN I WAS THINKING ABOUT WRITING A BOOK ABOUT THE HABITS OF FAILURE AND SUCCESS, I FREQUENTLY SPOKE ABOUT MY IDEAS WITH MY MOTHER. My mother was a gifted writer in her own right and I enjoyed kicking creative ideas like this around with her. But even though I talked a lot about the book, I never actually got around to finishing it.

My mother kept after me about writing the book, and after she became very ill with cancer, I made a fateful decision. I wanted to give her something as a goodbye gift, something that I knew would mean a great deal to her. When she was literally on her deathbed with only a few weeks to live, I made a promise to her. I promised her that I would finish writing the book and that I would dedicate it to her memory.

We both fought back tears when I said this. We knew that she would not live to see the book published. But in that instant, the book became much more than an idea or a goal. It was now a tangible reality. I had crossed the Rubicon. There was no turning back, and she and I both knew it. The idea of having the book we had talked so much about dedicated to her memory meant a great deal to her. I could see it in her eyes.

My mother looked up at me with a determined look on her face: "You do that Matthew. You do that!" I'll never forget the look on her face when I made that promise. Her countenance lit up and she smiled brightly despite the terrible pain she was experiencing.

I'm proud to say that I fulfilled that promise to my mother. I published my first book a few years after my mother died, and the second edition of the book was released by Morgan James Publishing on March 1, 2009, my mother's birthday. I included the following dedication: *In loving memory of my mother, Virginia Hope (Ludascher) Butler.*

*

I did it, Mom! Finally! I can honestly say that this book would never have been completed without the promise I made to you.

I'm not especially proud to admit that it took a solemn promise to my dying mother to give me the inspiration I needed to finish that book. But there is a powerful lesson here, for me and for many others. When you make a promise to your mother, failure is not an option!

More generally, there is an important personal empowerment lesson here. Instead of setting a bunch of vague goals, I encourage you to make a few promises to people you care about. If you really want to make sure you accomplish a particular goal—to quit smoking, to lose weight, to stop drinking, or to write that book you've been talking about for years— make that promise. Your integrity will then be on the line, *big time*, and it's much more difficult to turn your back on a solemn promise than it is to ignore a goal or a half-hearted New Year's Resolution.

If you make that promise to someone who means a great deal to you, you'll get it done because you know in your heart that if you don't, you will be disappointing that person and yourself. You'll begin to close the gap—as I did—between your performance and potential, helping to jumpstart your personal journey towards change.

Take it from me: making a promise and fulfilling it truly is a powerful example of personal change you can believe in.

— FACING DIVORCE: HOW DO I TELL MY SON? —

by Rosalind Sedacca

❧

I'VE FACED MANY DIFFICULT MOMENTS IN MY LIFE. Who hasn't? But preparing to tell my son that I would be divorcing his father was absolutely one of the worst. The emotions were overwhelming: gut-wrenching fear, anxiety, incredible guilt—and the oppressive weight of shame.

My son, after all, was innocent. He was a sweet 11-year-old who loved his father and mother dearly. He certainly did not deserve this.

I struggled with the anxiety for weeks in advance. When should I tell him? How should I tell him? And most frightening of all, *what should I say?* How do you explain to a child that the life he has known is about to be disrupted—changed—forever? How do you explain to a child that none of this is his fault? How do you reassure him that life will go on, that he will be safe, cared for and loved, even after his parents' divorce? And, even more intimidating, how do you prepare him for all the unknowns looming ahead when you're not sure yourself how it will all turn out?

I needed a plan, a way of conveying all that I wanted to say to him in a way that he could grasp.

✳

While my son was still a child, he was old enough to feel the tension in our home that had been escalating for years. He heard the irritation in our voices when his father and I spoke… the arguments that would flair up suddenly in the midst of routine conversations… the sarcastic inflections as well as the deafening silence when we were beyond words, and engulfed in frustration and anger.

Silently, my son was experiencing it all and, not surprisingly, began to show signs of stress. Sometimes it came in the form of headaches. Other times it was his tears that revealed the pain he felt when helpless to stop what he heard. Often he acted out, showing us his escalating temper. Our son was quietly filling up with rage about controlling a situation that was out of his control.

Most frustrating of all was that his father and I knew better than to fight in front of our son. But as our unhappiness together grew over time, we lost a handle on what we knew and gave in to what we felt. It was a mistake I will always regret because my innocent child, the person I loved more than anyone in the universe, was paying the price.

✳

I wrote a list for myself of what was most important for me to convey to my son, Cassidy, when I—or both his father and I—spoke to him. Six points stood out as most essential:

1. This is not your fault.
2. You are, and always will be, safe.
3. Mom and Dad will always be your parents.
4. Mom and Dad will always love you.
5. This is about change, not about blame.
6. Things will work out okay.

But… how do I say all that? Everything I tried brought up more questions than answers: How do I begin? How do I prepare myself to answer all his questions? How do I cope with the inevitable tears? What happens next?

One night in bed at 4 a.m., while my troubled mind rehashed my insecurities, a thought came to me that resonated in a powerful way. I remembered that my son always enjoyed looking through the family photo albums, primarily because they were filled with photos of him. He liked seeing his baby pictures and watching himself change as he grew. The albums were like a storybook of his life.

What if I prepared a photo album for my son that told the story of our family in pictures and words? The storybook concept gave him something tangible he could hold on to, and read over again and again, to help him grasp what was about to transpire. It would explain, in language he could understand, why this was happening and what to expect.

Rather than rehearsing a conversation that felt like a minefield of possible mistakes and detours, the storybook would give me a written, pre-planned script that was well thought through in advance. The idea still had merit the next morning. The more I thought about it, the more it seemed to be the best option, both for my son, and for us, his parents.

✳

When the storybook was completed, I showed it to my husband. It was important to me that we both agree about the message we were conveying to our child.

While my husband was angry with me for initiating our divorce, he understood that the point of our storybook was not to air our differences, but to show as much support to our son, during this difficult time, as was possible. He agreed the book was well done and important.

On the evening we set aside, my husband and I sat down with Cassidy and told him we had put together a storybook photo album about our family. He was immediately interested.

As I started reading about changes in the family, tensions, disagreements, and sad times, I watched as tears pooled up in my son's eyes. By the time I reached the end of the story, he was weeping uncontrollably.

And then, as a family, we talked, cried, hugged, answered questions, and consoled one another.

The deed was done. It was awful to go through. But somehow, having the book as something to reread was helpful for my son. We talked about the impending divorce many times in the next weeks and even after the divorce itself. Sometimes we'd refer back to passages in the book as a reminder that Mom and Dad will love him forever and everything will be okay.

The book also helped my husband and me remember that, despite our differences, our frustrations and disappointments, we were still both Cassidy's Mom and Dad, and always will be.

✳

It has been more than a decade since I prepared that storybook about our family. I have since remarried, and my son has graduated college and embarked on an exciting career as a veterinary cardiologist.

As a grown young man he is still very close to both his father and me. He tells us, much as he hated our decision at the time, he now believes we were wise to get a divorce and move on with our lives, both of us choosing more suitable mates.

When I approached him with my idea about sharing our family storybook with others who are facing divorce, he enthusiastically agreed it was a great idea. I am proud to say he wrote the book's introduction.

― THE UNEXPECTED JOURNEY ―

by Alberta Sequeira

IN 1990, LIFE THREW ME A CURVE, WHEN MY FATHER, ONE-STAR BRIGADIER GENERAL, ALBERT L. GRAMM, SR. OF SOUTH DENNIS, MASSACHUSETTS, WAS DIAGNOSED WITH TERMINAL CANCER. I called my place of employment and took an immediate two-week leave of absence. I joined my mother, four siblings and the hospice professionals in caring for my father's everyday needs.

Dad had been one of the commanding officers of the 26th Yankee Division during World War II. He fought throughout Europe in some famous campaigns. He had been at Lorraine and Metz, and had taken part in the Battle of the Bulge, to name a few. He had promised Our Lady that if he came home safe to his family, he'd say the rosary every day for the rest of his life. He was struggling to keep that pledge to her.

After his passing, I came to understand that this remarkable man, with his military background, had more interesting experiences for me to explore than I had realized. His service background had been hidden from us. While growing up, I looked at him as just being my dad.

Without any planning on our part, our destiny in life can sometimes change direction. I was supposed to be enjoying retired life, relishing the opportunities to travel to tropical islands that offered warm weather, beautiful, clear, blue-crystal waters for swimming and boating, and white sandy beaches on which to soak up the sun, and maybe adventuring out to try snorkeling. This spare time would give me the long neglected chance to visit distant relatives to reminisce about our memories of days of laughter and craziness we had shared so long ago.

I had planned to spend my cold, winter Sundays cuddled in a warm blanket on the couch watching the continuous, televised football games, or finally having the time to read that special book that had been put aside for months—it was going to be *my* time. But everything changed after my father's death. Numerous incidences, which I consider to be miracles, began happening to me.

✳

After my father's passing, I wanted to leave my children, grandchildren, and any future generations, a small biography of his life. I e-mailed the 26th Yankee Division's website on the Internet and asked if anyone had known my father. Servicemen replied with letters, pictures, e-mails and personal telephone calls.

I slowly started to put together my first memoir, *A Healing Heart: A Spiritual Renewal*. It describes my relationship with my dad and my trip in 1998, after his death, to the tiny, remote village of Medjugorje in Bosnia. This was the location where six visionaries had been claiming since 1981 to have daily apparitions with Our Blessed Mother. My father had wanted to travel to this holy land to pray for a miracle since he first heard about the apparitions taking place, but had been too ill and weak for the trip.

After being in the presence of the visionaries while they witnessed the apparitions, I came to feel the unconditional love deep within my soul that God has for all of us. I returned home with renewed faith and came back to the Church.

✳

I soon began a memoir of my own story, called *Someone Stop This Merry-Go-Round: An Alcoholic Family in Crisis*. I had kept this story hidden for over seventeen years, living in an unhealthy and alcoholic marriage. Our once happy and secure life with two beautiful daughters turned to a life of fear, confusion, and abuse. I watched a wonderful, loving father and husband turn into someone completely foreign to me. And in 1985, at the age of forty-five years old, my husband died at the VA Hospital in Providence, Rhode Island due to cirrhosis of the liver.

While I was writing, tragedy again struck my family when I came to realize that my daughter was following the same path as her father, and after three alcoholic rehabilitation stays, she died of cirrhosis of the liver in 2006 at the heartbreakingly young age of 39. She was laid to rest at St. Patrick's Cemetery in Somerset, Massachusetts, and her name was added to her father's tombstone, which faces a huge, white statue of Our Blessed Mother, her arms extended; it was the statue that Lori had said gave her peace while being at her father's gravesite.

✳

I became a public speaker in order to help other substance abusers and their families suffering in silence from the same heartbreak and feelings of hopelessness caused by this demon. And though I mourn my husband and daughter, if they had lived, I would not be speaking out about this worldwide disease that is killing so many people, or writing about my life to share with readers. Through God's miracles and love, He has turned me around and returned me to the holy city of divine accomplishments.

~ MY WAKE-UP CALL ~

by Clarence Reynolds

I WAS IN THE ELEVENTH GRADE WHEN, ONE DAY, MY FATHER CALLED. My parents had been divorced since I was a toddler, but he, for unknown reasons, decided to take a sudden and active interest in my academic development.

"Let me speak to your mother," he said abruptly. "And I want you to stay on the phone."

I was both curious and relatively unconcerned with whatever he had to say because his presence in my life, up to that point, had been inconsistent. By now, my second semester of eleventh grade, my father and his irregular input were unwelcome.

Even my expert sense of apathy didn't prepare me for what I was about to hear. Essentially, my father told my mother that a "friend" of his, who works in academia, reviewed my high school transcripts and concluded that I was not college material.

"This guy knows his stuff," he told my mother as I listened on the other phone. "He suggests we send Clarence to the military or, if we want to waste money, to a junior college for a year—but he'll probably flunk out."

I was stunned. I have nothing against those who choose military service as their path. In fact, I think it's a noble calling. And I believe junior colleges play an important role in bridging the education gap in higher learning, but I knew that neither was my fate. As he hung up the phone, I became determined to prove my father and his "friend" wrong.

Five years later, on the morning of Sunday, May 18, 1987, was graduation day at American University in Washington, D.C. I had earned a bachelor's degree in communication, with academic and campus service honors. But before the ceremony, I went to confront my father at the hotel my family was staying at. When he opened the door, I hardened. "I think you have a phone call to make," I said, while trying to contain the anger that I had harbored for many years. My father looked puzzled. "You need to call your 'friend' and tell him where you are," I barked. He suddenly remembered the day, just five years before, when he told me that my options in life were limited. He made the call. I listened as he told his friend the details of the achievements in my life—many of which I didn't know he knew. As he spoke, his voice trembled and he wiped tears from his eyes.

That afternoon, as I walked across the stage at Constitution Hall to accept my diploma, I decided that I was going to aggressively pursue a relationship with my father in an effort to know him and myself better. My efforts were successful. My father became my mentor, confidant and motivator. I continue to wonder, however, how many other young people get cut by harsh words that infuse doubt, fear or surrender at times when they need someone to believe in them most.

As a speaker, I encounter a lot of young people who have big dreams. In the eyes of each one I see myself. I let them know that they have the potential to change the world. This is what I know: in their own way, each one will.

CHAPTER FIVE:

Facing Adversity

> "THE DEEPER THAT SORROW CARVES INTO YOUR BEING,
> THE MORE JOY YOU CAN CONTAIN."
>
> —— *Kahlil Gibran*

Adversity can make you stronger than you dreamed possible or it can crumble the basic framework of who you are or who you want to be.

Sometimes it's expected and sometimes it's a surprise but it is always a challenge. You will dare yourself to direct how your life will unfold from that point forward.

Always remember… you are the one who decides what is carved in your spirit.

> —— *Beth Henry,*
> *author of "Delivered to the Gates of Hell"*

~ Delivered to the Gates of Hell ~

by Beth Henry

ॐ

It was one of the most beautiful mornings I had even seen. Puffy white clouds were rolling by against a crisp blue sky. I was in New York City, and the city was in its full splendor.

I came out of my hotel room early so that I would be able to find a cab that could bring me downtown where I would be teaching a class for New York State employees in the financial district. I didn't even really know where I was going, so I handed my cab driver, Juan, the address, and watched the meter tick the distance as we drove.

I asked Juan about the weather, and about the area to which I was traveling that morning, and he replied in short bursts and smiles, clearly somewhat less than proficient in English.

After an awkward goodbye, I paid Juan his fare and tip, and turned to look up at the towering buildings around me as he pulled away. He dropped me off at Rector Street, in front of the Department of Motor Vehicles.

The class I was to be teaching was held on the second floor of the building, so I stepped out of the loud New York streets and into the forced air of the DMV. I was immediately greeted by a true New York woman named Irma, who had lived in the city all of her life and was a goodwill ambassador for the Big Apple. I looked the part of a motivational speaker, in a work suit and wearing my smile on my sleeve. She escorted me upstairs where my class would be held, and showed me around the various offices and rooms.

I was already reviewing the material I had planned to go over that day in my head, and I was happy when Irma left me to sit in my conference room alone to prepare. The room was set up for the program, but not one participant had yet arrived. I thought, It must be a New York thing…

The first person to arrive was a woman named Jackie, who had traveled all the way from Long Island that morning and had left early since she wasn't very familiar with Manhattan. We began to chat and quickly realized that we were both psychiatric nurses. Besides that and having been lost in lower Manhattan, we also had several other things in common.

As we sat there talking and waiting for the others to arrive, we heard a loud noise. I immediately turned to Jackie, somewhat alarmed, and asked her, "What was that noise?"

She pointed to the window and told me that the streets were so narrow in the financial district that two garbage trucks had probably collided. There were two garbage trucks when I jogged over to look out the window, but there was not the tangled metal and debris I had expected from such a loud noise.

Within moments, Irma came hurriedly into the room and said, "Hey Beth, you want to see something? The World Trade Center is on fire!"

In hindsight, Irma seemed fairly cool and collected for what was actually going on only a couple of blocks away. But it was as if we were watching television or something; it didn't seem that this was truly happening in front of us.

We ran down the stairs with Irma, flew out the front door, and we couldn't believe what we were seeing. We stood on the corner in front of the Department of Motor Vehicles, and we watched the black smoke billowing out from the building. A plane had hit. One girl ran towards us with blood on her face and no shoes on her feet.

Dozens of people began grouping around us, wanting to see what was going on. I remember thinking the fuel from that plane was dripping into the basement of that tower. I thought that the whole island would blow up.

Perhaps in an attempt to rationalize what we were seeing, Irma explained to me that a pilot had a heart attack while taking people on a plane ride to see NYC. She told me to go back upstairs and see how many people had arrived for class.

As my heart pumped faster and faster and I started to feel the impulse to run, Irma tried to convince me to go back upstairs. It was only a few minutes until the class was supposed to start, and she believed that the participants would still arrive. When Jackie and I said there would be emergency vehicles that would need to be in the area, and that many of those scheduled to be in the course were nurses or other health care providers, Irma disagreed: "This is New York City, honey... We can do anything. This will be cleaned up in no time."

Jackie and I ran upstairs to get our purses. We knew that the class would be cancelled, and we wanted to decide what to do and where to go once we got out into the street. I left my class materials there in case I would be able to come back there and teach in the afternoon. We were scarcely out the door when the second tower was hit.

At that moment, Jackie and I knew we had to get out of New York City, but we had no idea how. We barely knew where we were. It took hours and days to find our way out of the deathly smoke and horror that enveloped lower Manhattan that morning. I arrived home to Buffalo several days later, to the grateful hugs of my friends and family.

✳

A few weeks after 9/11, I received a phone call from the dispatcher of the car service that had brought me to the financial district that morning. He told me how happy he was to hear my voice, and to know that I was all right.

The dispatcher explained that Juan, the driver who had dropped me off the morning of 9/11, was having a very hard time. He was very upset and kept telling everyone that he drove me to the gates of hell and left me there to die.

The dispatcher even told me that Juan tried to drive back into the financial district to save me but all the streets were blocked.

The next thing I knew, Juan was on the phone with me and we were both crying our eyes out. He is a very quiet man and didn't say much, but words weren't necessary.

Three months later, I returned to New York City and I asked if Juan could be my driver. He pulled up outside my hotel and ran to greet me. We embraced and then we headed onwards to our destination.

As I spoke to Juan from the backseat of the car, he nodded his head, agreeing quietly with a big smile with everything I said. Then I asked him a direct question. He turned just a little bit towards me, looking back at me in his cab with a twinkle in his eye. He said, "I don't understand English..."

We both laughed for the rest of the ride, thinking about my one-sided conversation, and overjoyed to be alive.

— ONE THING AT A TIME —

by Nancy Bauser

IN NOVEMBER OF 1971, I WAS AN ACTIVE, LIBERAL AND REBELLIOUS COLLEGE STUDENT. I was fiercely independent with just the right touch of passive-aggressive resistance against authority figures. I remember laughing a lot and handling stress without much thought of anxiety. The ability to manage multiple demands came easily to me.

That same month, my world collapsed. In a split second, my career-path changed from one of a special education teacher to an entry-level position in the field of brain injury recovery.

One beautiful afternoon, an impressive set of credentials was awarded to me. I was a passenger in a head-on collision in Ann Arbor, and my right wrist was crushed, both my eyes would never work together again and I sustained a severe brainstem injury. Fortunately, the driver of the other car was a physician and he immediately began mouth-to-mouth resuscitation in order to restore my breathing. After being rushed to the University Hospital in Ann Arbor, life support was administered to me.

From November 1971 until February 1972, my memory did not exist. I don't remember anything of my friends' visits or the daily vigil of my mother who spent her days talking and reading to my comatose form. I can recall nothing of my transfer to the Rehabilitation Institute in Detroit that December.

✳

My first recollection is waking up in my bedroom at my parents' house, wondering why I wasn't at the University of Michigan, where I was a student. I had scars on my body and a cast on my arm. The words, "rehabilitation center" and "catheter" were suddenly in my vocabulary. Confusion set in and I was terrified. My surroundings were unclear to me and everyone was continually asking me, "Nancy, how are you feeling?" The sad thing was, I had no idea why.

I continued outpatient physical, occupational and speech therapy at the Rehabilitation Institute for three months. I was frightened by that place because I hadn't yet realized that I had been in a bad car accident. I insisted that my mother sit where I could see her while I was in therapy because I was afraid of being abandoned.

The doctors and therapists did all they could and told my mother that she could expect to see my condition improve over the next five years. My mother then took over. Guided by her own beliefs, she developed a program. She took me shopping, where I had to make choices about clothing, which she later returned. Three days a week, she took me swimming to strengthen my body and reestablish my coordination and sense of balance.

In 1972, I learned to walk without using furniture for support. I also needed to relearn other life skills, like going up and down stairs, cooking my own meals and setting my hair. Things that I unconsciously do today were very difficult and required deliberate efforts. "One thing at a time" became my new mantra. I couldn't have a conversation and eat at the same time.

I used to hesitate between groups of words so often that I was told that I sounded retarded. As you might expect, this did not make me very happy. So I started listening to how people in the mainstream talked and I copied them. I also had no idea how to interact with people after my trauma, so I watched how others did wherever I could. My role models were chosen from the people I liked and respected. I set a goal to become the type of person who got treated the way she wanted to be treated. I knew I had to respect others in this way in order to be treated well in my new post-trauma circumstances.

✳

Nine months after the accident, I returned to school. In 1973, I earned a bachelor's degree in education. A teaching certificate was not awarded to me because I did not do regular student teaching, and I knew that I couldn't deal with all the sources of stimulation—students—coming at me at the same time in a classroom. I continued to live in Ann Arbor and, by simply doing that, learned to care for myself. After graduating from college, I held countless jobs and had difficulties in just about all of them. Then I went to get my master's degree in social work, and eventually opened up my own private practice.

✳

I accept myself with all of my limitations. I do the best I can with what I've got and I know that recovery is not only making progress, it is one step. Making progress is simple, but not easy. It requires commitment and a single-minded sustained determination to overcome obstacles and improve. Doing anything to try to make a change is positive. The simple act of making a steady effort is making progress. I have learned that this has got to be enough for me, on a daily basis.

Every morning, I get a new opportunity to be better than I was yesterday. I put a lot of small accomplishments together and find that I've realized a huge goal. My ability to reintegrate into the mainstream is a product of many small accomplishments tied together in a neat bundle. I work very hard every day to live as well as I can.

— My Inner Voice Speaks Health —

by Dr. Tom Potisk

I BELIEVE EVERY EXPERIENCE WE HAVE HAS A LESSON BEHIND IT. I've also come to know that if one ignores the lesson, you're likely in for a more dramatic experience.

On a cold afternoon in January 2007, my daughter, Emily, then age nine, our dog, Lou, and I took a snowmobile ride (yes, our dog likes snowmobiles). We were riding back and forth on a small pond near our home, gleefully exhilarated by the fish-tail turns made possible by the 1 inch of snow covering the ice. We had enjoyed many such rides on that pond, and on this particular day, we were celebrating Emily's return from school with no homework.

As I slowed the snowmobile to round the bend one more time before heading home for the steaming hot cocoa my wife would have waiting for us, my life changed forever.

For over 20 years I had been one of America's busiest family doctors. Patients came to me with their families in tow from far and wide, seeking the holistic type care I was well known for. Being a doctor of chiropractic, most of my care was hands on and very personalized. I focused on helping all ages with the principle that real health comes from within, and that with rare exception, the body heals if given everything it needs, like sufficient rest, nutrition, free-flowing nerve supply and positive state of mind. My skill at finding the need and delivering it was what my patients admired. I found answers for babies with colic, toddlers with ear infections, teenagers with acne, ladies with migraines, and even seniors with arthritis. They called me "the- down-to-Earth doctor" because of my organic/holistic lifestyle and my easy-going, practical nature. I was comfortable and content, except…

Slowly and gradually over the years, I had felt a calling to share my knowledge and skills on a larger scale, so I hired more doctors to assist me, and expanded the practice not once but several times.

Although that was enough for me, somebody had other plans.

✳

I had always been a sound sleeper, in bed by 9 p.m. and arising by 5 a.m. But then, mysteriously, I found myself waking up at 2 to 3 a.m., feeling uncomfortable. Not in pain, not ill, just uncomfortable, perhaps closer to restless. Tossing around in bed led to getting up to read, which led to turning on the television, which led to quickly turning it off (there is a lot of junk on television at those hours). After several weeks of this annoying disruption, I started paying closer attention to what was going on—there were profound words in my head!

Upon closer scrutiny, I found the words made up sentences, and those made up paragraphs, and, "Oh my!" I said to myself. "Only crazy people hear voices!" But I calmed when I discovered they were not really "voices"—they were words and sentences in my mind, and they were about health, and they were profound. It was information that could help people get and stay healthier, lots of people.

"So what do I do with this?" I pondered. I already was living a life to be admired by most, and already helping hundreds of people per week through my office.

A colleague steered me to a jolly lady called Sunni, a life coach, and self-proclaimed "joy manager." After explaining my plight to Sunni, she put her hand over her heart, gasped and said, "You're supposed to be an author!" Shaking my head vigorously, I explained that it could not be possible, that I had gotten lousy grades in grammar and composition, and worse yet, only typed with one finger.

She laughed heartily and shook her head opposite of mine, saying, "Yep, great authors don't search for their text; they receive it, usually waking up with it!"

I'd love to tell you that I then took a typing class, or a writing seminar, but no, most of us doctors receive a harder skull with our diplomas—I did nothing, except notice that the words and sentences were becoming like shouts, and sometime later I was waking up with the words on my lips. Still, I did nothing. Until that dreadful experience I call the day of "motivational terror."

✳

As we rounded that last turn on the pond, I felt the back of the snowmobile make a slight but odd drop. Hesitating briefly, I then gunned the engine, but already it was too late. The snowmobile's track was spinning rapidly, with water splashing wildly around us.

"No," I droned in my deepest voice, as if I had some influence on the power of who's ultimately in control of our destiny.

"Daddy!" screamed Emily repeatedly, as the three of us found ourselves bobbing in the icy death trap up to our necks.

We were wearing the heaviest of clothing—big boots, bulky coats and thick mittens.

In an extreme panic, I clawed and grabbed my way to some solid ice with one hand as I towed Emily with the other. With all my might, I boosted her and her now nearly saturated heavy clothing up onto the ice shelf, exclaiming in my shrieking voice, "Go tell mom to call 911!"

As she slowly crawled away screaming and crying that she could not stand up due to the weight of her wet clothing, I next grasped my whimpering dog by the nape and boosted her up and out.

Managing to get both elbows up onto what I thought was solid ice, my hands now numb, I just began to get my chest high enough when the ice broke once again. This time I submerged up to my eyeballs in the 12-foot deep water.

By the grace of God, and with a boost that I'm sure was from angels, I found myself out but hyperventilating, while wiggling my way across that ice to the shore, with words on my lips again, but this time words of prayer. I crawled home knowing without a doubt that I'd been given a second chance to write and teach, perhaps globally, the health and wellness information with which I'd been gifted.

✳

The next morning, still traumatized, I awoke again at 2 a.m.

This time, I sat at my laptop, extended one finger and started to peck at the keys. The words, sentences, and paragraphs poured out like water over Niagara Falls, soon becoming pages, then chapters, then a book, and then seven books over the coming months, all about health.

My sleeping is normal again and I've progressed in my typing skills; I now use two fingers.

Without that horrific, near-death experience, I believe I'd still be wallowing in that semi-content, semi-uncomfortable existence I stubbornly maintained for so long. I now place more value on guidance that I am sure comes as a gift from heaven, and pray that neither you nor I ever take it for granted. As part of my wellness teaching, I explain the importance of listening to one's inner voice as a guiding spirit from God.

— CONFRONTING CROSSROADS: —
A SUGGESTION FOR SANITY

by Lars Clausen

WHEN PEOPLE SAY "LIFE'S A JOURNEY," I GO BACK TO THE TRIP THAT MADE ME AN AUTHOR AND A SPEAKER—9,163 MILES BY UNICYCLE THROUGH ALL 50 STATES; STILL A STANDING GUINNESS WORLD RECORD FOR THE LONGEST-EVER UNICYCLE RIDE. I kept my head down and pedaled for six and a half months. But what do you do when you come to the end of the road?

After the speaking and authoring gigs for my first book, "One Wheel—Many Spokes," I vowed to use all that gained experience for at least one more book. I pedaled and then published "Straight Into Gay America—My Unicycle Journey For Equal Rights"—one thousand miles by unicycle and hundreds of roadside conversations. For five years of publishing, selling, and speaking, I kept my head down and lived the life of author and speaker, searching out the next sale and the next podium as if they were the food of life.

The end of my author-speaker road came when I recognized a simple truth—my book was really just the final escalation with the battle against my dad over gay rights. All my riding, all my research, all my conversations, and all my writing didn't change the character of our argument one bit. A year later, I tried loving my dad just for who he is, and that has made all the difference for the two of us. It also took the charge and the being right out of my speaking. What do we do when life quits working in the manner to which we've become accustomed?

Mark Twain wrote how "we never really and genuinely become our entire and honest selves until we are dead—and not then until we have been dead years and years." In the meantime, how do we deal with transitions?

I'm sure most authors and speakers are better about game-plan changes than I am, but I bet plenty of others also handle transitions sideways—finding that next thing to do, that thing that keeps us from asking, "Who the hell do I think I am?" and, "Is the only real way to find out going to be when I'm as dead as Twain?" If a group of us sat down together we might find at least a small circle of us admitting we're scared out of our gourds.

I got some "Dark Night of the Soul" rush when I stopped speaking and some "I'm gonna die" dread too. It has been three years since the dreads started, but also now more than a year since they stopped.

Somewhere in the process, I started to understand that the *journey* is the gift, and I'd be better off pulling my head up from the rut and considering being grateful for the mere gift of a beating heart.

I might just be lucky that this accumulation of appreciation came to me in due time—it did not arrive by my working at it or figuring it out. This means I don't have a step-by-step plan for trekking the dark valley. I do have some ideas, and I do admit that I'm tempted to tuck my head down and just start working the new ideas. However, now I'm taking my time, waiting to see what appears if I give these ideas some freedom before I jump on them. Somehow, strangely, the world seems a more expansive place because I slowed down for it and let my days catch up with my life.

I believe what Mark Twain said. I'm just a bare shadow of becoming my genuine self. But I'll take that—with thanks.

— WHAT DYING TAUGHT ME ABOUT LIFE —

by Teri Rose

I can't remember the sound of screeching tires, breaking glass, or the crunch of metal as my car flew into the air, hit a telephone pole and landed in a ditch. My friend was able to walk away but I was not.

Somewhere in all of the commotion, I died.

When I awoke in the hospital days later, the only memory I had was of the time I spent outside of my lifeless body that had remained in the car. I vividly remembered the sensation of being pulled into a vacuum. I could see lights flying by me as if I was traveling at a very high speed, even though it felt like I was in a vacuum at the same time.

Suddenly, I emerged from the tunnel into an indescribable place of peace and tranquility where I was met by a beautiful Being of White Light.

Being in this place caused me to feel like I had come "home," and I experienced a feeling of comfort and wholeness like I had never known. I saw that my true essence was also this energy of pure love. But as we reviewed my life, I received the understanding that I was the one who removed myself from the benefits and bliss of love by harboring anger and negative feelings because of some experiences I'd had growing up.

✳

I learned then what science has now validated: that everything in existence is energy, including things that appear to be physical. I felt the difference between energies that fall into the category of love, such as gratitude, appreciation and peace, and those that fall into its opposite category, fear, such as anger, resentment and an unforgiving nature. I saw how important it is to project feelings of love instead of the energy I was projecting through my emotions and feelings about life.

I also came to an understanding that heaven isn't a place you are admitted to, but it is a frequency that you attain. Being in the presence of this White Light *was* heaven. It was better than the greatest feeling I had ever experienced or dreamed was possible. Having that feeling again was what I wanted to strive for, not going to a *place*. The feeling, the energy I was experiencing, *became* the place.

When I came back to the hospital days later with the memory of that experience, I had the distinct feeling that the life around me, the physical objects and things I could see, were very inconsequential and unimportant. This physical life I found myself back in could be compared to a speck of sand on the beach—just a very small part of something much bigger.

Things that once had all of my focus and attention now seemed miniscule as I thought about the big picture. All I wanted to do was to get back to where I had been during my near-death experience. And to do that, I knew I had to change.

❊

I determined that I would keep my near-death experience to myself and search for ways to change myself. It took about 25 years of constant dedication to that purpose before I found the missing pieces for my permanent change. I made slow progress over the years, but I had some very deep-seated wounds and anger that it seemed no amount of willpower and determination would help. I hadn't yet learned about the power of the subconscious and how to work with more of my brain.

But the more I studied the way the brain works, the way memories are stored and accessed, the power of the subconscious, the energetic system of the body and so on, the more pieces came together for me. And thankfully, many new scientific studies have come out that have validated the power we have to change things from what they are to what we would like them to be. I have become very consistent in my ability to create change in the physical world out there by changing things inside of myself. It happens as soon as I am able to shift my feelings about the situation, my perception of it through my thinking and the way I see it in my mind's eye.

There is something very powerful and magical that comes about when the brain waves are slowed down, a mental vision of attaining success with a goal is held and positive emotions are felt, all simultaneously. Love enhances and amplifies the experience, and brings about infinite possibilities for improving life, while fear creates barriers that make it almost impossible to attain what you fear you will never have.

We are meant to constantly strive to love and to act out of love in everything we do, from our own health to our attainment of life goals. Negative emotions, like anger, are toxic to the body, and positive emotions, like love, hope, and joy can truly heal.

Love is very powerful medicine.

— From Beverly Hills to Homeless Shelter —

by Shari Rightmer

WHEN I LANDED A JOB IN BEVERLY HILLS, CALIFORNIA, I KNEW I WAS GOING TO MAKE THIS THE OPPORTUNITY OF A LIFETIME. With a complete identity makeover, I began to live the life of the rich and famous. The doctors I worked for were world-famous and many of our patients were celebrities such as Elizabeth Taylor, Danny Kaye, Howie Long, and too many others to mention. I had the world at my fingertips, and soon, I met my husband of 17 years, a well-established rock and roll musician from the 70's. It was a story of good girl meets bad boy.

He was in the film industry at that point, and with his computer savvy, we invested in our business in creating high-end computers for film sets. But then things started turning for the worst. In 1999, my husband was diagnosed with Hepatitis C and we found out that he was already in the fourth stage of Cirrhosis. My dream world disintegrated quickly.

My husband and I started pulling away from each other, our four-year-old son started becoming angry and violent, and our finances started changing. We lost our home and my husband's income. We stopped talking. My husband seemed not to care whether or not he lived. And our son became more out of control each day.

When my husband died, I seemingly lost myself at the same time. But soon I fell in love again–with a childhood friend. I moved, hoping my new knight in shining armor would take care of my son and me as I healed from my loss. I was in love again, but after more troubles with my son, he kicked me out.

So there I was. No money, nowhere to go. All I had was part of a tank of gas, and that was it. I cried and thought to myself that this can't be happening to me. I am from Beverly Hills.

When I finally found the Bakersfield Homeless Shelter, a building surrounded by tall blue metal gates, I pulled in and saw people smoking, sitting with unmatched clothes on, teeth missing, no makeup on; all seemed as if they were waiting for someone to come for them. But no one did. And no one came for me either.

As I sat parked in front of the shelter with no gas and no money, I cried and said to myself, "There's no way I can stay here." But I also knew that I would be dead if I remained on the streets in my car. I cried but tried to compose myself with dignity; tried to rise above this as if I were not homeless, not like them—dirty, druggies, parolees, welfare trash, not caring about themselves... I just needed to sleep as best I could until I was able to figure things out with my life.

I entered the office and stood in line to be helped as I stood behind a black woman with a beautiful baby crying in a stroller. She asked the assistant "Is the nurse in? I have a bad toothache and I need something for the pain." I couldn't help but wonder what was going to happen to her baby and now I was thinking about my son and how I remember him at that age holding him in my arms with the warm glow of a mom.

I gave the assistant my name and she took me back to another room to speak to Dan. This man was gruff and rough in the face and had a long ponytail. He loved Harleys and had probably been doing this job for a thousand years. He showed no emotion, didn't speak much, and only asked questions. He didn't even flinch at my answers as he asked for replies. I couldn't help the tears from coming down my face as I relived telling him my story and the events that led me to his office.

He looked up at me when I was finished as if he had heard every story and said, "We are all full and have a waiting list of people to get a bed." Then he showed me all the people hanging on or sitting by the big blue gates, all hoping to get in. I went back to my car, locked the doors, and waited. With great luck, late that afternoon, the shelter was able to find me a bed for the night.

When I entered the dorm room at the shelter, I tried not to look at anyone; after all, they all seemed worse off than I was. I still saw myself as a Beverly Hills princess.

The noise was loud and the dorm echoed. The floor was dirty, but there were shelter inhabitants cleaning everywhere. Clearly that was part of our assigned duty.

All that first night, I tried to figure out who would be the first to jump me, steal from me, or try to rape me. I sat on the nasty couch that was sticky and smelled. I prayed this was all a dream and that it would all go away. I also thought of all the others that were outside the gate waiting to get in. Though I hated every moment of my anxiety and terror, I was grateful I was in here instead of outside those blue gates.

I had never seen so many metal bunk beds in my life. There were wall-to-wall people; forty-eight total and I have no idea how many on the families side. I was issued the top bunk, which I noted, was Bunk #11.

✳

I made the bed and jumped up as fast as I could and rolled in the blankets as I stuffed my purse under my pillow. I cried for a while and everyone seemed to leave me alone. Slowly, I sat up and looked around to assess my new surroundings.

My life needed to change. I had lost everything and all I had left was my soul, my essence, and myself. I went back to the shelter and was never late. I did my chores with pride. As I sat in my car watching the kids in the playground, I started thinking about my spirituality and God. Every evening, I would meditate and write in my journal. With this and all of the other inner work I had been doing, I was given something that would change my life and would be my gift to give to others.

I have always considered myself very spiritual ever since I was a little girl, even in the abusive childhood. I have studied most religions to some degree. I became a Christian in 1976 and started studying the Old Testament, which then led me, deeper into Hebrew history. When I worked Beverly Hills I found myself working for Jewish doctors mainly and loved the religion. Before my husband passed away, I did not want to get out of bed and found myself wanting to give up. I had succumbed to drinking alcohol to relieve the pain of my past that was colliding with my present.

I asked myself, "Why am I really here? What am I supposed to be doing? What is my true purpose in life and what really makes me happy and unique?"

One day when I was gardening as part of my daily duties, as I was daydreaming and thinking about my life, a fellow homeless person, a black woman who had aged far beyond her years, her hair in cornrows, came to me and remarked how beautiful I looked every single day. She asked me how I was able to wake up each morning and look so good.

I also saw her great beauty in that moment, and I told her so. She had made my day wonderful, and I did my best to return the favor. Life is about sharing these small gifts with one another. That is the gift of Bunk #11 for all of us.

CHAPTER SIX:

❧

On Friendship & Love

"YOUR TASK IS NOT TO SEEK LOVE, BUT MERELY TO SEEK & FIND
ALL THE BARRIERS WITHIN YOURSELF THAT YOU HAVE BUILT AGAINST IT."

—— *Rumi*

We are living in strange times. Websites with cleverly-developed software have given us the ability to choose a mate as easily as we order a customized laptop. We tune into *The Weather Channel* instead of looking at the sky. We learn to play simplistic musical instruments on *Rock Band* instead of learning to play a real instrument. We socialize with our social network instead of talking with our neighbors. If bored we can text, blog or tweet our friends while standing in line at a movie theater. Our cell phones can do a hundred different programmable things besides making a phone call. Today's devices give us the ability to do things we could only imagine in science fiction stories. We can even see our planet from space, all from the comfort of our living rooms.

All of these cool gadgets have shifted our communication styles, but at their core, we are using technology to do what we have always done best—connecting to friends and family. No matter how much technology advances or changes, there is nothing that can replace the craving we all have for connection; to be understood, to be accepted, and to be loved; that connection is the divine and spiritual within us. Love is, as it always has been, when we seek and find the best in ourselves and in others.

—— Brad Szollose,
author of "The Strength of a Mother"

⌐ Hannah Montana vs. the Kentucky Derby ⌐

by Kate Sheridan

❧

My daughter Olivia is a precocious and beautiful six-year-old. Her fair skin, blond hair, crystal-blue eyes and prominent dimples can be deceiving, and behind her girlish exterior beats the heart of a feisty Irish lass.

I have witnessed her spiritedness since the day she was born. She refused to be ignored in the delivery room and hasn't changed too much in that department over the years! Time has shown me that Olivia has few, if any, unspoken thoughts. She calls things as she sees them, and rarely leaves a conversation without leaving behind something to be considered by her unwitting listener.

Nothing in my life has shaken my belief system more, time after time, than having to look into those crystal-blue eyes and be forced to answer my daughter's constant question: "Why?"

Olivia currently aspires to be an actress and, in an attempt to introduce her to the finer side of the arts, we attend live theatre, art galleries and benefits, including, this past year, the Kentucky Derby. She joined a large group of adults to watch the 134th annual event, and though she was the only child present for the event, she seemed nonetheless fully absorbed.

As we waited for the race to begin, she asked, "Mom, do you like horses?"

Thrilled that she had asked, I told my daughter about the horse, Charley, that my parents had given me on my 12th birthday, and how I had spent every weekend riding him through the mountains near our home. I told her how great it had felt to me as a child to race home through the meadows, jumping streams and fallen trees. I told her how I had to dig my fingers into Charley's mane and close my eyes so that I wouldn't get scared and fall off. I told her that the love of riding will never leave me.

Her eyes ignited with excitement. Olivia said with a wide smile, "Wow, horses are great!"

✱

Our conversation slowed as race-time approached, and I shifted the talk back to the Kentucky Derby and focused on the ladies in their designer dresses and regal hats. When I glanced at her sidewards, Olivia pushed back in her chair and seemed to be unimpressed.

After the two-minute race was over, Olivia began to tug on my sleeve to remind me that we had planned to go together to the newest Hannah Montana movie that evening.

Frustrated that my daughter was distracting me from the award ceremony, I got down on my knees to come face-to-face with her and said, "You know Olivia, this whole Hannah Montana thing isn't real life!"

She brazenly stared me down and with a glance at the television screen said, "And neither is this!"

She had done it again. I was again stunned and overjoyed by Olivia's insight.

✳

I said my goodbyes and got her to the movie theater just in time for the premiere. The movie's theme was amazingly fitting for our evening. It was a story of a small-town girl struggling to find out what was "real" and important to her now that she was living a big-city life.

As the movie played on, I began to think about the relationship that I enjoyed with my daughter. It was one of honesty and mutual growth. She was born possessing a gift that I desperately needed. I pondered destiny, purpose, and ultimately, the genetic material that we shared.

Her physical resemblance to me had evoked many comments over the years. Tonight was the first time that I looked beyond the surface to discover that she was like me in many other ways. Though Olivia has been raised her entire life in the fast-paced city of Atlanta, she has instinctively loved everything country. She loves waterfalls, hiking, bugs and tree-climbing. And when she is in her element, her laughter is contagious.

There was no mistaking the lesson here. I had been trying to force my daughter to conform to my—or the world's—view of an "elegant young lady." But I was fortunate to have a child who would have no part of it.

✳

When we arrived home, I looked up the definition of "elegance" as Olivia dressed for bed. I found brief definitions like "understated," "delicately displayed," and "exuding a sense of class." There was no mention of frilly dresses or imposing hats.

As I sat on her bed watching her drift off to sleep, Olivia reached out and wrapped her small hand around mine. The last thing that I saw was the twinkle in those crystal-blue eyes.

I spend my public speaking career sharing insights, unlocking human potential, and doing my best to inspire greatness in others. At the heart of each of these things lies the bit of wisdom that Olivia taught me on that day.

Nothing can be more important than following our hearts.

~ THE STRENGTH OF A MOTHER ~

by Brad Szollose

❧

MY MOTHER HAD A TENDENCY TO BE A HYPOCHONDRIAC. Every six months it was a new ailment, a new disease, or some sort of pain in a weird part of her body. If it was on television or in a magazine, she had it. My dad and I couldn't keep up.

Even though every doctor visit ended with, "You're fine, Diane," my mom would find something else that was wrong.

In the winter of 2006, I received a phone call from my mother, informing me that she had a pain in her wrist. She thought it might be carpal tunnel syndrome, but since she had never worked at a computer or employed her wrists in a way that could cause such an ailment, I chuckled, thinking it was another one of her episodes.

A month later, I saw her for the first time. As she walked towards me, from the kitchen to the front door, I went cold. She was dragging her left foot while holding her left arm close to her body.

What had at first seemed like carpal tunnel syndrome now affected far more than her wrist. My mother's entire left side was slightly paralyzed. But as parents often do, she was attempting to stoically hide the severity of her condition from me. My mother could barely walk, yet here she was, trying to protect my feelings, perhaps not wanting to face the fear that was now evident in my eyes.

The three of us, Mom, Dad and I, decided to go out to dinner as a family. Little did I know, it would be our last time out together.

That night, my mother's shoe kept coming off, since she no longer had feeling in her foot, she was unaware it had come off. This was serious.

✳

My mother was a devout Christian, spiritual but not religious. She knew the Bible but never forced her beliefs on others. Nor did she judge anyone. As a professional singer, a nurse's aid, a mother, and a wife, as well as through her service in the army and within the local community at soup kitchens and shelters, my mother always cared for others with her songs, spirit and hands. Her motto was, "In service to others is our reward."

My mother did not have an easy life, and many of her experiences would have crushed a person of lesser character. The strength she gained from such a full life was present in every decision she ever made. She passed that strength on to me, and I am forever grateful for that.

I am also grateful for her deep sense of humor. My mother had an immense capacity for compassion and love, and a wonderful sense of humor. As her son, I would always try my hardest to make her laugh. She was my best audience!

✳

A few days after the dinner when Mom's shoes came off, we brought her to Hershey Medical Center for a biopsy.

Her doctor informed us that her mysterious wrist problem wasn't carpal tunnel; the pain and weakness was caused by a tumor on the right side of her brain. The tumor was malignant, and it was in an area of her brain that was inoperable. If surgeons had attempted to remove the tumor from my mother's medulla oblongata, she might have become blind, deaf or incapable of speaking; or worse, all three.

Once she had recovered from her biopsy surgery, Mom was wheeled into a tiny examination room. She sat in the center of the room as my father leaned into the counter to one side. My wife and I pressed ourselves against the wall as two oncologists entered and shut the door behind them, enclosing all six of us within the airless room.

One doctor was a chemotherapy specialist, and the other was a radiation expert. They gave us several options, but no matter how they explained it, therapy would only extend her life for a few weeks or months at most. The inevitable was going to happen. Mom was dying.

✳

The year I turned seventeen, my mother spent several months in a local rehab center for what they used to call a "nervous breakdown." When it was time for my mother to return home, I was naturally resentful of her time away, and I felt abandoned and angry.

On the day my father and I returned home from the hospital, he assigned me the job of bringing Mom inside and putting her stuff away while Dad parked the car. The medication she was taking left my mother docile and in a state of childlike wonder. For some reason, she wanted to go out to the backyard to see our garden. In typical teenage fashion, I was impatient with her.

It was a beautiful sunny day. It didn't cross my mind that my mother had spent most of the summer locked away in a strange place. Although Philhaven was a beautiful place, the first thing she wanted to see was her own home, with its imperfect banister, timeless wallpaper, and our tiny backyard.

She wandered off the back porch and down the steps. As she stared into the garden, I noticed the bluest butterfly I had ever seen flitting around the garden over thirty feet away. When my mother spotted it she couldn't help herself: "Oh, I wish I could see that butterfly up close."

My frustrated teenaged-self made fun of her: "Are you kidding me? Butterflies don't just come up to you bec…"

Before I could finish my sentence, a miracle took place. The butterfly flew straight towards her and landed on her fingertip.

Until this day, I have never seen another butterfly fly in a straight line. But on this day, this bluest butterfly did. He landed on my mother's outstretched hand, and I stood with my mouth hanging wide open.

Then the second most amazing thing in the entire world happened. That bluest butterfly stayed on my mothers hand for over two minutes, its wings pulsating in the sun.

My adolescent cynicism was destroyed in those two minutes. Here was a small miracle.

"Oh, you're so beautiful." My mother just looked at this butterfly as if it were the only thing in the universe; the greatest of God's miracles right here in her hand. And the butterfly responded like a proud child being admired by its mother. She not only cherished this small wonder, but admired its grace with a love reserved for the saints.

In those few moments, the miracle of the bluest butterfly showed me that the miracles of life are in the little things.

Now I leave room for miracles... because they are there. We just need to get out of their way in order to allow them to happen.

✳

In the crowded examination room thirty years later, everyone had an agenda. The doctors wanted to keep my mom alive, my father didn't want to face the fact that his wife and companion of over forty years was dying, I wanted my mom to just get better, and my wife was there to lend support.

In the midst of that cacophony of noise and facts, I kneeled in front of my mother and asked, "What do you want to do, Mom?"

My father shot back immediately, "I think the chemo pill is your best bet, Diane."

I looked at him as sternly as I was able and then directed my question back to her: "Mom, don't listen to everyone else. Of course we want you to live, but this is your decision. What do you want?"

My mother looked up with her soft green eyes, her shaved head hidden by a blonde wig, and she said gently, "I don't want to fight... I want to go home."

I completely understood what she wanted. Despite everything, she didn't want to go through months of painful therapy that would render her bald, clinging to what little life she had left.

In that moment, kneeling on one knee as if I was praying in church, I lowered my head and cried. My wife put her hand on my shoulder.

Then I stood tall, looked the two doctors in the eyes, and I explained with as much unwavering strength as I could muster, "If my mother is to die, I want her as comfortable as possible."

✳

Over the next five months I put over 6,000 miles on my car making the trip back and forth between New York City and my hometown of Lebanon, Pennsylvania. We were able to get my mother into Cedar Haven, a nursing home in Lebanon, and soon hospice took over her pain management.

This was not an easy time for any of us, especially for my father. At one point he broke down and said, "Brad, I can't do this."

"What do you mean, Dad?"

"I can't watch your mother die like this. This is how my mother died... a brain tumor."

I summoned up as much strength as I could as I told him, "Dad, your job in this moment is to help Mom get ready to leave Earth. I think that is the greatest gift you can give someone: to help them cross over."

That Sunday, the last week in August, I knew my mother was gone. At 4:30 in the morning, during a brief trip back to New York City to get some clothes, I woke up, sat bolt upright in bed, and said out loud, "My mother just died." At that moment, I didn't feel sad. I was filled with joy. Mom was now relieved of her burdens here on Earth. My wife woke up as well, and then we fell back to sleep.

When I checked the messages on my cell phone in the morning, sure enough, my dad had left a message that Mom died at 4:30 that Sunday morning.

✳

As I began driving the long three-hour drive to my hometown the day of my mother's passing, I thought of that day in the sunshine when the bluest butterfly had perched itself on my mother's hand. And as I passed from New York into Pennsylvania on the interstate highway, butterflies began to cross in front of my car.

There was one butterfly, amd then two. And soon, hundreds of butterflies of different types and colors flew in front of my car. Yellow, orange, purple, pink, green, and even black butterflies. I had made that trip from New York to Lebanon a hundred times before, and I've made it a hundred times since, and I have never seen more than a few butterflies. But on that Monday in August, they were everywhere.

I called my wife that morning from the car, as butterflies were all around, and I smiled as I said to her, "You are not going to believe what is happening!"

Together we laughed, knowing that Mom was letting me know... She was home.

A HANDFUL OF RICE

by Deborah Chamberlain

"TAKE, I WOULD, A HANDFUL OF RICE
AND SCATTER IT OVER THE SEA
WOULD BUT THAT SLIGHT ENDEAVOR
CHANCE BRING YOU NEARER TO ME.
BETWEEN US AMERICA'S TRAGEDY
A CIGARETTE AND A CUP OF TEA
I FIND SOLITUDE QUITE MISERABLE
WITH ONLY MYSELF, WITH ME."

- Michael

THAT POEM WAS WRITTEN BY A YOUNG MAN WHO DID NOT, AND WILL NOT, KNOW WHAT AN IMPORTANT PART OF MY LIFE HE CAME TO BE. It was a miracle that I even met him in the first place.

My family moved often while I was growing up: several places in Wisconsin; fourth grade in California after my parents packed five kids and a German Shepherd into our station wagon filled with snacks and dog tranquilizers, while we drove west for my dad's new job with Mattel Toys. When that didn't work out, we made plans to relocate to Australia—had the shots, passports, and tickets—until my mother got sick. So we returned to Wisconsin— but not for long.

When I heard that we were going to move again for another of my dad's job changes, to a new town in a different state, I could not believe it. "Not again!" was all I could think. But little did I know it would be the path to meeting Michael.

After about a month of ninth grade in Wisconsin, we moved to Homewood, Illinois, where I met my still-best friend, Buffy, after being stuffed into the middle aisle of the school bus, packed as tightly together as modesty would allow. We spent as much of our free time together as we could, doing stupid things like playing tennis in our bare feet or tanning for hours. The summer before our junior year, we both turned 16, the age our parents found appropriate for dating. Our attention turned to boys.

Buffy was the first to catch the eye of an older (by two years) man. She met him at the Newgate, a small, cozy coffeehouse that was located across the street from her parents' house. His name was John. We three would sit around the coffeehouse for hours, sipping coffee, watching the cigarette smoke from John's French cigarettes swirl about the room while we listened to folk songs being sung and poetry being read on the tiny stage.

I began to notice a tall, good-looking blond guy during my visits to the Newgate, but I was too shy and insecure to get up any nerve to even try to attract his attention.

A week or two later, I was sitting alone with John, waiting for Buffy to arrive. While looking around the room, I suddenly spotted the blond man walking toward us. My heart did a little flutter. When he got to our table, he gave me a quick glance then leaned over towards John as he greeted him. I dropped my eyes and pretended to read the menu.

Their talking stopped for a few seconds. Our visitor must have walked away. It was safe to look up, or so I thought. My heart skipped when I saw the blond man looking right at me.

"Hello," he said softly, with a gentle smile and a slight nod.

"Hi," I returned his greeting, a little breathless from the shock of unexpectedly meeting his eyes.

After a second or two, he quickly glanced at John, then turned and walked away.

Thereafter, I looked for the blond man during my visits to the Newgate, watching him from afar when he was there, strangely disappointed when he was not.

A couple of weeks later, I met up with some friends at the Newgate. They were sitting at a table that was close to the one where the blond guy was seated with a couple of his friends. I spent my time watching his friends flirt with mine as I secretly watched the blond guy sip his coffee and smoke his cigarettes.

Then it was time for me to leave. Very slowly and reluctantly, I pushed back my chair and stood up so I could shove my arms through my coat sleeves while giving a final, quick glance at the table so near. Then the blond man got up, standing close to me in the crowded space.

"Couldn't you stay?" he asked, looking down into my eyes.

"No, I really can't," I told him, silently cursing my strict curfew.

"Then," he continued, "perhaps another time? I'm Michael. What is your name?"

"Debbie."

"No, your formal name."

"Deborah."

"Ah, Deborah. Well, good night, then, Deborah," he said softly, gently, pronouncing my name in three syllables instead of the customary two.

Well, that was it. I was in love and very, very happy. One spring day, Michael and I celebrated our six-week anniversary with our very own orange picnic, and on another day, I cut school so we could go fishing. There wasn't anything I wouldn't do to spend time with him.

But the cruel Vietnam War intervened. Michael received the "Order to Report for Physical Exam" to determine his eligibility for the draft. I could not imagine my kind and gentle boyfriend pointing a gun at anyone. Some months later, Michael got the results: 1-A.

Time plodded on, colored gray with fright about what lay ahead. We continued our lives that suddenly seemed empty, even as we tried to fill the hours with our mundane responsibilities, cheerlessly observing the winter holidays that could not be avoided.

And then it came.

Michael received the "Order to Report for Induction," the letter every young man I knew dreaded. We had only four weeks left. Time's pace quickly changed from plodding to racing along, going by too fast and crazy for me to capture the details of what was happening—precious, irreplaceable time. Those four weeks passed as if each day was less than a second. Time was no longer holding its breath; it was released in a furious, ferocious funnel-cloud.

Within a five-month time span, both Michael and John were dead. They both committed suicide. Buffy and I were only 17 years old.

✳

I wrote about the events as they swirled around me, then after decades, I decided to preserve my penciled notes to fill the empty hours after my daughter went off to college.

Writing my memoir became my passion with one major goal—to put a finished copy of the book in the hands of Michael's mom before she died.

Sharing my story has shaped a new career path as a speaker to talk about the circumstances surrounding Michael's and John's deaths, that of suicide. I've volunteered for the National Survivor's of Suicide Day, been a panelist and am involved with grief and bereavement studies.

Along the way, I made a major discovery in my thinking about suicide. We will never know what kind of pain suicidal people experience, can't feel what is inside their hearts. How selfish would it be if I had "saved" Michael or John and forced them to live a life of unendurable suffering?

So my stance is this: if you love them, let them go. Honor their memories, cherish the time you had with them and love them for the rest of your life. But peacefully, lovingly—let them go.

I put a finished book in Michael's mom's hands on Mother's Day.

— A Chance Meeting —
With the Greatest Generation

by Lewis Harrison

WE RAN FROM THE VAN INTO THE DINNER, HOPING TO AVOID THE POURING RAIN.

As we ordered our food from the waitress, two men walked by. One was in his fifties and the other was energetic but clearly up there in age. As they passed us on the way to the next booth, I noticed that the older of the two was wearing a baseball cap that said "Purple Heart."

Assuming this gentleman had won a Purple Heart in some foreign war, I commented sincerely, but off the cuff, "Thanks for your service."

He responded quickly, saying clearly, "I have three Purple Hearts."

My thoughts scanned my knowledge of movies, articles and television shows that told me what a person would have to do to get one Purple Heart, let alone three. He must have either killed a lot of people or saved a lot of people, having gotten three Purple Hearts for being wounded in battle. We watched the wizened old man step into a nearby booth with his younger companion.

While I played with the potatoes on my half-empty plate, I wondered which wars he had fought in. Had he been in Vietnam? No, he was too old, unless he had been there in his late forties.

I was more than curious now. I turned over my shoulder and tried to get his attention.

"Excuse me. Sorry for interrupting you… Were you in World War II or Korea?"

"Both," he replied. "I flew helicopters and trained new pilots to fly 'em."

"Is that how you got your Purple Hearts? Flying helicopters?"

"No. I parachuted behind enemy lines two days before the landing at Normandy!"

Huh? I said to myself. This guy parachuted into the middle of thousands of German soldiers two days before the landing at Normandy?

Then I asked him a question with an obvious answer, but I needed to ask it anyway: "Weren't you landing in the midst of thousands of Germans?"

"Yup. Made my first kill in less than five minutes. Was there to blow up key targets before the landing."

I heard him say the words about blowing up targets, but I couldn't help but picture the soldiers on the other side who were killed while fighting for their country at the hands of this man, the valiant American soldier.

I imagined an old German woman somewhere whose son had been killed in Normandy. Maybe this old woman had not even been a Nazi, and had hated them, but sent her son off to war anyway. She had lost her son in that awful war, and this man in front of me had killed him. At that moment, good and bad blurred in my mind, and I thought about the horrible cost of war in human lives.

My attention returned to the war hero sitting only a few feet away. This was a man who had won Purple Hearts for being wounded in battle three times!

"Landed by parachute into Holland, too." he said. "Behind enemy lines… My brother at my side."

"How did you get that job?" I asked.

"All volunteers," he replied. "We volunteered."

"My brother got shot up pretty bad," he continued. "Machine-gunfire to his legs and knees… He had a real hard time getting benefits from the VA when he came home."

I knew about the trouble some veterans of the Iraq wars were having getting benefits from the Veterans Administration.

"My brother. So sad. One day he called me over his troubles with the VA. He said to me, 'I just can't take it any more.'"

Then the old war veteran told me something that I will never forget. He remembered that for his brother, "that was it." And then he shaped his hand into a fist and extended his middle finger towards his own head and pulled his trigger-finger.

"That was it." He said it matter-of-factly and without emotion.

"I'm so sorry," I said, but he continued speaking.

"My son was in Iraq, the first one, and Vietnam too. He's retired. My grandson is at West Point."

"Was your father military as well?" I asked.

"Yup." Then the old man laughed. "He only saw three days of action and then they shipped him home!"

"Wounded?"

"Nope, they just shipped him home."

Old Purple Heart and his friend got up and put their coats on.

"Nice talking to you," he said as he prepared to pay the check.

As he walked to the cash register, his younger friend stopped and said to me, "When we spend weekends together, I get to hear all of his war stories."

Then they left waving to me one more time as they walked past the diner window.

— THOUSAND DOLLAR BILL —

by Bill Crow

ॐ

"IF IT WASN'T FOR THE PAIN IN MY BACK AND THE PROBLEM WITH MY EYES, I'D FEEL LIKE I WAS TWENTY-NINE AGAIN," SAID 81-YEAR-OLD JAZZ LEGEND CLARK TERRY. My wife and I were visiting him at his home in New Jersey. It was the first chance we'd had to spend some time with him since his recovery from an ileostomy.

We waited in Clark's living room while his masseuse finished giving him a rubdown. Then we heard him coming down the hall singing, to the tune of *The Battle Hymn of the Republic*, "Som'p'n's gonna jump out the woods and graaaab you!" As he turned the corner into the living room, dressed in a white terry bathrobe and leaning on his cane, I joined him in the song. It was one we used to do for laughs at the old Half Note when I was a member of the quintet he co-led with Bob Brookmeyer.

After hellos, we sat down on the long, curving, white leather divan that filled most of the room. I asked Clark how he was feeling after his operation. "That's all healed," he said, "but right now I have a pinched nerve in my back, and the pain comes and goes. When it comes, it's unbelievable. I'm taking a course of 36 chiropractic adjustments for it. I've had about 19 already."

"Are they doing any good?" I asked.

"Well, at least I can sit here without crying like I used to do. Sometimes I'd have to scream. It hurt so bad."

I asked the trumpeter, "But your lip still works?"

Clark's eyes lit up, and he announced proudly, "'Yeah, the chops work!" To demonstrate, he played a series of amazingly agile phrases, just buzzing his lips. "That's the only way I can keep in shape, man. This is the sort of warm-ups we prescribe for the students."

I told him about the tuba mouthpiece I keep in my car for warm-ups, and he laughed and said, "We used to do that, driving in to the studios. I'd be in my car, buzzing my mouthpiece, and I'd look over, and there'd be Bernie Glow with his mouthpiece, and over on the other side, Snooky (Young) with his. I think Bernie had his connected so you could hear it outside the car... *To-doot, to-doot, to-diddley doot!* When you walked into the studio and they put that drop on you, you'd better hit that note 'cause nine thousand other dudes would be peeking over your shoulder, waiting for you to miss."

✳

I first met Clark Terry in November 1960, when he and I joined Gerry Mulligan's Concert Jazz Band at the Village Vanguard. Conte Candoli and Buddy Clark had gone home to California after the band's European tour that summer, and Clark and I were their New York replacements. That same year, Clark became the first black musician on NBC's payroll, becoming a regular member of Johnny Carson's Tonight Show Orchestra when Skitch Henderson was the conductor. Since they taped the show in the afternoon, Clark was free to play at jazz clubs at night.

Among many other prestigious jobs through the years, Clark toured several times with the late Norman Granz's Jazz at the Philharmonic, playing with Oscar Peterson and Ella Fitzgerald. Remembering the tour, Clark said that Granz always treated his musicians well, paying good wages, and providing first class accommodations.

Granz once cancelled a sold-out concert in a huge auditorium in Europe because the promoter failed to provide Ella Fitzgerald with a private dressing room. The promoter threatened to sue, and Granz said, "I hope you do. And when you come to court, be sure to bring that section of the contract near your thumb there, where it says that Miss Fitzgerald must have her own dressing room." As the promoter began refunding thousands of tickets, Granz took his touring musicians to dinner, never complaining about what the cancellation had cost him.

On another tour, Granz had asked Clark to "not bring that funny horn," meaning Clark's flugelhorn, an instrument with more curves than a standard trumpet. Clark obliged, playing only trumpet on those concerts.

At the end of that tour, when Clark went into Granz's office to get what he described as a generous paycheck, Granz said, "…and thanks for not bringing that funny horn," and slipped an extra banknote into Clark's hand. As Granz walked away, Clark peeped at the denomination and was surprised to see it was a thousand dollar bill.

Just then, Granz returned and said, "What did I give you?"

Clark replied, "I knew you'd made a mistake. This is a thousand!"

Granz nodded. "I did make a mistake. I meant to give you two." And he handed Clark another one.

~ LOVE LINES ~

by Judi Piani

WOULD ANY OF US BE WILLING TO GIVE UP WHAT WE HAVE LEARNED SO FAR IN OUR LIVES TO BE YOUNG AGAIN? Sure, I would love a young agile body, but would I ever give up the wealth of knowledge and wisdom I have accumulated for that young body? Would I want to make the same mistakes again? Would I want to relearn all the lessons over again? I can say without a doubt or hesitation, I would not.

The richness of aging is in the gathering of experiences and learning, and the quiet peace of knowing things while the young still struggle to understand.

The richness of aging is in the accumulation of loving friends.

The richness of aging is in having been present as our family grew with each new child and then the joy of adding each new grandchild to our circle of love.

With this in mind, I have a short story to tell you.

One day my sweet little five-year-old granddaughter climbed up onto my lap. As we were talking, she looked up at me and said, "Grammy, what are those lines on your face?"

My reply was quick. "Those are love lines, Anelyse."

"What are love lines," she asked.

"Well Anelyse, every time you love someone you get lines, and the more people you love in your life, the more lines you get."

Her reply was, "I love people. Do I have any lines?"

"Well, let's look," I replied.

So we started to look at her feet and found a few tiny lines on the side of her heel. "See, these are some love lines on your feet. They start at your feet, and the more people you love in your life, the more they begin to cover your body. If you are really fortunate, by the time you are old, you will have lots of lines right up to the top of your head. Then you will know that you have had a full and love-filled life."

Many months later, as Anelyse again sat on my lap; she looked up at me and gently said, "Grammy, I can see your love lines."

I replied, "Yes, I am so fortunate to have loved so many that the lines are up as far as my face and still increasing. Aren't… lucky Grammy?"

✳

I am hoping that Anelyse will never see wrinkles as ugly or bad, but that she will always see them as a sign of love and the fullness of life.

Perhaps at least for her, we have changed the negative perception of aging and wrinkles to a positive one. Maybe we can change the negative perception, one grandchild at a time, one love line at a time?

Perhaps as a society, we can begin to look at the outward signs of aging as confirmation that we are alive and have experienced joys and sorrows. We have learned from these experiences and moved on with wisdom to a place of peaceful knowing, surrounded by love and covered in love lines.

I think I will just flaunt my love lines and be grateful for all the people I have loved, while I anticipate the next new learning experience.

⁓ A MAGICAL TEN-YEAR ANNIVERSARY ⁓

by Sarah Jane Cion

❧

TEN YEARS AGO, MY HUSBAND AND I WENT TO A LITTLE SHOP IN CONNECTICUT TO SHOP FOR OUR WEDDING AND ENGAGEMENT RINGS. I found a setting that had a pearl in it, with a teeny tiny diamond attached to the side, around 10 o'clock from center.

I immediately fell in love with the ring, and I asked the staff at the little shop if the large pearl in the center of the setting could be replaced by a diamond. They looked intrigued, and said that no one had asked for that before, but they could do it for me. I also asked whether a band could be designed to fit the ring as part of a set, with a twist in each one, as if each had matching tiny waves.

Around one week later, I had two rings that fit around one another like puzzle pieces. The rings were beautiful, and were unique to me and would represent my special marriage. I loved them so much, and of course being in love and in anticipation of my wedding added to the magic of the rings.

I wore those rings on special occasions, but I was always careful to put them in my purse when I played piano (which is what I do for a living). After I had my two children, I would lovingly put the ring into a small red sparkly container in a very specific place on my bureau when I would pick them up or change their clothes, careful not to scratch them with the diamond or rough edges. But the ring was always in the red case, on my finger or in my purse. I loved the ring as much as I did the day I first saw it, and whether I was wearing it or not, it was always in my heart as a symbol of the young love my husband and I had felt.

Last year, on our ninth wedding anniversary, my husband suggested that we go to a restaurant in Greenwich Village in New York City where we used to play jazz together as young people in love; he is a bassist and I am a pianist, and we would play sweet duets during the jam sessions there. On this occasion, we ran into musicians who we knew and after dinner they asked us if we wanted to sit in with their band.

In the excitement of the night, I hastily took off my two rings and placed them on top of the piano. It had been a long time since I had played gigs regularly and I had forgotten to put my rings into my purse as I had always done before. I made a mental note to myself to be sure not to forget the rings on top of the piano, and I placed them within my eyesight.

After we played a couple of tunes, the adrenaline was running high, and we thanked our friends for the great time on our anniversary. I remembered the young love that I had felt a decade ago in that same club, playing that same piano. We said our goodbyes and we went on our merry way, my husband and I.

My husband and... and my bare finger.

✳

When we got home, I went to put my ring away for the night into its box on the bureau. I panicked. It wasn't on my finger! Immediately, I called the restaurant. I told them to please, please find my wedding ring that I had left on the piano. But there was a lot of noise in the background and when the person came back to the phone, they said they had not seen any rings there. The next day, I called the bass player who had requested for us to sit-in to ask him if he had seen it. He said he had not seen a ring, and couldn't remember seeing one. I knew in my heart that someone had taken it.

I was depressed for the next few days, feeling a lump in my stomach like I had lost a best friend. I couldn't believe how foolish and careless I'd been!

I even went so far as to call a renowned psychic from Los Angeles. I left a message for him and he called me back a few days later. He could hear the distress in my voice. He said, "Listen, I'm not going to charge you a dime for this because it's such a cut-and-dried case." The psychic continued, "Your rings were taken by someone in the restaurant. They were sold the next morning to a pawnshop in the area. The woman who bought them was so delighted because the rings were so beautiful. I'm so sorry to tell you this, but your rings are gone, and you won't be getting them back."

I couldn't accept this! I tried all of the pawnshops in the area, to no avail. Slowly, the reality that I had lost the rings began to sink in.

Last year, on December 22, my husband and I celebrated our ten-year anniversary, one year to the day after I lost my ring set. When my husband asked me what I wanted to do for our anniversary, I told him that I wanted to go back to that shop in Connecticut and see if I could find a replacement ring set.

He said, "I wonder if they will have the same one."

"Me too," I said. "That's the one I want."

I wanted to replace the feel of those rings on my finger, and the comfort of their twisting bands.

On that same day, we drove up to the ring shop in Danbury, Connecticut, where they had my ring on file with a picture and everything, the exact diamond cut, carat count and so on. They didn't have the setting on hand, but they said they could make it within the week. I was so excited!

After looking at all of the rings on the shelves of their shop, we ended up liking a different ring so much that we purchased that one instead of replacing the exact one I used to have. We chose a .38-carat diamond for the setting and, with the increased prices over a decade, this new ring was quite a bit more expensive. The total for the ring came to just about $2,300. I paid for the downpayment with $935 that I had found in an old business bank account just days before. We put the rest on layaway, and would pay it off when we could. We both knew it would be a financial burden, but I was so happy to be putting a ring back on my finger.

✱

Two days later, an unexpected check came in the mail—it was for a song that I had written called "Cat in the Hat" that a company in Los Angeles had signed up to license five years ago! It turns out that the show Beverly Hills 90210 had used it for three minutes. The check came out to $1,500, exactly the amount of money we needed to pay off the ring!

That was a magical moment. My husband and I jumped up and down like little kids when we opened that envelope! It truly was meant to be. It felt like a new beginning for us. Of course, it wasn't about the money. All along, it had been about our love, and we hadn't let money stand in the way of replacing the beautiful twisting bands of my engagement and wedding rings.

The new bands on my finger, with their polished gold and small diamond, remind me each day of the special relationship that my husband and I share, and each day I am grateful for my life and my love.

PART III

❦

BUSINESS STORIES

"QUALITY MEANS DOING IT RIGHT
WHEN NO ONE IS LOOKING."

—— *Henry Ford*

"THE FUTURE BELONGS TO THOSE WHO BELIEVE
IN THE BEAUTY OF THEIR DREAMS."

—— *Eleanor Roosevelt*

"WHY JOIN THE NAVY
IF YOU CAN BE A PIRATE?"

—— *Steve Jobs*

CHAPTER SEVEN:

❧

Business

"THESE ARE THE GOOD OLD DAYS."

In these times where everyone seems to be in perpetual *busy-ness*, these true business leaders always have more time, always get more done, and always have the fewest excuses.

In recent years, we have seen failure of the old-model for-profit businesses, from General Motors to Citicorp, and even the American economy itself. All of these busy entities are struggling in the new world.

Indeed it *is* a new world. In the last ten years we have seen the rise of the social entrepreneur: Richard Branson, Bill Gates, Warren Buffet. These figures and countless more ascribe to the mantra of social entrepreneurs: "Business for more than profit."

It is time for all business to embrace a new methodology with real social conscience and heart. The era of business from 2010 and onwards should be christened "Business with Heart."

— *Mike Handcock,*
author of "Asking Better Questions"

— LET YOUR NATURAL HUMOR SHINE THROUGH —

by Kristin Arnold

❦

A SEASONED SPEAKER WAS ONCE ASKED, "IS IT NECESSARY TO USE HUMOR IN A PRESENTATION?" The speaker responded, "Not unless you want to get paid."

I would take that one step further and add, "Not unless you want people to listen."

Except for the guy whose car you just rear-ended, everyone likes to laugh. When you make your audience laugh, they feel more connected not only to you but also to each other. Research has shown that we like to be around people who have a sense of humor. It's a human quality that breaks down tension and resistance, and enhances communication and relationships. Plus, it makes the presentation more fun.

If you are naturally funny, then good for you! This article will reinforce what you already know. If you think you are funny but you really are not, keep reading; you may discover some valuable information. And if you are like most people, who don't think they're funny at all, you will be surprised at how you too can succeed at creating a humorous experience for your audiences.

I never considered myself to be funny. Humorists and comedians are funny. My brother is funny. Some of my friends are funny. But funny is not a quality I would use first to describe my presentation style.

But truth be told, some people find me witty, which brings a soft chortle, a gleam in the eye and a smile to the lips. And I sometimes get a few chuckles from observational humor and stories that come from my own life experiences. I'm just not a laugh-every-six-minutes kind of speaker. But I have found ways of strategically using humor that can help even the most humor-impaired among you (defined as those of you who never quite understood The Far Side cartoons).

✳

The most important principle of humor is that it be natural to your style and personality. David Letterman doesn't try to be Chris Rock. Chris Rock doesn't try to be Ellen DeGeneres. And Ellen DeGeneres doesn't try to be Joan Rivers. In fact, with all the plastic surgery, it appears that Joan Rivers isn't even trying to be Joan Rivers.

The point is that professional comedians are successful because they have found their own style and voice. The same holds true for speakers. So, before you start to add humor to your presentations, consider these basic principles about finding your own natural style.

Pay Attention.

What makes you laugh? Chances are, you will find out more about your own style by taking note of the things that make you laugh. The converse is also true. Don't pursue humor that you don't find funny.

Use Humor Role Models.

Perhaps you have a friend who is particularly funny. Or there is a humorist on television, radio or the Internet who makes you giggle. Watch them for what they do and observe how they do it. See if there is something from their style that you can adapt to your own.

Seek Out Humor.

Be a sponge. Read anthologies, collections of jokes for speakers and other books on humor. Capture the techniques that work for you, and adapt the material you like and that resonates with you. Just like anything else in life, the more you expose yourself to something, the more you will understand it, and the more competent you will be in the execution.

Keep Track of the Humor You Find.

No matter how funny something is, you won't remember it unless you write it down. When you find something that tickles your funny bone, write it down, clip it out, take a picture of it or sketch with charcoal if that's your gift—and save it for future use. Create a system (a file, box, and notebook) where you keep your found humor in one place to pull out just when you need it.

Practice.

Practice your bits of humor on a friend, your spouse, or your coworkers. If you're a member of a Rotary club, Toastmasters, or some other organization, take advantage of this ready-made audience to try out your new ideas. If it works, you've got a keeper; if not, good that you found out before trying it during an important presentation!

Believe!

It's trite, but true. If you believe in your material, if you believe that it is funny, and if you believe that you can make others laugh, you will be more humorous.

✳

What do we do when humor bombs? Every professional humorist and comedian has dealt with failed humor. They wouldn't be successful if they hadn't. But what they know that most of us don't is that a "saver line" can help the pain of the bombed humor. A saver line is something you use only when the humor bombs. For instance, if you tell a joke and nobody laughs, you can say, "It's a good thing that wasn't supposed to be funny." The saver line gets the laugh. The audience has recovered and you can move on. You can find books that will give you examples of various saver lines. Most pros have a dozen such lines in their back pocket.

The only thing worse than bombing with humor is bombing without humor! These days, it's practically impossible to engage an audience without some form of humor. So, start with the right frame of mind and assume that humor is necessary for your success.

- Find the humor that works for you. Your humor must fit you.
- Trust that once you've found the fit, it will work.
- Use a type of humor that fits the topic, the situation and the group.
- Use subjects to which everyone can relate by enhancing your observational skills.
- Find humor in your own life, the newspapers, a funny joke, or from a friend.
- Take advantage of humor to make your presentations come alive.

So, should you use humor in your presentation? Only if you want to be effective!

— Success in Marketing Today: — It's Not About Force; It's About Building Trust

by Terry L. Brock

A while back, I remember going to a seminar that had a variety of speakers. One of those speakers advocated using pop-ups on a website to "grab people" and get them to buy. He bragged about a new technology that used these invasive advertisements to essentially block people from leaving his site without buying. I guess his idea was that by annoying the daylights out of people, you'd get more sales.

I don't like that approach—at all!

You might agree with me that it is more important to build trust and a strong relationship with buyers rather than to annoy the daylights out of them or force them into buying from you. Too much of what we see in many areas of business today employs the principle of force rather than persuasion through trust.

*

Long-term relationship marketing and building a solid business require trust, which can best be built by consistently watching out for your customers' best interests.

Trust is required even for quick transactions. I could run into a convenience store and quickly purchase a bottle of water without the transaction taking a lot of time. Sometimes that is what I want. If I've just filled my tank with gasoline, am in a hurry, and want to grab a bottle of water to drink on the next portion of my trip, I don't want to stop and talk at length with the clerk.

However, even in that situation, trust has to exist. I can trust the manufacturer of the bottled water. For me, I like Aquafina bottled water and trust the people who make it. This is based on past experience with many good bottles of Aquafina I've consumed! I also have a relationship with the convenience store because I've been to that chain before.

Too many people in business try tactics like the Internet marketer I discussed above. He giggled about how he "tricks" people into buying and using these pop-ups. Well, the marketplace has a way to stop that. Most browsers now have a pop-up blocker. The techniques will change. What matters is the attitude of the marketer. Successful relationship marketing is interested in a long-term, mutually beneficial tie between buyer and seller.

I'm reminded of the sites on the web where you see someone walk out from the edges of the web page and begin shouting at you. Yes, it seems like nice technology, but it is annoying at best and disgustingly irritating in most cases. When something is forced upon us, we tend to avoid it in the future. Let the user choose to play that or any other video. Don't start it automatically!

A good example of how to do it right is *Amazon.com*. They don't shout and yell at you when you come to their site. I particularly like that they keep a record of what I've purchased and what I've reviewed recently. They do this (most importantly) with my permission and are there to help me as I make selections. They are serving me as their customer, and I'm glad to shop with them and spend lots of money with them. I often find that I purchase from *Amazon.com* because of the high level of trust I have with them and their affiliates— even if the price is a little more than the competition.

Trust is the key to building quality relationships in business. You begin by helping people know you as someone who is trustworthy. This is demonstrated in all you do.

The next step after someone knows you is that they grow to like you. They have favorable reactions to what they have seen. They like the way you run your website. They like the content you create. It is your job to create lots of ways for people to like you. After they know you and like your business, you want them to trust you. If you've done your job properly, they will see that trust as the next logical step.

There is another critical step after they begin to trust you. You want them to become engaged with your business. You can start small with a lower-price sale and build from there. This is the ladder that all businesses must ascend.

✳

Know. Like. Trust. Engage.

These steps have to take place. The speed at which they occur varies, but they have to take place in order for relationship marketing to exist.

What can you do today to get more people on your ladder? Think through the strategic process and involve your prospects and customers at the appropriate level. Remember that the steps are repeated and you have to continue to let people know about your products, like what you're doing and trust that you're still dependable.

Somehow, this makes a lot more sense than the force and trickery method employed by that Internet marketer I mentioned at the beginning. Somehow, I think his website visitors used a "blocker" on his marketing style and methods.

― Asking Better Questions ―

by Mike Handcock

Looking for the key to wealth? Then look no further. This is it. Ask better questions.

My philosophy is that if you ask poor questions, you get poor answers, have poor information, and therefore make poor decisions. As soon as you ask a great question, that all switches.

Example 1. I'm out to dinner with my friend.

We look at the menu, and the waitress comes to tell us the specials. We listen and are tempted to ask: "So what's good?" But instead, I ask a better question: "If you were eating here, knowing the chef who's cooking tonight and what he or she does best, what is the one thing you would have to have?"

"That's easy," she replies. "The lamb."

We have the lamb, and it's sensational. Maybe that chef was great at lamb and couldn't cook fish at all. Asking a great question gives you great information.

Example 2. My friend, Terry, is retired.

He is sitting on his yacht in the Hauraki Gulf outside of Auckland when he gets a call from an old client in Sydney who has a major computer problem. He tells Terry that if Terry can fix it inside a week, there is a $500,000 fee in it for Terry. So Terry asks himself this question: "Who in the world can fix this problem?" Not "who in Sydney?", or even "who do I know?", but "who in the world?"

Terry makes calls and eventually gets put through to a guy in the United States who can fix the issue and will complete it before the end of the week. Terry agrees to pay him a success fee of $250,000. Terry banks $250,000 net without leaving his yacht.

Example 3. I need to get some tertiary qualifications.

At age 30, I really don't want to attend university, but I think I need the qualifications. I sign up, pay up, and then ask every head of their respective departments the same question: "I have little time available to study due to work and family commitments. What is the absolute minimum I need to study to pass with straight A's?" Every single person answers me.

Two years later (by correspondence), I have my qualification with mostly straight A's, including two academic prizes for topping the country.

Example 4. Most financial salespeople ask for referrals.

They ask poorly: "Who do you know who you can refer me to?" They get poor quality referrals, and their future is left up to the judgment of the person they ask. By changing to the awesome question, "Who is the best business person you know personally?" they now get great referrals to people who have money and are concerned for their future. Bigger sales and fewer problems.

✳

Everything you want in life will result from the quality of questions you ask. Decide what you want. Decide whom you need to ask, and to whom they can in turn lead you. Plan when is the best time to ask and just leave the "how" up to the person you have asked to guide you.

So many of us get stuck by asking ourselves, "How can I do this?" when the right question is, "What do I need to do next?" or, "Who can help me reach my objective?"

Focusing on asking great questions will really help to lift your game and bring you close to your ultimate objectives.

When you are faced with a problem, sit down and write out the questions you could ask to get answers to that problem. Actually write down the words *what* or *who* and frame your question from there. You will find that in no time you are getting better results.

~ KEEPING CUSTOMERS FOR LIFE: ~
11 PROVEN SOLUTIONS

by Arnold Sanow

IN TODAY'S FAST-CHANGING AND COMPETITIVE ENVIRONMENT, CUSTOMER SERVICE IS NOT ONLY NICE, BUT IT IS ESSENTIAL FOR SUCCESS. In the words of Tom Peters, "If you are customer-oriented, you're ahead of 98 percent of the other businesses, because they are not." The bottom line for you and your company is that customer service is one of the only ways you can differentiate yourself from the competition.

1. Reward your customers.

You can either help them increase their business, or help them on a more personal level. It can be as simple as sending them a gift or helping them find leads or opportunities. One client of mine makes it a policy that when he goes out to dinner and sees one of his clients and their family eating, he goes over, says hello and picks up the check. Unexpected extras show appreciation and build relationships.

2. Kill them with kindness.

A recent USA Today article stated, "Americans are ruder than ever." Studies show that simple kindness is the deciding factor in many cases when people choose where to purchase a product or service.

3. Be a resource.

No matter what your customer needs, try to find it for them—even if it has nothing to do with your business. And, if you can't provide the service or the product when and how they want it, recommend your competition. Also, let your competition know that you referred them. They may return the favor in the future.

4. Have a goof kit.

If you make a mistake, it's not enough to say, "I'm sorry." In a recent encounter at Starbucks Coffee, I ordered one beverage and received the incorrect one at the end of the counter. I mentioned this to the barista, and immediately the employees made me the drink I ordered and gave me a coupon for any other drink I wanted in the future.

5. Give your customer what they want and how they want it.

A few years ago there was an inventor who developed a mousetrap that was made of steel that would last for 20 years. He spent a million dollars advertising it, but then went out of business. He realized that what the customer really wanted was a trap that they could throw out with the mouse.

6. Give back to your best customers.

If you run a special price or make a special offer, make sure your best customers are given the opportunity to get the same deal. For example, one major cellular phone dealer lowered its price for new customers only. Long-time loyal customers were not allowed to get the same deal. Many of those loyal customers felt left out in the cold.

7. Don't show an attitude of indifference to your customers.

In a recent study on why people move on from a certain company's products and services, 68% left due to the company's indifference towards the customer, and only 14% left due to dissatisfaction with the product/service provided.

8. Have a customer advisory panel.

If you are a one-person company or major corporation, make sure you get some of your best customers as your advisors. The best advisory panels consist of six to ten people who are the types of customers you want to work with in the future. Every six months, have a meeting to share your ideas, concerns and challenges about your business.

9. Treat your employees well.

Three key ingredients for providing great customer service to your employees are: A. Recognize and appreciate them, B. Let them know what is going on and make them feel part of the team, and C. Show sympathy for their personal problems, giving them the time and understanding to handle those problems.

10. Do what you say you are going to do.

Keep your promises no matter what the cost in agony or overtime. A colleague of mine who lives in Ohio was scheduled to deliver a speech at eight a.m. in Florida, but had forgotten. Around 10 p.m. on the night prior to the speech, he received a call from his brother who reminded him of the presentation. He searched for a commercial flight, but had no luck. But instead of giving up, he kept searching until he found that he could charter a medical transport jet. The fee for the jet was double the fee he was getting for his presentation. He not only won praise from the people who hired him for his willingness to do whatever it takes to keep his promises, but he also received many referrals.

11. Do it when you say you're going to do it.

If you promise to have something to a customer on a certain date, make sure you're on time. Better yet, have it to them earlier than expected. In a recent study, 76% of professional purchasing agents stated that the number one reason they would not buy a product or service, or deal with a salesperson, was because they were late for appointments or meetings.

✳

As we've seen, customer service is more than just smile-training; it's really about treating people the way you want to be treated, and knowing how to treat them the way they want to be treated. It's also about giving the client what they want, when they want it and how they want it. And it really comes down to the fact that:

GOOD COMMUNICATION + HR SKILLS = GOOD CUSTOMER RELATIONS

— THREE STRIKES AND YOU'RE IN! —
HOW MY LOVE OF BASEBALL HELPS IMPROVE
WORKPLACE PRODUCTIVITY AND PROFIT

by John R. Schaefer

❧

I'VE ALWAYS LOVED BASEBALL, BUT I NEVER REALIZED THAT IT WOULD COME TO DEFINE MY STYLE AND PASSION FOR HELPING COMPANIES OPTIMIZE THEIR MOST IMPORTANT ASSET—PEOPLE! Let me give you an example of what I mean.

When I began speaking to groups, I quickly realized that when I was in the audience and the speaker began sharing the 10 steps, or the 12 secrets, or the 25 tips to something or other, by the time they got to step five or six, I'd forget what they were steps of!

I decided to deal with everything in threes, which of course gives me the freedom to talk about my first love, baseball.

✳

Baseball is a simple game; not easy, but simple. It all began for me when I was nine years old. As the smallest guy on the team, they gave me uniform number "1" (the shirts were sized from smallest to largest back then). I was little but spunky, fast, and absorbed the game like a sponge! They put me in center field where I soon earned the nickname *The Vacuum* because I sucked up everything that went past the infield.

In one game, I surprised my team, the coach, and all of the parents in the stands by catching a fly ball on the right centerfield wall, and proceeding to throw a one-hopper to third to catch the guy on second tagging up. Not only was it a great play; the coach didn't even expect a nine-year-old to understand that aspect of the game. This was the beginning of a love affair that would last a lifetime.

By the time I was 12, I was the biggest guy on the team and got to wear number 15. That year I pitched, and in one game struck out 17 batters. The last out was a dribbler back to the mound, so I made that play too. We lost the game (I guess I walked some guys), but I still got the game ball.

In seventh grade, we had a guy at school that had us all bowing at his feet. Curt was bigger than everybody else, hit the ball so far that we didn't even go looking for it, was dating a tenth-grade cheerleader, and scrimmaged with the high school basketball team on the weekends. He even had facial hair: not stubble, but the real thing!

I'll never forget the day when the call came in… I'd been called up to play on the (Little League) White Sox, Curt's team, and his dad was the coach. I got a base hit the first time up and will forever cherish the high-five from Curt when I came in to score.

Well, just when you guys are beginning to whisper about who is lucky enough to have my rookie card, I should tell you that things took a hiatus for about 20 years. All of a sudden, everybody else grew up, I lost my nerve, went to work, began raising a family, and baseball became something I just watched on television. Like every fan, I always hoped to go to a game and catch a foul ball. *Sigh*—the dreams of the fan and not the player.

✳

But, the story's not over yet. When my kids were young, we went to the school carnival and there was this big dunk tank right next to the ticket booth. For five dollars, you got three balls, and if you hit the bull's eye, the principal took a bath.

"Go for it Dad, you can get him!" they shouted. They'd heard the stories of my youth, and I didn't disappoint. On the second throw, *whoosh*, I nailed it and down went Mr. McKinney. Hero again! I thought about this feat for a couple of weeks, and sure enough, as luck would have it, ran into a guy who was playing men's over-30 baseball; real baseball, with metal cleats, wood bats and 90-foot base lines. I thought, "Heck yeah, I can still do this." So I told them I was a pitcher. I got my chance, and after balking twice, I got to strike out a couple of guys with the high hard one, but my elbow and hamstrings just didn't hold up.

Most of these guys had played college ball, some even had some minor league experience. They never did find out that I hadn't pitched since I was in little league. But hey, I got to run, hit, throw, and smell the grass and the leather; I was a ball player again! This, too, was short-lived, as my 40-year-old body just couldn't do it week after week.

✳

Fast forward to this year. Still the baseball freak, I go to opening day at Chase Field to watch the Arizona Diamondbacks every year. This season, my buddy (who always gets tickets for my birthday) found us front row seats halfway down the first base line in shallow right.

We did the whole deal: hot dogs, beer and peanuts, and watched the Diamondbacks take the lead over the Rockies. In the seventh inning, we got texted by two friends and found out that they were in our same section, about 20 rows up. We stood and waved so they could see the cool seats we had. It was a warm April day—the perfect day for baseball.

Top of the ninth, first pitch, and Ryan Spilborghs sliced one down the right field line. It was tailing foul, coming towards our section. We were all on our feet, a couple of us braver souls stretching out over the wall as this screaming liner hooked our way. I, of course reached the farthest. Smack, ball against leather.

It seemed like an eternity... somebody had caught it. I thought I felt something, so pulled up my mitt and *holy cow,* there was a ball in it. I was stunned, then ecstatic. I jumped up, pulled the ball out of my glove and turned to show it to my friends up above. 3,000 people went nuts and jumped to their feet. Imagine that feeling! I'd seen this happen on television, but never thought it would be me!

Wait, there's more! They played it back on the Jumbotron and the analyst Mark Grace voiced his approval: "That's why you bring your glove to the ball game. Nice backhand by the veteran!" I was in heaven!

✳

What does my foul ball catch have to do with recognizing employees and getting high performance in the workplace? So glad you asked. There are three lessons here:

1. I was prepared to make the play. I'd spent my whole life learning the skills to make a catch like this: I had my glove on; I was paying attention and had the instinctive ability to make the play without thinking. I was trained, focused, present, and capable.

2. **I had the confidence** to go for it while others pulled back or ducked. Anybody can bare-hand a little pop-foul, but to snag a tailing line-drive, you must have a combination of experience, confidence, and guts.

3. **I got immediate recognition** and it felt great. I took a chance, used my training, came through and got the pat on the back I deserved. It made my day!

I certainly was engaged in that ball game, and so were all of my peers, who were as excited and energized as I was.

Now, I know what you're saying: That was a lucky break, because I was in the right place at the right time. But what if we could create an environment in your workplace where this happened regularly, on purpose! Use the same three strikes I used when I caught my foul ball with your employees:

1. **Prepare:** Hire talent and help them be the best they can be.

2. **Increase Confidence:** Allow them to take calculated chances to improve the company.

3. **Give Recognition:** Be there right away in force to congratulate them when they succeed. It will make your day and theirs.

How to Make Your Marketing Work Harder for You

by Ted Janusz

HAS THIS EVER HAPPENED TO YOU?

I was riding along in the car with my teenaged son and started to say something I had vowed I would never say, "When I was your age..."

Stephen's eyes rolled to the back of his head. You see, Stephen doesn't particularly care to hear his old man's reminiscences of the good old days.

Yet count the number of times a sales letter begins, "Our Company was started by my great-grandfather back in 1905. We now have 10,000 installations and 25,000 satisfied clients."

As a marketing consultant, I was recently asked by an accounting firm, after the fact, to review their new marketing materials. They handed me a professionally-designed, glossy folder that profiled each of their partners—where they had gone to school, degrees they had earned and achievements for which they had been recognized. The accounting firm was very proud of this slick, new—and expensive—materials.

Guess what? A prospective client doesn't really care about the number of degrees conferred or awards won. Rather, it's all about, "What can you do for me? How well do you understand my pains and my issues? What steps can you take to solve them?" That's what prospects truly care about—*What's In It For Me.*

Many companies will attempt to secure new business by mailing out marketing pieces. Americans now receive close to two million tons of third class or bulk mail per year.

There are two reasons for this:

Americans have more printing machinery than any other country on earth.

Despite recent rate increases, Americans have one of the lowest postal rates in the world.

Unfortunately, unless targeted recipients are specifically on the lookout for your material, it will likely get mixed up and lost in those two million tons.

The average white-collar worker now receives 160 e-mails daily. To be sure that your intended recipients want to open your mailing, include a *What's In It For Me*. Entice them to open the e-mail by including the name or your association in the subject line, and then provide something of value in the body of the e-mail.

Consider the words of David Meerman Scott, author of *The New Rules of Marketing and PR*: "The vast majority of e-mail newsletters just serve as advertising for a company's products or services. Each month you get a lame product pitch and a 10-percent off coupon. No wonder that house e-mail lists suffer from significant opt-out numbers."

Consider using a different type of e-mail newsletter, one that focuses not on your company's products and services, but on simply solving buyers' problems once per month.

In an increasingly competitive marketplace, companies able to demonstrate *What's In It For Me* win business.

— Social Media and You: — You Are Your Brand!

by Kathy Perry

DID YOU EVER GET ONE OF THOSE POSTS, TWEETS, OR STATUS UPDATES THAT WAS A LITTLE INAPPROPRIATE, ABRASIVE OR TART? You know the one where you immediately said to yourself, "What were they thinking?"

As a social media marketing specialist and coach, I am always being asked, "How do you deal with social media in regard to the personal and business aspects of posts and profiles?"

You can never remove *you* from the social media equation. You are your brand. What happens when you try to mix a business profile into an already existing personal profile, when the personal profile has things in it that you don't want shared with the business community of clients and prospects, or even an employer and co-workers?

Do you really want those posts and pictures of you in compromising situations on display for your clients, prospects, vendors, business associates, bosses, or co-workers?

❋

Can you afford to offend some of your following? Be careful when you are posting something, and make sure that the content is a good representation of the brand image you want to portray. Remember, once it's out and you've shared it with the world, you can't get it back to change it or delete it. It's now a part of online history—your history and your brand.

What happens when something you have posted goes viral? Viral marketing can be a blessing or a curse depending on what it is that goes viral for you.

A viral blessing is when something you've put together positions you as an expert, showing you in a positive light and reaching millions with your message.

A viral curse is when something that you don't want shared shows you or your company (your brand) in a bad light, again, reaching countless people. Now millions of people see it and develop a bad opinion of you.

❋

Think "backyard barbeque" when approaching your online audience on the social networks, forums or membership sites. You wouldn't walk up to someone at a barbeque and start pitching him or her immediately about your products or services. People don't like it, offline or online.

And yes, there will always be someone who is obnoxious or annoying, and who will try to blast out their ads all over the social networks, but sooner or later they'll get de-friended, hidden, un-followed or deleted.

❋

Just as people you meet on the street judge your appearance, your brand image is on display every time you interact online. It's more important than ever to be aware of how everything we do, say and post.

You are your brand, so treat your online experience and exposure with the utmost care.

— Do you Have the Right Attitude — for Customer Service Change?

by Wendy Gillett

DID YOU KNOW THAT PRIOR TO 1954, NO ONE HAD EVER BEEN ABLE TO RUN A MILE IN UNDER FOUR MINUTES? They said it could not be done. They thought that a human being simply could not run that fast. Well, in 1954, a man by the name of Roger Bannister ran the mile in three minutes and 59 seconds. Guess what happened after that? Everyone started breaking the four-minute mile. All of a sudden, athletes realized it could be done. Their brains caught up with what their bodies could already do. It just took an attitude change.

So this is it. This is where the rubber hits the road. Change the way you think and start providing the kind of service your customers will remember forever.

The reality is, we decide how we feel about someone in about five seconds. That first five seconds is important to every one of us. It is human nature. In that short amount of time when we meet someone on the street, we decide if we want to continue a relationship with that person. The same is true for a business. Consumers know instantly by the look of your website, the first telephone call, and the first moment they walk into your business whether or not this is the place for them. So you have to work to define yourself and your business, or you will be allowing others to define you. We will look at the *Who*, *What*, and *Why* of your personal and corporate identity.

First, who are you? Are you the surfer dude wanting to live the casual beach lifestyle? Are you the guy taking over the family business now that your father has retired? Are you the stay-at-home mom trying to start a home-based business? Decide who you are.

I have a friend who used to be a gourmet chef. Not only did she prepare every kind of meat but also ate it. After she says she saw a series of signs, she opened her own restaurant serving only vegan fare and now lives a lifestyle reflecting her beliefs. She is clear about who she is.

Next, what is your message, and what does your business represent? It is important to know what you and your business stand for because customers will size you up in those five seconds. You need to be ready to fill those five seconds with the correct first impression.

Now, why are you here? Why are you in business? Why do you get up every day? Are you in business to make money, change the world or because you saw a need for a product? Whatever the reason, you need to know why.

After Hurricane Katrina devastated portions of the French Quarter, a business owner was asked by a news reporter if he would rebuild in New Orleans. "Of course," the man replied with a confused look. "There is no other place like New Orleans." He knew his *why*.

✳

Years ago, I saw a documentary about the art of movie making and someone said something that changed the way I look at life. He said that the first moment of a character's screen time is the moment when we either "buy into the character" or we do not. That split second of how the director chooses to introduce the character to us will determine whether or not we like the character.

In Saturday Night Fever, we see John Travolta, first just by his disco shoes, strutting down the street to the music, and we completely buy it. Scarlet O'Hara is introduced to us surrounded by eager suitors at Tara. We know instantly who she is. We first see Harrison Ford with his fedora and whip as he searches for the treasure, and we believe that he is Indiana Jones.

Now think of movies that did not work for you and the characters that, at first glance, just didn't sell you. The same is true in your business. If you spend your entire life with a look of defeat and boredom, then that is what you will receive in return. And if you manage to reach out to your clients and customers right from the beginning, they are more likely to buy what you are selling.

Are you that guy who does not even look up when I walk into your store? Are you the gal with the lackluster, uninspired response to the question, "So what do you do?"

Just like a dog can smell fear, a customer can smell indifference. And they don't like it. Customers will get as enthusiastic about your business as you are. They will meet your level of excitement. So get excited!

⌐ PSYCHO GENERATIONS: ⌐
WE ARE DRIVING EACH OTHER CRAZY

by Dr. John B. Molidor

⚘

THEY ARRIVED FOR A WEEKEND AWAY FROM HOME. MY OLDEST BROTHER'S FOUR KIDS. The boys were 15 and 13 and the twins were nine. They came to visit me, their Uncle John, during the summer.

"Take us out water skiing!"

"No problem…" I said, and out we went in the boat. I would do the driving.

They had never really water-skied, so they brought their camcorder with them. The oldest went out first, and one of the siblings videotaped him, and then the next, the next and then the next.

Usually when you take somebody out water-skiing for the first time, there's laughing, there's hollering, and there's screaming. But out of these kids… nothing!

I thought to myself, "Whoa, what's the deal here?"

As I docked the boat, they abruptly leapt out and made a beeline back to the house. And I thought to myself that this trip was a total bust, and that my 'Uncle' status was probably in jeopardy.

First thing they did in the house was turn on the television, and they plugged the camcorder into the front of it. Then they played the video, and guess what happened? *That* was when they started whooping, hollering and screaming. I thought, "This is clearly a different generation than the one I came from."

They told me that they had taped every major event in their life. And then they watched what happened. It seemed to me that the event wasn't real for them until it was captured and viewed on video. They also seemed extremely comfortable in front of a camera, unlike their parents, and mugged freely and unabashedly.

I knew I had to learn more.

❋

As a psychologist, I have always been fascinated by the mysteries of human nature, and among the most interesting are the differences among the generations. Every generation is stymied by the actions of the previous and next generations. They share things in common, but they just don't understand one another… in so many fundamental ways.

These generational differences range from the basics (such as musical tastes, language, and clothing) to the more complicated (e.g., work habits and work ethic, how information is obtained and the role of technology).

But the way the other generation operates isn't necessarily wrong—it's just different. Sadly, though, when we say a generation is different, we are usually saying that they are deficient. Different is just different, neither good nor bad in and of itself. How people act upon these differences, though, makes a huge impact on each other.

In thinking about the demographics of the people who will pick up a copy of this Anthology, you, the reader, are very likely to be a Baby Boomer as I am. We were born between 1946 and 1964, and we just don't understand why Gen Y comes to the workplace in flip-flops, chronically late, and inappropriately dressed. If you're a member of Gen Y, who just happens to be reading this article at this very moment, you will likely get bored, and jump to the next article, because I haven't provided you with enough interesting material. This is the way of our generations.

Each generation has its own quirks and strengths, and that's why we should get to know each other, psycho or not.

The word "psycho" has been used to represent "psychotic" people in horror movies, and has been picked up in culture to mean "crazy" or "insane." Indeed, each generation thinks the other generations are *crazy*, so it's a fitting way to describe all of the generations.

But the word "psycho" also precedes my title as a "psychologist," and it's very important that we understand the psychology of one another before we decide that the other generations are *all* psychos.

There are four generations in our workplaces and we are dealing with increasing amounts of tensions there. And there is certainly a lot craziness currently going on in our institutions.

The most important thing that every generation can do, in the workplace and everywhere else, is to understand where another generation is coming from, what the key events were that have shaped their lives, and to figure out why they act the way they do.

And only *then* are we first able to decide what to do about it.

— How to Get the Laughs Started —

by Brad Montgomery

As a professional speaker, I see the great value of humor each time I go to work. And there is a similar need for humor in every meeting and at every workplace. Here are some tips for presentation skills, whether from the big stage or from the front of a small room.

The best way to make a connection to your entire audience, whether in a classroom or a stadium, is to start a dialogue with one audience member in order to make a connection with the rest of the audience, putting them immediately at ease. Think of it like an interview of this certain audience member. Here are a few ways to connect.

✳

Choose a "helper" from his/her seat in the audience to join you to make a point. Or, take an informal poll: "How many people have ever had that happen to them?" or even, "How many people think the cookies on that break were awesome?"

While hands are up, single out somebody and ask a follow-up question. "What was the worst part about it for you?" or "When is the last time you had cookies that good?"

When they know they are planning to talk about jobs, comedians first ask the audience, "Who's got a job they love?" Somebody yells, "I do—I'm a courier."

Now the comic has a real reason to talk to that guy. "Courier, no kidding. How did you get that job?" The conversation goes from there. Eventually, the comedian will roll into the prepared material about jobs.

Couldn't you do the same, no matter what you talk about? Perhaps you're a sales presentation speaker. Instead of launching into your section about IRAs, you could say, "How many people have an IRA?"

Then turn to somebody and follow up. "What is your dream for retirement?" The connection is made with that person and the audience. It's lively and interactive, and many times it gets a laugh.

You can also follow up on whatever interaction you are already doing. Interview the volunteer for an exercise or a game. Or, ask someone to help write on an easel chart or to "report back" on what her group did in a small-group exercise.

Another great way to transition into an interview is the boldest, but works great. Imagine you have three points to your message, and you've just finished up the second one.

Point to an individual in the audience and interview them. You can do it from the stage or as you come down into the audience, but just start asking questions.

"Hi, thanks for being here today. What do you do?"

"I'm in records."

"What is the most exciting or surprising part of your job?"

Now, again, this is where you cannot lose, because any answer they give you will be good. They will say something heartwarming like, "I work with people I love." Or maybe they'll say something funny like, "I get to steal all the post-it notes I need." Either way, you get further connection—and the chance for easy humor.

And nearly always you can find a way to transition from this interview to your third point in your presentation. It might be something like, "Well, the fact that this person loves her workmates is going to make my next point easy for her. My next point is... blah, blah, blah." (Note: please insert your "next point" for the "blah, blah, blah." If you don't, your audience will think you've lost it.)

It might sound scary, but the interview technique is easier than it seems, and the rewards are huge. Pick some transitions, go with some prepared questions, and you'll be surprised by how much closer your audience feels to you and how many laughs you get without writing a single punch line.

CHAPTER EIGHT:

Leadership

"ANYONE CAN TAKE THE HELM WHEN THE SEA IS CALM"

—— *Publius Syrus*

Leadership often invokes thoughts of famous leaders: Martin Luther King, Gandhi, Oprah Winfrey... But I have also seen strong leadership qualities in a production associate who is at the lowest level of an organization or a shipping clerk who has no formal authority.

Leadership is a state of being that is built upon the thoughts, actions and daily habits that become our character. In times of difficulty, true leaders appear whether they have the power of their position or they are just stepping up to lead by example.

—— Paula Shoup,
author of "Using Your Internal GPS"

~ YES... IT IS REAL ~

by Ngahihi o te ra Bidois

※

IT HAPPENED IN A MARKET IN CAMBRIDGE, ENGLAND ON A BEAUTIFUL SUNNY SUMMER'S DAY. I was looking at T-shirts with my wife, Carolyn, and our two children. A couple of young men slowed as they walked towards me. My whole family heard their conversation as they took glances at my *ta moko*, the traditional Maori tattoo on my face.

This was not the first time my *ta moko* had attracted attention from strangers and as usual I pretended not to hear their conversation. As I continued browsing through the T-shirts rather than look at them, their conversation went as follows:

"Wow, look at that guy's face man. That tattoo is really cool."

His companion replied: "Yeah, but it's not real."

"Yeah I think it is, man. Have a closer look." They took the courage to walk closer to me.

"No way, man. That's not real."

"I think you're wrong, man. That looks pretty real to me."

"Nah, that's definitely not real."

My wife's patience and grace ended and she turned around to the guy and said: "Yes... it is real."

At this stage I looked at them and smiled and they took a good stare before both looking away sheepishly. As they disappeared into the crowd and the myriad of stalls, one of them punched his mate as he said, "See, I told you it was real, man."

Yes, my *ta moko*, or traditional Maori tattoo, is real. It is not a stick on, it is not painted on, it is not makeup—it is permanent. It is a gift I have received from my ancestors as an outward sign of my inner development and journey of identity. My *ta moko* is also part of my development as a leader that I am privileged to share with you.

✳

How do leaders develop? I am convinced from my personal leadership experiences and working with many leaders that our leadership begins and ends with ourselves.

I alone must decide to develop inwardly, so people see my leadership on the outside. You determine your leadership. You choose to lead—or not. My presentations encourage people to lead.

As a speaker, I share my stories, outlining aspects of ancient wisdom from my Maori culture. Ancient wisdoms that are also modern solutions developed from the ancient world of my people, the Maori. Ancient wisdoms I have had the privilege of receiving and sharing with many people.

Yes, my *ta moko* is real, and so are the leadership gifts inside of you. They are like hidden treasures waiting for you to unwrap and present to this world. A Maori wood carver once told me that when he looks at a block of wood he sees beyond the bark outside of the wood to the gift waiting to be revealed. His role was to slowly unwrap that gift one chip at a time.

Such carved gifts are a part of my Maori culture. They are carved *taonga* ("treasures") that stand in ancestral houses and important places to encourage and inspire us all. Each one of these carvings tells a leadership story and so do you. A block of wood that may have been lying dormant for many years awaiting the carver's arrival now stands in its rightful place. I hope that sharing my leadership story with you will inspire you to continue making the chips to reveal your gifts.

You were born for things such as these—to take that first step, and then the second step, and the next until your leadership journey becomes as real for you as it has been for me. And just like the gift of *ta moko* that was lying dormant inside of me for many years, I know there are gifts waiting to be revealed through you. Gifts that will make a difference in peoples' lives—leadership gifts that only you can give.

✳

One of my mentors and a close friend called me to his home for an important event. In our Maori world we call this event his *ohaki*—his dying speech to me. This would be our last conversation together. His name was Busche King and he had helped me through many situations and truly inspired me. He was one of my "eagles," a leader who was walking the talk and occasionally stopped to encourage me during his own leadership journey.

During his *ohaki* conversation, I mentioned that I would miss him sincerely and that I did not know what I would do without him. In typical Busche style he looked me in the eye and said, "Well, Nga, look in the mirror. Every answer you will ever need can be found in the person looking back at you if you look hard enough and ask the right questions."

Throughout my presentations I utilize my academic background to present to the visual, auditory, and kinesthetic learning styles of audiences to provide opportunities for you to stop and look in your mirror and ask yourself tough questions. Questions that will encourage you to look deeper into your being so the gifts lying dormant, like those which were lying in that carver's block of wood, will be revealed by you to you. It will then be your choice to chip away like that carver, one chip at a time.

I often have question and answer sessions at the end of presentations and was once asked a very interesting question. "Do you have tattoos anywhere else on your body?" My reply was, "No, I do not. I could have placed this gift from my ancestors on my arms or legs, chest or back where I could cover it with clothing each day. I decided to place this gift on my face so that I could not do that." I hope you choose to do the same with the leadership gifts you have received. There are times when we can choose to lead or not—I hope you choose to lead.

— CONTRACT TO CONFRONT —

by Dr. Paul Radde

DO YOU EVER HAVE CONVERSATIONS THAT TRULY ASTOUND YOU? For me, one recently came in the form of a phone interview with Lt. Col. John Spain, Director of Pharmacy at Walter Reed Army Hospital in Washington, D.C., for a speech I was to give.

Walter Reed Hospital's pharmacy operates 24/7. At the height of the Iraq war, some 60-65 new casualties came in daily from the hospital in Rammstein, Germany. Today, casualties are flown in from Afghanistan within 36 hours of their injury. Combat wounds and infections are treated; trauma is stabilized. The staff is on continual alert. Life and death issues are dealt with every shift. Effective response is essential to the entire Walter Reed operation; no less so for the pharmacy.

Here is what that interview revealed to me, which has taken a great deal of time to understand:

Lt. Col. Spain has what he calls a "contract to confront." That means that he "stops soap opera in his workplace dead in its tracks."

"I tell my people that they do not have the time to be concerned about how I look when I come in at the start of a shift," he said. "I may have had some concern at home, with one of my kids or a tough commute. That is none of their concern. They have a job to do. Don't waste your energy trying to figure out what I am thinking."

"I take one hundred percent ownership for communicating with you if I am upset about something that involves you or a situation in which you are at fault. If I don't tell you, then it doesn't concern you," he said.

John also makes sure his people know what his intent is at the end of the day, in order to get results and quash speculation.

What I found, which happily turned over my mental apple cart, was the initiative that John Spain was taking. That was a rare commodity to find coming from the high-ranking person in an organization. After training well over 5,000 supervisors, managers, leaders, and working with another 5,000 hospital pharmacists, this was an exceptional example of side-by-side leadership initiated by the person in the high status role.

It opened up a plethora of possibilities that I had not considered. Soap opera obtained no foothold in the workplace and simply went away, which reduced energy drains and increased efficiency. Stress was reduced in the workplace when the person in the status position took one hundred percent responsibility for providing timely feedback—the grapevine dried up. Essential professional communication was assured from the top down, with responsibility for it initiated by the higher-ranking individual, rather than hiding behind his status, rather than being venerable, becoming vulnerable.

❋

There is a major paradigm shift happening today, and this is one good example. The major shift is from a "power over," top down assertion of power in relationships, to a "power with," or side-by-side exercise of power in relationships. Relationships include the full range of vital relationships: professional and personal, organizational, institutional, governmental, and international. It's simply happening everywhere. We're all in it. There is no parallel universe to escape to where things will stay the same.

Each one of us does have the option to hold out, ignore, deny, and resist it. We can find pockets of reality where people stick with business as usual, where the old "power over" script is adhered to and where one finds comfort in the familiar. But the tide of the new practices is moving toward exercising "power with" in side-by-side relationships.

Meanwhile, top down practitioners grasp for high ground based on status alone, seemingly secured by their gender, age, sexual preference, skin color, position, physical attributes, wealth, family, tribe, and national origin.

Supremacy, as a state of being, is wilting; it is no longer an entitlement of birth. As a trait of being, it is attainable based on merit. Of course, vestiges of supremacy will continue. They are a part of our way of life. And these practices have found their way into our mentality, personal and professional practices, expectations, and competencies throughout all of human history.

It is well to recognize that people do not change! Things change. People transition, meaning that they move on, shedding prior practices—it is two steps forward, one step back. The roller coaster trajectory of transition carries us ever higher and onward. We are in the early recognition stages of this power paradigm shift. It needs to happen in the workplace, between nations, and between individuals.

❋

On the floors of Walter Reed Army Hospital, injured troops are being attended to in an efficient and professional manner. Total focus of attention from the pharmacy assures the safety, accuracy, and timeliness of their medications. The solutions and formula need to have healing properties. What better way to begin the healing process in the pharmacy than with an open, inclusive, reduced tension, professional atmosphere backed by solid communication practices?

Lt. Col. John Spain provides one vivid example of a person and professional stepping up and leading our evolution as a people and individuals. This person is having an impact every day with a better life for his staff and recovering patients. Such leadership requires sufficient maturity to take complete responsibility for one's actions, replacing brash exercises of "power over" with "power with" practices, infused with humor and humility.

— LEADERSHIP SHOULD START WITH C —

by Karl Mecklenburg

CAPTAIN, COLONEL, CHAPLAIN, COMMANDER AND CHIEF, CARDINAL, CHIEF EXECUTIVE OFFICER, CHAIRMAN OF THE BOARD, COUNSELOR, COACH, CHIEF FINANCIAL OFFICER... There are so many leadership titles that start with the letter C that "leadership" should start with C.

Fortunately, you don't need a C title to be a leader, but you do need the three Cs of leadership. These Cs are community, commitment, and consistency.

When I became a leader for the Denver Broncos, it wasn't when I was selected to be a captain. I became a leader when I decided to get to know all of my teammates better by sitting at a different lunch table every day.

In a similar way, true leaders are community-centered. They know their team; not only their names, but their likes and dislikes, strengths and weaknesses, their family situation and their hobbies. There is nothing more important to a team than relationships. The anonymous worker bee is a thing of the past as Generation X and Y teammates become a higher percentage of the workforce. And with the explosion of technological tools available to teams and leaders, there are no more excuses for a lack of communication, explanation, and relationships, within and throughout your team.

Communication must be a two-way street for the community to thrive. Opportunities for input in decision making across a team brings ownership and accountability to team members. These input opportunities strengthen a team by allowing team members to demonstrate their strengths and helping to prepare future team leaders.

My favorite leader has a name that starts with C: Christ Jesus. Isn't it amazing that God, the supreme leader, decided to come to earth as a dependent child and to live his life humbly, teaching through relationships, rather than coming in like a Greek god on a flying golden chariot with lightning bolts strapped to his back? That's because *dominance* isn't leadership. True leadership demands that the leader puts him- or herself in a position to serve his/her teammates and the team.

A leader's absolute commitment to the team's mission placed over his or her own short-term interest is vital. A leader thinks "we" instead of "me." The football coach who cuts a veteran teammate and friend when it's best for the team is a leader. The parents who send away the rebellious teenager they love in order to remove his influence on the other children in the home are leaders. My wife's commitment to staying home for our children, rather than using her many gifts in the working world, is a sacrificial act of leadership on her part. She is a brilliant woman who has made a conscious decision to put our team's needs, our family's needs, before her own. Mom should start with C, too.

Consistency in making tough decisions for the good of the team, repeatedly over time, is the mark of a great leader and essential to motivating the team to buy into the team mission. It takes time to build a reputation of consistency in followers' minds.

As my old coach Dan Reeves was fond of saying in his southern drawl, "You're either gettin' better or gettin' worse. You can't stay the same." When problems become apparent, making no decision and hoping the problem will go away will undermine your position as a leader. If you are not consistent, you will quickly lose your followers. Followers will question a leader's decisions, but if they see that the leader is consistently trying to do what's best for the team, they will continue to follow.

Remember the three C's of community, commitment, and consistency, and you will become a competent captain for your team.

— HUBRIS OR HUMILITY: —
FOUR LESSONS OF PHILANTHROPY

by Richard A. Marker

IT WAS DURING MY INTERVIEW WITH EDGAR M. BRONFMAN WHEN I LEARNED PHILANTHROPY'S FIRST LESSON. "We need someone who will know how to say no to all of these wonderful causes in a gracious manner," he told me. There are so many worthy and deserving causes, caring and thoughtful people, genuine unmet needs and powerful but untested ideas. Many more than any philanthropist or foundation can possibly fund. Indeed it is clearly important to say "no" graciously.

In the case of most requests, it is intellectually easy to say "no," since they simply don't fit. Emotionally, it is much harder. Individuals' destinies and dreams are in your hands. Institutions' missions are on the line. Social welfare and the social weal can be influenced by a nod or a "no." Cutting-edge thinking can be legitimated by an endorsement, or relegated to triviality by a rejection. There is a power in the role of the founder, which I experience on a daily basis in my work, which reinforces these lessons:

Lesson #1:

Our answer has an impact on the lives of so many. The more one must say "no," the more humility one must have.

If it is hard to say "no" graciously, it is even harder to say "yes" wisely. In reviewing eligible proposals, the decisions become even harder. In my career, I have been an executive in the not-for-profit sector, taught at the university level, consulted in the for-profit sector, and served on a wide variety of boards. Yet, as a foundation executive, I am continually struck by how little I know. There are seemingly wonderful projects which we cannot adequately evaluate because we lack the expertise, and whose worth cannot be proven unless a funder takes a chance. Some ideas and projects might change the world, or at least some small part of it; others will be failures, glorious or otherwise. Some are prestigious and safe; others might become the next great thing. With limited funds and more limited prophecy at our disposal, each approved grant is a well-placed bet. With all of the analytical abilities that trustees, program officers, and evaluators bring to bear, it is always human judgment that is the final arbiter. Thus,

Lesson #2:

Every grant reminds me that nothing is guaranteed. With humility, we rely on our best judgment to decide and on others to implement what only the future will demonstrate to be true.

If I am aware of my limited expertise, others are always telling me how wise, insightful, thoughtful, helpful, and unique I am. When I first moved to this side of the table, I was convinced that they must be correct. It felt wonderful that all of my fine attributes were finally being recognized. Fortunately for our foundation, flattery didn't guarantee a grant. And I quickly learned that my much-heralded attributes were less appreciated when a grant was not forthcoming. Ah, humbling.

Lesson #3:

Don't confuse who you are with what (or whom) you represent.

The last lesson is the most important and transcendent of all. It is an extraordinary blessing to be in a position to make a difference. It is all too easy, with so many wanting so much, to take our good fortune for granted, to become insensitive to real need, or worst of all, to become haughty with the power in our hands. That would be both sad and wrong. It is important never to forget, as the one on whom luck, skill, or destiny bestowed the bounty of this world, or as their professional representative, that it is a rare privilege to engage in philanthropy. Its very meaning, the love of humankind, must inform all of our actions and affect.

Lesson #4:

Our vision, therefore, must be dictated by the mandate to make the world a better place through the resources we dispense.

History will judge us by how well we respond to this unique challenge and gift. And that is the most humbling lesson of all.

CAPE TOWN—GUIDED BY THE LIGHT TO A LIGHT IN AFRICA

by Dave Rogers

FLIGHT SQ 480 ARRIVED AT 7:30 A.M., A PLEASANT THIRTEEN-HOUR JAUNT FROM THE ISLAND STATE OF SINGAPORE TO CAPE TOWN, A CITY THAT I AM CALLING "A LIGHT IN AFRICA."

Surprisingly, I smoothly and simply picked up my luggage, then gracefully whisked through customs, immigration, and easily found my awaiting event manager in South Africa, Lluwellyn Diedericks, at the arrival areas of the International Airport.

The freshness, lightness and chilly air of Cape Town filled me with excitement, energy and a sense of vibrancy. I felt invigorated to have arrived in South Africa; this was my first visit and I was looking forward to connecting with Mother Africa, the children of Africa and the entrepreneurs of Africa.

We were quickly joined by Lluwellyn's event collaborators, Lisa and Greer, and chose to have our first lovely informal connection in Camps Bay, an amazing spot where the Atlantic Ocean, the beach, and the 12 Apostles Mountain range co-mingle with majestic grace, vibrational delight and divine flow that shifted my body, mind and spirit to an altered state of cellular serenity, bliss and awareness that I had yet to feel, experience or recall anywhere in the world.

Breakfast flowed for several hours as three South African entrepreneurs shared some of their stories of the ups and downs of entrepreneurship in South Africa, the economic challenges, the political climate, and their mostly upbeat outlook for entrepreneurship in

South Africa. I felt humbled to be in their presence and truly felt that their belief, courage and action would see them through the terrain that spirited entrepreneur must face to endure, experience, and embrace the greatness that is possible through entrepreneurship.

With social entrepreneurs looking to align their business enterprise with the spiritual purpose, I was thrilled to share a promise in South Africa, a promise that is resonating with social entrepreneurs around the world. The promise is "to share the playground for extraordinary lives to grow and to build the foundation for world wide wealth to flow."

World Wide Wealth is the 2020 vision of aligning social entrepreneurs worldwide. The vision sees for the eradication of extreme poverty globally and sets steps for connection, collaboration, and creativity to increase value for aligned enterprises by at least one billion dollars per year that will translate into effective giving initiatives of at least one hundred million dollars per year. It is felt that entrepreneurs will be the effective change agents to set in motion sustainable, practical, and collaborative methodologies in the fields of health and wellness, the environment, education, peace, and prosperity.

✳

Following a stimulating breakfast, my kind hosts chose to give me a short tour of the Table Mountains and highlighted some sights including Robben Island where Nelson Mandela was incarcerated for more than 20 years from June 1964 to April 1984.

It made me smile to think that I was born in 1964, and I lived in Canada for twenty-one years before moving to Japan to set out on my global adventure. The comparison with Nelson Mandela was stalled there but then my curiosity started to play.

As I stood there facing Robben Island, the place where Nelson Mandela resided for twenty years, rain gently massaged my face. In the majestic glory and eternal vibration of the sea, the wind, and the mountains, I asked myself, what do I see as the similarities of Mandela's life and legacy and my life and legacy as an entrepreneur? Could it be the opportunities, the vision, the passion, the purpose, the conviction, the certainly, the uncertainty, the luck, the timing, or the talent? Does the comparison inspire or frighten?

I left Robben Island that day a little bit different. A little frightened and a little more inspired. There was a reason after forty-four years on this planet, I had been guided to Cape Town, I was certain of that, and I felt unbelievably blessed that a light had guided me to Africa, a light had guided me to Cape Town, and a light had guided me to come face to face with Robben Island and to the man called Nelson Mandela, which led to the next questions: As Robben Island is to Nelson Mandela, is there anything in my life that is keeping my in prison? Is there a specific belief, a rule, a conviction that is holding me back, keeping me down?

If I answered the question today, I feel that it is my relationship with racism, my relationship with equality, and my relationship with myself. I will be exploring racial discrimination and racial equality as an area that may allow me to add some insights, to share some distinctions, and perhaps make a difference to someone, somewhere.

— "FIFTEEN MINUTES OR LESS, — FIFTEEN DOLLARS OR LESS"

by Andy Masters

I ONCE PRESENTED AT AN EVENT HOSTED BY ONE OF THE UNIVERSITY OF MICHIGAN CAMPUSES, AND ENJOYED DINNER WITH MY CLIENT AFTER THE PROGRAM. During casual conversation while deciding what to order, she mentioned she goes *hog-wild* for A&W Root Beer.

Good thing she didn't say Dom Perignon, since dinner was on me.

I made a mental note of her affinity for A&W Root Beer, and pondered a few alternatives on my flight back. When I arrived home, I jumped online for less than fifteen minutes and ordered a case of A&W Root Beer for less than fifteen dollars, to be delivered to Marilyn's home address within three days.

Pretty cool.

The moral of the story?

I was re-booked there the following year, right?

Ehhhhh… no.

I was referred to a colleague who booked me the following year, right?

Ehhhhh… no.

In fact, over three years went by and I didn't hear anything from Marilyn.

Sad. But I was used to that from women.

Until one day when I received a phone call.

"Andy… Hi—It's Marilyn from up in Michigan. Do you remember me?"

"Sure I remember you, Marilyn. How are you doing?"

"I'm great! Hey, I wanted to tell you that I'm so sorry I hadn't kept in touch. You're not going to believe this, but, less than two weeks after you presented up here… well, I quit my job! I'm doing something completely different now. But, guess what…"

"What?" I responded.

"I just became chair of the planning committee for our upcoming conference and we'd love for you to be our keynote speaker. Are you available on August 23rd?"

Excitedly, I replied, "Yes that sounds great. Would love to do it!"

After that program, Marilyn and I again enjoyed dinner together. I asked her a question.

"So, Marilyn, I have to ask… After three years, what made you decide to track me down to present this program for you?"

"Sure, Andy. I've been waiting three years to tell you this. You know, I love your program. You're really a great speaker. But, there are plenty of other great speakers out there who also present great programs, as well. Do you remember that case of A&W Root Beer you shipped to my home?"

"Sure… absolutely."

"Andy, do you know I still have one can of that A&W Root Beer in my refrigerator that I show my friends and family when they come over? That was the greatest small gesture that anyone has ever done for me when it wasn't my birthday or Christmas."

❋

As great as we think we are at what we do, there is another person, or another company, who can probably perform the same function or service just as well as we can. So, what makes the difference? The little things which take fifteen minutes or less and fifteen dollars or less.

The excuses we subconsciously tell ourselves are, "I don't have enough time," and, "I don't have enough money." Sure we do. Fifteen minutes per day is just one one-hundredth of our time.

We should always have fifteen minutes or less, and fifteen dollars or less, to spend on the most important people in our life and career.

I once shared this story during my program for a chapter of Meeting Professionals International in Richmond, Virginia. During casual conversation at lunch, I mentioned to one of the event organizers that Fanta Orange was my favorite drink. Three days after my program, I had a box waiting for me outside my front door. It was a collectable Fanta Orange glass purchased from Coca-Cola.com.

I had a smile on my face from ear to ear. This totally made my day.

Then I thought to myself, I have to include this in my program! So, I visited Coca-Cola. com to download a photo of the glass, and discovered this product was just $4.97—on clearance for $1.97!

Awesome!

What amazing impact can you make today with your special client, significant other, employee or new contact, using just fifteen minutes or less and fifteen dollars or less?

— Using Your Internal GPS for Stronger — Relationships and Increased Sales

by Paula Shoup

LEARN HOW TO USE YOUR INTERNAL GPS TO INCREASE YOUR QUALITY OF RELATIONSHIPS THAT WILL MAKE YOU MORE SUCCESSFUL BY CLARIFYING YOUR DESTINATION, UNDERSTANDING YOUR CURRENT LOCATION, USING A MODEL TO NAVIGATE OBSTACLES, ESTABLISHING A STRONG MAINTENANCE PLAN, AND ENJOYING THE JOURNEY.

Clarify Your Destination

A GPS device will not work without a crystal-clear destination, something you are excited about and believe in; it evokes such strong positive emotions that you can't help but want to go there and the people you are relating to will feel your positive energy and want to help you go there. It is a big destination, not a trip across town.

Imagine you want to improve your relationship with your boss. Do not make this your destination; it is too small and boring. An improved destination is something like, "I am in a position of freedom and flexibility that allows me to use my strengths and talents to make a significant difference to the bottom line and increase prosperity for me, my boss and everyone in our business." It is unique to you and includes values that will keep you inspired and motivated.

Creating a clear destination will keep you on track. Your customers, peers, team or boss will feel your excitement and strong belief, which will naturally increase their levels of trust and collaboration.

Understand Your Current Location

Of course, GPS devices constantly re-calculate your current location in order to keep you focused on your destination; "Make a U-turn here..."

If your destination involves increasing sales with a current customer, where do you stand in your current relationship with your customer? Are things going well or not? Or is it unclear?

Research and understand the tools available to assess your current location. This may include customer surveys, personality and/or communication style assessments for improving peer-to-peer or team relationships, market analysis tools, etc. Do your homework in order to utilize a tool that fits your needs and then put an action plan in place to use the data gathered to take you to your destination.

Navigate Around the Obstacles

It is unrealistic to think that no obstacles will appear; the key is to have a plan in place to minimize them and get back on track quickly. In my many years of experience in the corporate world of working with suppliers, the best suppliers understood that problems will occur periodically and they had processes in place to handle them extremely well.

Over and over again, the best suppliers were using this model:

Early and Clear Communication + Action Plan + Timeline

Communicate that there is a problem early and clearly; don't wait until the delivery is overdue or, worse yet, the customer has complained. A big caveat: have the next two steps in the model clear in the communication before making the call or walking into their office. Just blurting out that there is a problem with no course of action is like bringing them a big mess with no plan to clean it up.

Understand the timeline of resolution, even if it is: "We need to do more investigation into the issue and will have an update in two days." Of course, ideally you will have a clear timeline that shows the complete resolution of the issue in your initial communication, but if this is not possible then be prepared to give regular updates until the issue is resolved.

Maintenance: Keeping Focused for Growth and Performance

All of the earlier actions are dependent on a good maintenance plan. Think about it—if your vehicle has not been well maintained, then you may break down before you even get to your destination. Or you may get there but it will take you more time and use more resources.

How do you maintain strong relationships with your colleagues, customers and overall network? Actively maintaining your relationships is critical to increasing your ability to be successful and increasing your sales.

Your sales and success will multiply beyond your imagination when you focus on what you can do to help them with nothing expected in return. Helping them may even include sending their sale to a competitor if they are a better fit or connecting them to another person in your network for something that has nothing to do with your product or service.

Maintaining relationships in this way will grow your network and connections because many more people will be passing on stories of your helpfulness and referring to you wherever they can. Building this reputation in a business will attract more people to want to work with you and recruit you to be on their team or move you up to a higher level of responsibility.

Enjoy the Journey

Think of a time when you were working with a salesperson or colleague who came across as needy and frustrated. You wanted to get away from them as quickly as possible and may have avoided them deliberately afterward. Relax and let your internal GPS guide you to stronger relationships and more prosperity:

- Stay positive and energized toward your destination.
- Track your results and make adjustments.
- Keep focused on helping your customer, colleague or boss.

You will attract more business and success than you can even imagine. Enjoy your travels to the destinations of your dreams!

WINNING WITH PRIDE:
PERSONAL RESPONSIBILITY IN DEVELOPING EXCELLENCE

by Donny Ingram

SEVERAL YEARS AGO, AS MY WIFE, CHARLOTTE, AND I SAT DRINKING COFFEE IN OUR DEN, REMINISCING ABOUT THE PAST, SHE ASKED, "HOW DID WE GET WHERE WE ARE TODAY, AND WHY ARE WE SO BLESSED?" Her questions made me stop and examine the past, and evaluate our journey.

As we reflected, I began to remember people, events and books that helped us discover how to take *Personal Responsibility In Developing Excellence* (PRIDE) in every area of our lives. The greatest lesson I remembered was in making good decisions. We all make decisions, and each decision has an end result and will affect our future.

The decision that began to totally alter my future was to attend a reading lab for four hours each day until my speed and comprehension reached a 12th grade level. You see, I graduated high school in the half of the class that made the top half possible! I finished high school with only a sixth-grade reading level which did not allow for a great many quality career choices. Furthering my education was definitely out of the question. I knew that being able to read better would allow me to open avenues in my mind that could change how my world would develop. That decision was essential in my being able to live life to its fullest and fulfill my dreams.

Another decision was to think differently, which was also vital to my success and the success of my family. I began to realize that as a human, I was born to succeed. Even my body is designed to succeed. When I get a bruise, puncture or break, my body begins immediately to heal itself. It will fight foreign bacteria, begin to regenerate itself, and create the chemicals necessary to sustain life. This is a great example to help us understand where success starts—on the inside.

I discovered that my thoughts produced feelings. Therefore, in order to feel good, I had to think correctly. Medical science has proven we have the ability to get the feeling we want, when we want it. I began to realize just how my mood changed when I would view a movie, one that made me cry or an action movie that excited me. I discovered my feelings changed because of my action to view and listen to something that my brain responded to and that my brain then began to produce the chemicals, hormones, and endorphins that gave me the resultant feeling. That is the beauty of how humans are designed: we are in control of how we feel.

The decision to set higher standards began to propel me forward. Setting standards meant being careful about the people I surrounded myself with. One such person in my life was a gentleman named Norm. Norm was an exceptional individual and an encourager of the greatest kind. He pushed me every day to go back to school and work on completing a college degree. Through his support and daily counsel, I gained the confidence to actually start and see myself completing the degree. Even though he was there only a short time, the words and confidence he instilled in me stayed in my heart, and helped me to finally earn my degree and even continue further.

✳

The most important decision in my life was choosing to have a positive attitude. Let me share a perfect example of how I learned the power of a positive attitude.

An organization in Nashville, Tennessee had an office just southeast of town that had never been successful. In fact, the director of operations decided to terminate the last two representatives in that office and close the office down because of non-production.

After several months, the director got the idea that he could make someone successful if he could do the following: instill a positive attitude and an optimistic perspective in the person he hired for that office. He called a company meeting that included every person in the organization. At that meeting, he told them of his plan to re-open that office, and that he needed their help in making it successful. He went on to explain how they would be involved in helping. He said, "Every time you speak to the person I hire, leave that person with the impression that their office has more potential than any in the organization. Tell him you don't know how he got such a great office; you wanted that office. All he needs to do to be successful is just show up for work." He received full participation because no one wanted to experience his wrath.

It wasn't long before he found and hired what he thought would be an ideal candidate. On the first day at orientation, the young man was approached by the trainer and asked, "How did you get that office? I wanted that office. I was willing to go back out into production to get that office. That location has more potential than any in the state. All you need to do to be successful down there is just show up for work."

Every time he talked to another branch or to someone at corporate, they left him with the impression he had one of the greatest opportunities in the entire organization. Even when he was having a slow month they would tell him, "You better hang on to your seat, because a slow month for you means you'll triple next month." He never saw failure.

You can imagine the results. The first year, he was 150 percent of his goal. The second year, he was over 200 percent. He was winning awards and contests he didn't even know were possible. He was just having fun going to work. After the third year, at the annual awards banquet, he was winning most of the yearly awards, and it was then that the director of operations decided it was safe to tell how this happened. He stepped to the podium and began to tell the story. I was sitting about four tables back, and I became very embarrassed and probably turned several shades of red because I suddenly realized that I was the man who had been hired. I remember thinking to myself, Have I been manipulated? Have they given me a worthless office and expected me to make it work?

✻

After a few minutes, I really began to see that what they had done was to teach me a life lesson. If I could maintain a positive attitude and outlook, I could be successful doing almost anything, anywhere, anytime. However, being able to work in a perfect environment, around perfect people who will give such encouraging feedback is almost impossible, but I discovered it could be done through self-communication. I began to tell myself what I wanted to see happen in my life, and I did it day after day after day. Only then did it begin to manifest.

Anyone willing to take personal responsibility in developing excellence can enjoy a life of significance and success. Begin now to make good decisions, and communicate the right message to yourself and build a positive attitude. Once you begin to see the results, you'll never turn back.

~ ALWAYS KNOW WHO YOUR ~ MOST IMPORTANT AUDIENCE IS

by Dr. Andy Neillie

৯৫

WE BOUGHT OUR FIRST HOUSE IN AHWATUKEE, ARIZONA, A BEDROOM COMMUNITY JUST SOUTH OF PHOENIX, IN 1984. No more apartment living! Close to the freeway, close to the mountain preserve and, most importantly, with a backyard. A fenced backyard—large enough for a dog.

Unfortunately, it wasn't very long into the dog discussion that Lynn and I reached an impasse in our marriage. "Dog" to me meant big, happy, and goofy—the kind of dog you could roll on the floor with, take on long runs, put in the back of a pickup truck to take to Home Depot. A real man's dog.

Conversely, "dog" to Lynn meant small, gentle, and polite—the kind of dog that never dug in the mud that sat quietly on the couch while we watched television that waited to be asked before it crossed from the tiled family room into the carpeted bedroom. A lady's dog.

Despite my best persuasive power, I wasn't winning this argument. According to Lynn, we were not going to have the kind of dog " …that puts its paws on the kitchen counter, brings mud in the house, and sticks its nose in impolite places!"

My vision of a Golden or Lab was quickly losing momentum to a small, scruffy thing that you would never take with you to Home Depot or a pick-up football game with the guys.

Despite our lack of agreement on the "dog-ness" of a dog, we moved forward with the process. We had a family friend who was a vet, and we put the word out through him that we were looking for a good dog that needed a good home. Several weeks went by, and then we heard that a dog had been found in the desert north of Phoenix. A couple who loved dogs had taken him into their home until a permanent home could be found.

Here's the bad news: Alex, the name this couple gave him, was a golden retriever—which I knew was a big, happy, and goofy breed; the exact kind Lynn was dead-set against. Here's the good news: their home was a full forty-five minutes from where we lived, so it gave me an extended time in the car with Lynn to ply my persuasive powers on her. After I convinced her to at least drive up and meet this dog, we arranged to head out on a Saturday morning.

I wish I could tell you my degree in communications made the difference on that drive. I wish I could tell you that my persuasive speaking abilities paid off in a big way. I wish I could tell you my powerful logic won Lynn over. I wish I could tell you I clearly wore the pants in the family that day! Unfortunately, none of that proved to be true during our drive to north Phoenix that day. We arrived at Alex's foster home with Lynn as dead-set against a big dog as she was when we started the trip.

I was crushed.

✳

As Alex's foster owners ushered us into their family room, I took a corner on the couch, trying to put a game face on for what was undoubtedly a wasted trip.

Lynn told me later that, at the same time as I was moping, she began to notice what a beautiful home we were in. These owners of two Goldens, and now foster parents of a third, had beautiful white carpet; we were sitting on a beautiful white couch, and had crossed over a clean and tidy tile floor to get there. This was not the kind of house she had imagined a big, impolite, dirty dog would live in.

After visiting for a few minutes, Alex was brought in. What a beautiful dog! Big, red, a wagging tail and happy eyes; he walked into the room like a prince among dogs. This was the dog I had hoped for, a dog to wrestle with, a dog to run with, and a dog to take to a tailgate party! Too bad he wasn't going to be our dog. Too bad my persuasive powers had failed on the trip north. Too bad Alex would be passed over in favor of some small, "harmless" dog.

I was more than crushed. I was devastated. The perfect dog. So close, yet so far. All because Lynn was opposed to getting a big dog.

While all this was racing through my mind, Alex walked toward the white couch where Lynn and I were seated. Slowly. Politely. Gracefully. Upon reaching the couch, Alex sat down on the floor quietly next to her and, ignoring me almost completely, gently put his paw on the couch next to her as if to say, "It is a pleasure to meet you." The perfect gentleman.

At that point, all Lynn's objections evaporated. Alex and Lynn connected, and Alex became our first rescued Golden and a wonderful addition to our family. Big and happy, he wrestled with me on the family room floor and went on runs with both of us. He took trips to Home Depot and showed up on the sidelines for pick-up football games. He slept beside our bed, welcomed Kaibab, our second Golden, as his companion when she joined our family, and he never once stuck his nose in impolite places.

Alex also demonstrated an uncanny knack for reading people. I don't care what others think; he made me a believer in a dog's sixth sense. In fact, his ability to "zero-in" on Lynn and woo her at that very first meeting was a clear demonstration that he knew what all wise leaders learn:

Always know who your most important audience is.

Alex knew whom he needed to reach. His uncanny ability to read the situation and see who needed convincing worked in his favor—and mine.

CHAPTER NINE:

❧

Entrepreneurship

"ENTREPRENEURS NEED TO SEARCH PURPOSEFULLY FOR THE
SOURCES OF INNOVATION, THE CHANGES AND THEIR SYMPTOMS
THAT INDICATE OPPORTUNITIES FOR SUCCESSFUL INNOVATION."

——*Peter F. Drucker*

The word "entrepreneur" originates from the thirteenth-century French verb *entreprendre* meaning "to do something" or "to undertake." Successful entrepreneurs understand that it takes more that just doing something to be a successful businessperson.

Over nearly 25 years in the speaking, training and communication coaching business, I have met many successful entrepreneurs (and yes, even coached a few) and most have followed a philosophy I call "making" a risk, which is different than "taking" a risk. "Taking" a risk involves stepping out with an idea and acting on it without much information. "Making" a risk involves stepping out with an idea in a proactive way.

There is always risk involved with entrepreneurship, but by exploring ideas in an innovative way, researching the market, mapping out the sales/marketing process, and doing some testing, entrepreneurs stand a better chance of managing this risk and increasing their potential for success. To me that is what entrepreneurship is all about.

—— *Patrick Donadio,*
author of "Common Mistakes Presenters Make"

⁓ Killed by Technology ⁓

by Scott Klososky

FOR SOME REASON, I HAVE HAD THESE VISIONS POPPING INTO MY HEAD OF THE THINGS IN LIFE THAT TECHNOLOGY HAS PRETTY MUCH ERASED FROM THE FACE OF THE EARTH. If you are under twenty-five years old, this article may not mean much to you. For the rest of us, this will be a bit nostalgic. The point is not simply to stroll back through the memories of our past, because the real goal here is to help us look forward into the future. By taking a look at the dynamics of days gone by, we may be able to apply the flow of what has happened forward to predict the future, and maybe even make a guess as to whether we will like what we see.

✳

I remembered carbon paper this morning. I am not sure why, but I had the distinct memory of the days when we actually stacked up sheets of clean paper with sheets of carbon impregnated wisps and then hit the keys extra hard to make sure that our words actually were copied onto all pages. Of course, this also made me think of whiteout, and the big step forward when we got NCR paper, which had that magical ability to copy words through without the actual carbon paper being in-between.

I have often recalled those cute little pink "While You Were Out" tablets that my admin used to fill out with the fifty or so calls I would get a day on the telephone. That was back in the day when I received that kind of volume of calls. Today, a busy phone day might be five to eight calls, and they come on my cell phone, which has a system that recognizes most callers by checking the number against my contact list. That means the caller is greeted by name, their message is taken, converted to text and sent to my e-mail and texted to me. No admin involved at this point.

I remember going to the library and using the Dewey Decimal System to look up a book so I could find the piece of information I was searching for in that large institution of knowledge. I remember having to be quiet, having to check out the books, which meant having a library card and being forced to have a deadline for the return of their property. Oh, and I remember the fines.

Of course I remember vinyl records, 8-tracks, cassettes, and CDs. That means I remember having to clean the needle on the record player and buying a new one every once in a while. I remember my kid brother scratching the needle across my favorite Elton John record, and I remember chasing him around the house after it started skipping—never to be repaired. And I recall the tape players eating the tape on occasion. I also remember sitting by the radio with my cassette recorder ready to go so I could tape a song I liked that I just could not get anywhere else. Then I would be the only one of my friends with the recording—even though it started ten words into the song.

OK, let's go to bullet points from here!

- When my news came from television and paper.
- When I lost touch with friends and co-workers never to be found again.
- When I had to memorize addresses, birthdays and phone numbers.
- When I could be by myself and no one could find me and make me work.
- When my kids communicated with the person in the room, and not ten people on their mobile device.
- When my rolodex was the most important contact tool I had.
- And finally, when I read books made with real paper, and I carried one at a time.

❊

The truth is, life has changed a lot and I am not just talking about the tools we use. The pace is changing—it moves much faster. The input has changed; it is now a fire hose of information, not just bits and pieces. The ways we communicate and are entertained are completely different now. The ways we have meals, and what we think is appropriate, has changed. So, how does all this looking back help us look forward?

The strange thing about us humans is that we most often get what we want. That is to say that when we seek advancement, we always seem to find a way to make it happen. We believe in a world of possibilities and for this reason it is safe to say that the tools we use today will continue to evolve to help us get what we want. That concept is always hard for most people to wrap their heads around because they can only see what is right in front of them and they believe we are *soooo* advanced that we simply could not invent yet another way to improve things. This of course is not true. Here is a list of what we seek:

- **More convenience**—life in general and work specifically should be simpler to handle
- **More connection**—we like to connect with others that think like us, are related to us or have some other connection to us. At times we just want to connect with famous people because it makes us feel important.
- **Easier communications**—the simplest form of connection is simply being able to "talk" to others. We crave easier, faster, and simpler ways to get in touch with whomever we want, whenever we want.
- **Better entertainment**—need I say more? We like to be entertained.

- **More productivity**—our bosses demand it, and we have found that our pocketbook is enhanced when we can get more work done in a 24-hour period. Anything that helps us get more work done faster is a winner for most of us.

With this list as a touchstone, and given the changes we have already seen from the past, what can we look for in the future? And maybe the bigger question is: will our lives be better when we get it? Is everything we want actually good for us?

The answers to these questions could take up five more articles, but let me make a few observations. There are lots of things that are still broken with how we communicate, connect and get work done. Think about how inefficient the keyboard and mouse are as interface devices. It takes me way longer to document these thoughts than just to think them. I need them to be stored in some kind of digital file as fast as I can think of them. When I want to send them to you, I have to just pick one method, or work really hard to guess what you would prefer. Wouldn't it be great if I could just tell my computer the people I want to receive this and my system would reconcile with your systems the best way to get the information to you?

✳

Productivity is still in the dark ages for the most part. We do not have an automatic system to update those around us when we complete a task, or even what the status might be. We still must do lots of tasks by hand, doing the same things over and over. We still gather information through long, painful meetings and discussions… You get the idea.

The point I want to drive home is that we are making an escalating amount of progress in applying technology to improve our lives. We are not done. Because we have a driving need to improve on the ways I mentioned, we are only halfway there, if that. So, the change from carbon paper to Microsoft Word is only a partial improvement. Get ready for much more to come.

And when you have some free time, think about the really big question concerning whether we will ultimately be happy when we get there.

~ COMMON MISTAKES PRESENTERS MAKE ~

by Patrick J. Donadio, MBA, CSP, MCC

ॐ

IT WAS THE NIGHT BEFORE MY FIRST PAID SPEECH AND I COULDN'T SLEEP. Tomorrow was my debut as a professional speaker.

I wasn't sure why I was nervous. I had done everything a professional speaker would do to get ready to deliver a great speech: I went to the library and found a joke in a joke book to open up my talk in a fun way; I wrote out my talk and memorized it word for word; I rehearsed it at least four times to make sure I had the timing down.

Yet, still I was nervous and couldn't sleep. I found myself getting up and jotting down some notes on a notepad I kept on the nightstand next to my bed. Two o'clock, three o'clock, four o'clock… I still couldn't sleep. Finally I fell asleep around five. After about an hour of sleep, my alarm went off at six so that I could get up early and rehearse.

I was scheduled to give my speech before lunch and they had me seated at the head table. It was about five minutes before I was to speak and the person who was going to introduce me asked me how to pronounce my name. I told her, "DOH-NAH-DEE-OH." I was finally beginning to feel better about the impending speech.

The introducer got up and started to read my introduction. As soon as she got to my name, I could feel my stomach start to roll, and the more she talked about me, the more I felt like throwing up. Finally she said, "Ladies and gentlemen, please help me welcome our speaker, Mr. Patrick Donadio." I thought, Okay, the worst part is over… The speech is finally here!

Well, I opened with that joke I found in the library. No one laughed. There was dead silence.

I thought, Oh no! What have I gotten myself into? But it was too late. I had to just keep plugging away.

The rehearsing had paid off because I was doing well at first. Then I started to notice a man in the back row with a bad coughing spell. I tried not to make eye contact with him so that I wouldn't be distracted. But his cough was getting worse. Finally he let out a loud mucus-filled "*hurruhsss…*" I looked over at him, and completely lost my place. I went blank.

My mind was as empty as a clean blackboard. There was dead silence for a full twenty seconds. It was like a bad dream; all of the audience members were simply staring at me. What am I going to do, I thought?

Luckily, I had brought an extra copy of my text, so I walked over to the head table where I had left my things, and I grabbed my notes. Then I walked back to the front of the room, and proceeded to read the last ten minutes of my presentation. It was awful. I kept thinking to myself that I should just stop and get off the stage.

I finally got to the end of my speech. I was so glad to be done that I forgot to let the audience know. I just stopped and waited for them to clap. Well, they just stared at me, wondering if I was done, and I stared back at them waiting for the applause. This went on for what seemed like an eternity, until finally, my introducer, seeing me in a catatonic state, got up from her chair and started clapping her hands as if to signal to the audience, "Hey, he is finally done… Let's clap so he will sit down!"

They clapped and I sat down. Now it was time for lunch, and I had no intention of staying around! I was way too embarrassed by what had just happened. So I made up some story on how another commitment had come up at the last minute and I would not be able to stay.

What a nightmare! But I learned a lot from that first speech; all the things not to do. I gave that speech in 1986, and since then I have given over a thousand presentations and have helped hundreds with their presentation skills.

Based on my experiences and those of my clients, I have compiled a list of the most common mistakes presenters make:

1. Trying to imitate someone else.

Be your unique self! Be authentic! Be the best you! Trying to imitate someone else only leads to second best. When you are connected with yourself, you connect with the audience.

2. Failing to project a sense of confidence.

You do this by talking too quickly or slowly, too loudly or softly, having poor eye contact, or reading word for word… Confidence is visual. Portray confidence through your voice, eye contact, mannerisms, gestures, and body language. Act confidently and you will become confident!

3. Speaking down to the audience.

Speak with the audience, not to them. Be careful of using jargon and technical terms or having a superior attitude.

4. Neglecting to prepare enough supporting information.

Many presenters fail not because they lack facts but because facts are all they have. Incorporate stories, real-life experiences, quotes, and statistics to keep your audience's interest.

5. Lacking a dynamic at the opening and closing.

The first and last things you say are very important to the success of your presentation. Openings should get their attention, introduce the content and establish rapport. Avoid apologies—the audience doesn't know what your problems are, so why tell them? Avoid a slow start—open with enthusiasm! Avoid the trite comments such as "Thank you for inviting me to speak with you today" (they are almost asleep by now...). Open with something different, unique and attention-getting! Lastly, steer clear of over-used clichés or jokes. The opening should be tied to the presentation. As far as closings, they are a way to wrap up your talk and leave them with a good impression. Avoid an irrelevant joke used just for a laugh. Don't end abruptly—just stopping or saying "Well that is all I have to say." Finally, stay away from long dragged-out endings. Plan your close. It should tie your presentation together.

6. Failing to rehearse.

Work out the kinks before you present. Rehearse out loud! Otherwise your presentation is the rehearsal.

7. Memorizing your speech word for word.

It's okay to memorize your opening, closing, and quotes. Memorizing your entire presentation could be trouble. As vaudeville comedian George Jessel once said, "The mind is a wonderful organ; it begins working the day you are born and doesn't stop until you get up to give a speech."

8. Reading your speech word for word.

It is okay to use notes but try not to read the speech word for word. Wean yourself away from reading by gradually placing less and less words on your notes. Learn how to condense your text into key bullet points. This will allow you to make eye contact with the audience and look more natural.

9. Forgetting to involve the audience.

Involve your audience mentally, physically and emotionally. If you don't tune them in, they will tune you out.

10. Not getting mentally prepared.

As I always say, "If you are not mentally prepared, you are not prepared." Take a few moments before your presentation to mentally prepare. Use techniques like visualization, tense and relax exercises, even listening to music in your car. These are all great ways to burn off some of the excess energy and relax before your speech.

— Change Your Image, Change Your Life —

by Sandy Dumont

❧

When I was a teenager, I was a withdrawn, unpopular grey mouse. At age 16, I sat down to perform a piano recital in my high school auditorium. Before I walked out, two boys behind the stage remarked snidely, "Hey, Boney Maroney, where'd you get that haircut?" I sat down to play and blanked out completely. I hated the way I looked so much I wanted to crawl in a black hole and disappear. My mother had made my dress and it was in an ugly style and dreary color. My hair was awful and I hated my skinny figure. There wasn't anything about myself I liked.

One year later, it was graduation time and my birthday, so I went shopping for a dress. It must have been my Guardian Angel who made me try on a red dress. When I looked at myself in the mirror, in that exquisite moment I could see my own self peeping through. I had found the real me. My new red dress changed the way I saw myself and felt about myself. In that wonderful moment, I caught a glimpse of the person I was born to be. I knew I would never be a grey mouse ever again.

The next week I spent my hard-earned babysitting money on a haircut and taught myself how to apply makeup from the pages of fashion magazines. For the first time in my life, people told me I was pretty. Armed with courage, I went to Washington, DC and enrolled in a two-year fashion and modeling school and soon became one of the top models in DC. It all began with that red dress; it gave me courage and revealed the me I was born to be.

✳

I was fortunate to learn something very valuable at a young age: when you change the way you look on the outside, people treat you differently, and then you change on the inside. It gave me the motivation to help others discover the remarkable person they were born to be. There are no unattractive people, only those who haven't learned how to be attractive.

Here's what you need to know in order to look attractive and wow your audience. Remember, all animals, including humans, are hardwired to seek out and give deference to the most powerful and attractive of their species. Attractive doesn't mean Hollywood glamour. It means a look that signals you are polished and refined.

1. Never dress to match your "superficial" appearance, as we humans are prone to do in an effort to look "understated." In other words, redheads want to resist rust, blondes

should run from baby pink, and brunettes with olive or brown skin need to banish beige and brown. It's okay to "stand out"—in fact, it's one of the tenets of branding. Powerful brands aren't packaged in plain brown wrappers, are they?

2. Some colors are flashy and some colors are classy. Food colors are flashy; think ketchup, mustard, orange, lemon and lime. Jewel tones and most floral tones are classy; envision ruby, emerald, amethyst, sapphire, violet, and rose red. Brand yourself as a Class Act.

3. Resist "grunge" colors; they make you look drab, tired and older. This includes olive and moss green, mustard, beige, brown and camel. In decades of tests with audiences, these colors are voted to be the least powerful and the least professional.

3. At least 80% of the population has cool skin and looks better in "primary" colors than grunge colors or pastels. Good colors for most people are navy blue, black, charcoal, royal blue, peacock blue, Chinese blue, emerald green, true red (not orange red), fuchsia, magenta, ruby, and taupe.

4. Hair is the number one area where most women let their brand down. Make certain you have a flattering and up-to-the-minute hairstyle.

5. Wearing a tie that matches the suit—or one that is totally washed out—is the number one area where most men let their brand down. Never wear a blue tie with a blue suit or shirt. Your tie should make a statement and stand out. Choose a bold power color and make certain the pattern is refined; resist floral prints and gaudy or abstract patterns. Remember, "Old Money" is discreet and "New Money" is loud or flashy.

6. Women: wear professional makeup. No turquoise eye shadow, please; and brown lips make you look drab and dreary. University studies have shown that women who wear professional makeup are judged to be worth up to 18% higher salary. Accessories also ramp up your credibility. A suit without serious earrings misses the mark in terms of authority. Skirted suits convey more authority than pantsuits because they are more formal.

✳

The way you look and dress announces the outcome other people can expect from you. It also announces how you feel about yourself, and you'll be treated accordingly. I learned that valuable lesson when I was 16. No one knew or wanted to know who I was. I was an invisible grey mouse with minimal personality. When I returned to my class reunion ten years later, everyone wanted to know who I was, literally and figuratively. Heads turned and I owned the room.

You can turn heads. Own the room and close deals, too. The secret is to dress to impress. When you dress "down" or dress for your own comfort, others notice. It's tantamount to hurling an insult at them because your image shouts, "My comfort is more important than impressing you."

There is one more reason to dress to impress. The way you dress defines who you are not only to others, but also to the person in the mirror when you leave the house each day. The person in the mirror will say either, "Aw, what does it matter?" or, "I'm going to conquer the world!"

You don't need a crystal ball to predict your future; your mirror does it for you.

— Why Your Website Shouldn't Be —
Like the Grand Bazaar

by Jamie Gough

Three years ago, before I formed Simple Site Guru, my website development firm, my husband and I were living in Turkey as English teachers. Needless to say, we love the thrill of new experiences—which is how we found ourselves standing amid the sprawling mass that forms Istanbul's Grand Bazaar, shoulder-to-shoulder with the nearly half-million other shoppers who were ready to partake of the 1,200 stores that constitute the marketplace. By then we'd lived in Turkey for nearly five months and were comfortable with Turks and bazaars. Or so we thought.

Shoving into the shaded depths of the bazaar, we made ourselves small by hunching our shoulders and sidestepping every few feet to avoid colliding with other vigorous shoppers. Inside, I clung to my husband for dear life as we tried to process the pervasive aromas of strong Turkish coffee, grilled lamb, textile dyes, cloying colognes and other overwhelming scents, all mingling boldly with the body odor of thousands of sweaty people who'd come in to escape the hot summer sun. Immediately, our ears were accosted by salesmen calling the Turkish equivalent of "It is here!" from every direction, and primarily at the tops of their voices whenever they spotted potentially-gullible *yabancılar* ("foreigners"). We'd been looking forward to a trip to the bazaar for months, thrilled at the thought of arriving back in America with some truly fabulous souvenirs from that 500-year-old marketplace, but even with thoughts of returning empty-handed to dissuade us, we barely managed to endure more than half an hour within that beehive of bartering. One bright blue scarf, and many pushes and shoves later, we escaped back to the open streets of Istanbul, absolutely craving some downtime at a nice quiet restaurant on the Bosphorus.

*

This sort of overload experience is not confined to Turkish bazaars. In fact, I'll bet you've endured something akin to this when visiting a really *loud*, bright, jam-packed website.

And the statistics show that, like my husband and me, most site visitors are quick to escape from such overwhelming experiences!

In fact, studies have found that website visitors typically read a pitiable 20 percent of a web page. And this number drops rapidly for sites with more than 600 words per page. The point? The fewer words you have on your website pages, the more likely it is that visitors will actually read your text. The best you can do is to tell site visitors what your company does, how it operates (if necessary) and why it's better than all the others.

And I'm not just talking about text: even if site visitors aren't overloaded by words, they don't appreciate having to scroll down web pages to get to the *good* stuff that they've come for. In actuality, while viewers will often go through the act of scrolling, they only spend an average of 20 percent of their time looking at the content on the lower sections of your pages. This means that they spend 80 percent of their time taking in the text and images you've got at the top of each page. So, point two: don't make your site visitors scroll, and if you've got to do it, make sure that your crucial information stays at the top.

Of course, there's the possibility that you need to communicate gobs of must-know information to your visitors. If that's the case, don't slog it all in one place. Make it easy on people and break things down into clearly-named menu items that link to separate pages. It'll make your site visitors' browsing experience a heck of a lot more enjoyable.

✳

Now that we're talking about actual design (versus content), there are a few more points that will help you make your site a virtual haven for visitors (rather than a grossly overwhelming, difficult to navigate, Internet nightmare).

"X" Marks the Spot - Give your visitors a clearly defined, simple to understand navigation menu so they can easily get where they want to go. Name each page something logical, and keep all of your navigation links in the same general area. Have you ever visited a site with a home page consisting of merely a large (albeit attractive) image, only to linger in honest perplexity wondering what to do next? When this happens to me, I sometimes have the patience to roll my mouse over the image, only to discover that there are "hidden" links all over the picture. But really, most people don't want to play hide-and-go-seek when they're looking for information on a web page, so give them easy-to-follow directions to the different areas of your site.

If They Can't Read it, it May As Well Not Exist - Keep your font style simple. Like many website owners, you may think that Arial or Times New Roman fonts are dull and overdone—but there's a good reason that these fonts are so ubiquitous. They're easy to read and they load on every visitor's computer. If you use a swirly, calligraphic font, there are three potential problems: your site may appear unprofessional; the font could be difficult to read (in which case, you might as well not write anything); and the site visitor's computer may not even be able to load the font. Stick with the basics.

White Space Rules - The *less* that you have on your site, the *more* your primary content will stand out. Take *google.com*, for instance. This hugely popular search engine's website is uncluttered. Users know exactly why they've come to the site, and Google has obligingly provided a simple search bar front and center, surrounding it primarily by some lovely and unobtrusive white space. That's not to say that you can't have numerous images on each page, but you must properly balance your images, text and other content against a comfortable pillow of white space to avoid overwhelming, and thereby scaring away, your precious site visitors.

So what does it all boil down to? Keep it simple. When someone visits your site, it's because they want to know more about your business or even purchase whatever you may be selling. Give them the information they seek in a clearly defined, easy-to-navigate format. Welcome them warmly, and then offer them a comfortable, open space to explore freely and without feeling harassed by excessive amounts of text, images or useless information. Let your site be an oasis in the Grand Bazaar of an often large and overwhelming worldwide web.

— COMMUNICATION IS NOT A FOUR LETTER WORD! —

by Roseanne D'Ausilio

IF I ASKED YOU, YOU COULD TALK ABOUT ALMOST ANYTHING AT A MOMENT'S NOTICE. In the computer of your brain, you have many programs—what you think, what you feel or believe about anything, even things you know absolutely nothing about! And you can go on and on about any topic.

However, much of this is empty communication. It's defined by the four–letter words "talk" or "chat" or "blab" or "tell."

Poor communication is the most frequently reported, single, major source of frustration in companies and relationships today. So what can we do to improve that communication?

Two simple means to better conversations at home and in the workplace are inflection and listening.

Your inflection and tone of voice are often even more impactful than your words. One study shows that we communicate only 7% of the time with our words and 38% of the time with our tone and inflection. Therefore, we need to learn to control our tone, tempo and volume.

Listening is possibly the most important aspect of communication. We all think we know how to listen, don't we? But the fact is that very few people truly know how to listen. In our earnestness to serve, we get pulled out of a conversation by preparing for the answer while the other person is still talking.

We wait for a pause, and when the person takes a breath, we jump in to take them where we think they want to go, or to improve or remedy the situation. The truth is that if we're not listening to what someone is saying, we won't even know the question or request, let alone the answer.

Our intentions are good. We want to give the best response we can, and hopefully the right answer. However, if we're not present to the conversation, the other person feels unheard and unimportant.

The more we can avoid the four-letter words of communication, instead shaping our inflection and listening to the other party, the better our ability to communicate becomes.

― ATTITUDE? BAH, HUMBUG! ―

by Ebenezer Scrooge (aka Roy Lantz)

I SUPPOSE I REALLY CAN'T BLAME YOU FOR CONJURING UP IMAGES OF A SELFISH, MISERLY, MISANTHROPIC OLD SCROOGE WHEN YOU READ THE TITLE OF THIS BRIEF NOTE. Even my creator, Mr. Dickens himself, described me as "a squeezing, wrenching, grasping, scraping, clutching, covetous old sinner."

Granted, I may have been a bit intemperate in a few dealings with my fellow man. When I suggested that the poor and needy should be led off to prisons and workhouses at the festive Christmas time of year and was told that "many can't go there and many would rather die," perhaps my response that "If they would rather die they had better do it, and decrease the surplus population" was a bit harsh.

However, as I was quick to explain to the gentlemen who were soliciting funds for the downtrodden, "It's not my business. It's enough for a man to understand his own business, and not to interfere with other people." Mr. Dickens pointed out that after that dialogue, "Scrooge resumed his labours with an improved opinion of himself." I must agree that my attitude toward myself was significantly enhanced by the exchange!

Ah, yes, my attitude toward myself. In obvious contradiction of everyone else, it was quite flattering, and deservedly so, in my opinion. I had become a very successful man of business and extremely wealthy. My nephew Fred was fond of observing that "His wealth is of no use to him. He don't do any good with it. He don't make himself comfortable with it."

And as far as people suggesting that I grossly underpaid my clerk Bob Cratchitt, my attitude was that if he can't raise six children on fifteen shillings a week, he shouldn't have had so many children in the first place!

After all, why should I have cared about the attitude of others towards me? As Dickens observed, "But what did Scrooge care? It was the very thing he liked. To edge his way along the crowded paths of life, warning all human sympathy to keep its distance..." And besides, as I told the Ghost of Christmas Present in what I consider to be the best film version of my life ever made, the 1951 classic starring Alastair Sim: "I'm too old to change!"

Speaking of different versions of "A Christmas Carol," since the first film version appeared in 1901 in Britain, there have been dozens of audio and video recordings of the story. Alas, having seen and heard every one, I must concede that I, too, will agree that my attitude was a humbug.

✳

Happily, you'll note that I said my attitude was a humbug. How I went from "an odious, stingy, hard unfeeling man as Mr. Scrooge," according to Mrs Cratchit, to "as good a friend, as good a master, and as good a man as the good old city knew..." as observed by Mr. Dickens, is a wonderful testimony to the human spirit.

In fact, as I myself said when I realized that by changing my attitude I could change my life, "I don't know what to do! I am as light as a feather, I am as happy as an angel. I am as merry as a schoolboy. I am as giddy as a drunken man."

When the final Spirit departed, my attitude conversion was complete. I remember laughing as I hadn't laughed for years. In fact, Dickens remarked, "... it was a splendid laugh, a most illustrious laugh. The father of a long, long line of brilliant laughs!" I especially recall the difficulty I had in dancing and shaving at the same time!

Humbug? Ebenezer Scrooge? No more! When my attitude began to change, my life began to change.

As Charles Dickens so eloquently put it, "May that be truly said of us, and all of us!"

～ GIVING ～

by Jeffrey Gitterman

๛

IN THE CONVENTIONAL SENSE, PHILANTHROPY MEANS "LOVE FOR MANKIND, USUALLY DEMONSTRATED BY GIVING MONEY TO, OR DOING WORK FOR, OTHER PEOPLE." When it comes to financial philanthropy, most people who give generously are those who already consider themselves wealthy. As a financial advisor, I've seen this time and time again, and this makes sense to a certain degree. If you can't support your own family and pay the daily bills, you probably won't be writing $10,000 checks to even the most worthy of causes.

A few years ago, I went on a trip to a Land Rover training school in North Carolina. It was quite an experience. You get to drive a car that is smarter than you are when it comes to driving on rough terrain. The instructor told me, "If you're going downhill and you start losing grip, don't brake." I thought he was kidding, but he wasn't. He explained that with this car, you actually had to step on the gas, which is so contrary to everything we are usually taught. If you're flying down a hill and you start losing control, your natural tendency is to step on the brake. But in this car, the trick was to do the opposite. The tires would then grab onto the dirt, engage, and provide the stability and grounding you needed.

Giving also sometimes seems counterintuitive, but it tends to work in the same way. Just when your instincts tell you to try to hold on to as much as you can get, experience has taught me (sometimes the hard way) that you have to do completely the opposite, and find a way to give. This may sound like a simple principle, but it is one that often goes against so many of our deeply imprinted habits. Contrary to what many of us believe, giving is not just an afterthought to success. It is, in my experience, the very key to true success, fulfillment and lasting happiness.

✳

When I think about giving, I don't just think of it in terms of money. I also think about it in terms of our time, energy, and attention. From firsthand experience, I've definitely learned that simply being concerned about my own selfish needs and desires is a certain recipe for unhappiness, while being of service and giving to others is where true fulfillment is found.

My understanding of the power of giving came about many years ago, when I was just starting out as a financial advisor. One of the initial appointments that I'd have with any new perspective client is what we call in the industry a "fact-finding session." The idea is that you are there simply to get information and gather data like their Social Security number, date of birth, place of work, the kind of house they live in, income, assets and so on.

One day, I was getting out of my car and about to walk into a prospect's house to try and sell some insurance. I was way behind on my bills, and my mind was going on and on about how much I needed the sale. Desperation poured out of me as I caught my reflection in the car window. I stopped and looked hard at that reflection and said to myself, "Who would want to buy anything from you? Look at how desperate you look!"

I decided in that moment that I needed to get rid of my desperate, needy attitude and walk into this prospect's house with the attitude of someone who was looking to give without expecting anything in return. I dropped my worry about having to make a sale, and began to listen very deeply to what these perspective clients really wanted and needed. And as I approached more clients this way, my meetings started to transform and my success as a financial advisor grew exponentially.

Although it sounds like a bit of a cliché, I was able to see firsthand as I was going through my own crisis around wealth and success that the more I gave to others, the more I received in return. I quickly began accomplishing more in the world and my income grew substantially.

✳

Nowadays, my frame of mind going into any meeting is, "How am I needed here?" Often, I go into business meetings and when the other person comes in, I can see that they are largely focused on what they are going to get out of it. And such a person expects to meet someone on the other side of the table who is coming with the same mentality, who is going to fight for "what's in it for them." But if you are able to approach this kind of situation with an unconditional mentality of giving, it completely defuses the situation and provides a better opportunity for a win/win outcome.

Unfortunately, too many of us spend our whole lives waiting to get something from the world so that we can show up as the person we always knew we could be. Deep in our hearts, we think there's something missing. But when we flip that mindset, we can discover that by becoming a giver rather than a taker, we can change the world, literally, one person at a time.

PART IV

❧

MOTIVATING STORIES

"THE IMPORTANT THING IS NOT BEING AFRAID TO TAKE A CHANCE.
REMEMBER, THE GREATEST FAILURE IS TO NOT TRY.
ONCE YOU FIND SOMETHING YOU LOVE TO
DO, BE THE BEST AT DOING IT."

— *Debbi Fields*

"MAKE IT A POINT TO DO SOMETHING EVERY DAY THAT
YOU DON'T WANT TO DO. THIS IS THE GOLDEN RULE FOR
ACQUIRING THE HABIT OF DOING YOUR DUTY WITHOUT PAIN."

— *Mark Twain*

"IF I HAD EIGHT HOURS TO CHOP DOWN A TREE,
I'D SPEND SIX HOURS SHARPENING MY AX."

— *Abraham Lincoln*

CHAPTER TEN:

✿

Motivation

"REMEMBER THAT THE MEANING OF LIFE IS
TO BUILD A LIFE AS IF IT WERE A WORK OF ART.
START WORKING ON THIS GREAT WORK OF ART CALLED
YOUR OWN EXISTENCE. REMEMBER THE IMPORTANCE
OF SELF-DISCIPLINE, STUDY THE GREAT SOURCES OF WISDOM,
AND REMEMBER THAT LIFE IS A CELEBRATION."

—— *Abraham Joshua Heschel*

Motivation is an inner experience. We begin this journey seeking motivation from outside sources: parents, friends, lovers, preachers, teachers, and the noise of ever-present media… And then Truth dawns on us: *we* are our own Source. *We* have the power to shift internal gears. *We* and we alone determine our motives, our attitudes, and our path.

We are the only one in our life who is 100% impacted by our choices.

Choose how you are influenced.

Choose your input wisely—honor your gifts.

Remember who *you* are.

—— *Beth Terry,*
author of "Motivational Mayhem"

— Your Choice: Stepping Up, or Stepping Out? —

by David C. Allen

It was January 1987 in Baton Rouge, Louisiana at the LSU indoor track and field invitation and I was standing in the doorway of where dreams become a reality.

I was recruited by Samford University in Birmingham, Alabama on a track and field scholarship to specialize in the middle distance events such as the 800- and 400-meters or half-mile and the quarter-mile, respectively. However, on this day, this launching of my collegiate athletic dream and beyond, I wouldn't be participating in either one of those. No, on this day I'd be running a grand total of 60 meters!

This was way shorter than the distances to which I was accustomed, and I had never even run the 100-meters, let alone the 60! But I did have one guarantee as I went into this, and that was the fact that when I crossed that finish line, I would be significantly less tired than I was when I ran either the 800- or 400-meter events!

As the day drew on and the event drew closer, you could hear the voice of the announcer bellowing over the stadium speakers—"First call! Final heat of Men's 60-meters"—at which point I started fine-tuning and working on my final bits of preparation. As I continued to prepare, I heard the announcer's voice boom: "Second call! Final heat of Men's 60-meters. Please report."

So I went over to the table and checked in with the "clerk of the course." They give me my race number and assigned me my lane. At this point, it was just about launch-time and I started shedding my warm-ups, and I really started focusing in on the task at hand.

I was totally in the zone, and I was determined to run the best 60-meter dash I had ever run in my life. Then I heard the announcer one more time, booming out over the coliseum PA: "Final call! Final heat of the Men's 60-meters. Report to the starting line."

I remember it like it was yesterday. As I reported to the starting line and found my lane assignment, the noise of the crowd began to fade as a result of my intense focus. As I stared down the green track, my vision narrowed by the white lines on either side of my lane.

✳

As I prepared for the start, I happened to take notice of some of my fellow competitors in my heat. Down in the second lane was a gentleman by the name of Cletus Clark. Now, for those of you who might not know who Cletus was, he was a silver medalist in the 110-meter high hurdles in the previous Olympics in Los Angeles in 1984. He was quick!

I thought to myself, "Well, that's cool, I'll get to run against a silver medalist!"

Then I noticed another of his teammates from the same Olympics; a gentleman by the name of Carl Lewis. I don't have to go into the gold-colored souvenirs he brought home from Los Angeles that year.

The starter said to us, "Gentlemen, take your marks," and the tension was so thick you could cut it. We wound ourselves up into tight balls of rubber bands ready to spring at the sound of the gun. Then we heard him say "Get set!"

The energy built and built and built like a space shuttle sitting on the launch pad with the rockets firing, smoke billowing out around it as it prepares for lift-off... Then "Bam!" Off we would go in an explosion of energy. And there I was with Carl Lewis, the great Olympian! This was the greatest moment of my life! Side by side; neck and neck... If you were watching from the side, you couldn't even tell who was in front!

I was thinking to myself, "Exactly how long am I going to hold onto this position? I'm side by side with a great Olympian!!"

And then the gun went off.

And they finished and...

Then I finished, and well, I wasn't exactly neck and neck at the end of the 60 meters!

✳

This memorable day was my first collegiate athletic experience. I climbed on the bus that afternoon for the long ride from Baton Rouge, Louisiana to Birmingham, Alabama carrying what felt like a burlap bag of shattered dreams and reality.

Now, I realize that this story doesn't involve a close call with death, major financial ruin or setback, family tragedy or overcoming all odds. It does, however, tell a tale of devastation. The devastation of a dream and a future I had planned for myself.

I had worked all my life up to that point, invested sweat and tears in dealing with the trials of training to be the best. To have this stellar collegiate career and set national records and hang medals around my neck and compete nationally and then internationally... And there I was, the guy who also ran. So what could I do?

For many of us, this is the landscape of either our personal lives or even business environment. Many start families with gleams of bright futures and bliss only to have that dream altered in the blink of a bad choice. Businesses large and small are dealt blows with changing environments, technologies, and economies. What can you do?

Find a way! We must adapt to the change and realize we have a new hand we must play. It's not what cards life deals you, its how you play the hand you're dealt!

As for me and my story, I had a choice to fold my tent or rise to the challenge. Later that spring, I was pitched another curveball when I was presented with yet another new event two days before a big meet: the 400-meter intermediate hurdles. I had never run a hurdle in my life! And I succeeded that first time out, and went on to hold the collegiate record at our school for the next four years I was there.

The best news is that you hold the key to your future and success through the choices you make. Will you step up or step out?

— MAKING MISTAKES —

by Craig Price

"ALL MISFORTUNE IS BUT A STEPPING STONE TO FORTUNE."

- Henry David Thoreau

MAKING MISTAKES IS A PART OF LIFE.

We all make them. You make them, your boss makes them and your employees make them. Everyone except my wife. I know she doesn't make any because she told me so. Oh, and everything is my fault. I have accepted this truth because I want to remain married and I hate sleeping on the couch. But mistakes are never in short supply.

The Myth: Don't dwell on mistakes. If at first you don't succeed, try, try again. The Reality: Making mistakes is not the problem. Repeating them is. If you constantly repeat the same mistake over and over, you're not learning. And if you're not learning, you're not helping.

Mistakes are part of the learning process. Often mistakes show us where we missed something in the planning process. When we make mistakes we need to evaluate what went wrong, not just what went right. After every mistake, it's vital that we sift through the ashes and identify the potential causes.

A mistake is only a problem if you repeat it. Treat your mistakes as learning opportunities. A mistake is a great way of finding out what's not working; a way to self-evaluate your abilities.

No one is perfect, but as we strive for perfection, our mistakes will lead the way. How we choose to recover from these mistakes is the key.

"WE CAN'T SOLVE PROBLEMS BY USING THE SAME
KIND OF THINKING WE USED WHEN WE CREATED THEM."

- Albert Einstein

Whenever you commit a mistake it's important you follow these simple steps:

1. Relax

If you make a mistake, calm yourself. When you panic you make bad decisions.

We hear survival stories all the time, and in them, the ones who don't make it always were the ones who panicked. They didn't think things through and made a series of rash decisions that only got them deeper and deeper into trouble. So when you make a mistake, don't panic.

Don't panic!!

Panic causes us to react, not think. Often, those reactions are mindless flailings that end up causing more mistakes. Sometimes, like running out of a burning building, they save your life. But in general, don't let panic set in. Relax. Take a calming breath.

2. Contain

Some mistakes are cut and dry. You made the mistake, it's done, you move on.

Some mistakes are just the beginning. They ripple out and cause more problems until you correct the mistake. You made the mistake and now there are consequences if you don't fix it.

Do your best to stop the forward progression of a snowballing mistake. No need to let it get bigger and more unwieldy. The smaller the mistake, the faster it can be corrected.

3. Decide

The fire's out.

The ashes and smoking rubble are all around you.

Time to start repairing the damage.

Now is the time to think your options over. Take some time to decide what the best way to fix the mistake is. Five minutes of planning can save you days of headaches.

4. To Confess or Not to Confess

This one is the toughest for most people. No one likes to admit they screwed up, especially if they can't repair the damage themselves. If you've screwed up at work and haven't found a solution to the problem, confess. Your boss may be able to save the day!

Lies and cover-up will almost always backfire. Time is not on your side. Sooner or later someone will find out.

The first time you're caught in a lie will be the last time those people will ever trust you. Besides, lies are tough to keep going because they require you to remember everything.

5. Keep it real

Be objective about the seriousness of your mistakes.

Don't over- or under-value those mistakes. Take the serious ones seriously and the little ones in stride. Look at every mistake and judge it honestly. Was it a serious mistake that could have hurt someone? Then, regardless of how quickly or effectively it was handled, regardless of the fact that no one did get hurt, take it seriously.

If you make a huge, monumental mistake that freaks everyone out and you just go "Meh" and think nothing of it again, someone in a position of authority may think it's a real big deal and your nonchalant attitude will only piss them off. Nothing irritates a person faster than when they think something is important and you don't.

Was it a minor mistake that was easily handled? People often blow little mistakes way out of proportion. They turn it into a morality play of life and death. They want to show how much they care by making it sound like it was the biggest mistake in the history of the world.

We know you care. You don't need to exaggerate to show how invested you are. We know every day, because we see how you act. Your character defines you, not necessarily your mistakes.

6. Everyone makes mistakes

You do it. I do it. We all screw up from time to time. You're not unique in your occasional ineptitude. Well, maybe *you* are, but most people make minor mistakes all the time. It's part of the human experience.

Once you understand mistakes are a part of life, the fear of making them should diminish.

Go out and make a few, a little one here and there, then graduate to big ones! The sooner you can learn to master mistakes, the less often you'll actually make them. Because taking the fear out of mistakes no longer makes it a mistake, just another opportunity to learn.

Wow, that sounds almost like a cheesy motivational poster!

Sorry, my mistake.

— WINE AND THE PODIUM: —
UNCORKING THE MESSAGE

by Gilat Ben-Dor

IF YOU'VE EVER STROLLED DOWN THE VAST AISLES OF A WINE SUPERSTORE, OR MEANDERED AMID THE DUSTY CAVES OF AN OLD WINE CELLAR, YOU PROBABLY NOTICED THE SHEER NUMBER OF WINE BOTTLES AMASSED IN ONE COLLECTION. At first glance, these all appear to be a similar product—a commodity, even: all glass bottles, displayed symmetrically with somewhat similar labels in indistinguishable rows; and all containing wine. But upon closer inspection, we come to realize that each bottle has arrived to this spot on its own separate journey. From grape to glass, there is a history of struggle, of development, of cultivation and ultimately, of blossoming—a journey that is strikingly similar to our own as professional speakers.

The development of a wine can often take years, and impatience and arrogance are the enemies of this careful process. As speakers—and individuals thirsting for learning and growth—we can take some cues from the wine world ourselves.

Signature Style

Like the maturing of a wine, our unique message as speakers takes time to cultivate, to grow and flourish, and finally, to harvest and share with the world. This expression unfolds over time and cannot be rushed. How do we know when we are truly "ready"? How does a vintner know when to release their special vintage of reserve wines? This is part art, part science, and a great deal of *je ne sais quois*, which in technical terms means "who knows." Our raw ingredient is our message that we want to uncork and share with others as we watch it evolve over time.

Even the great wines of the world had rustic—if not humble—beginnings, among dirt and stones. These world-famous masterpieces of grapes may have had a rather mundane start—after all, how distinct is a raw bunch of grapes from the rest of the grapes in the same field? But then the individual winemakers begin their creative process, and the unmistakable characteristics of one winemaker's mark can be felt against others. They all produce wine; that is a fact. But what will make some vintners develop a cult following, with waiting lists? It is all about their signature style—their signature story in a glass. Think about your own as you step up on stage.

Old World versus New World

For centuries, it was Europe that was considered Wine Royalty. From Burgundy to Tuscany, the *Vitis vinifera* grapes of the Old World were the most prestigious. But then, in historic moves such as California's triumph over French wines in a world-renowned competition in 1976, the face of wine began to change. "New World" wines—from the Americas, from Down Under, from South Africa—began to populate the scene, and the face of the industry has never been the same.

There has been a similar shift for the speaking industry. For a long time, hard-copy one-sheets, video demo tapes and marketing kits made their way through snail mail, stacking up at speakers' bureaus and on meeting planners' shelves. But then, the "New World" of the Internet emerged and with it electronic one-sheets, downloadable marketing materials and speaker websites became the new black. As we navigate through the world of social media, blogging, online videos, and search engine optimization, we need to step back and—like any good speaker—look for the message, for the take-away. Could it be that with all of these rapid developments, we are standing at the helm of a New World for ourselves? We may, in fact, be standing squarely at the intersection between tradition and innovation, the crux of creativity and inspiration. What new trails will you blaze? What will be in your bottle?

The Power of Terroir

Once in a while, we are treated to something magical. That giddy sense that there is something very special contained within. In the wine world, this mystique is often attributed to the *terroir* (ter-WAH) of the grapes. *Terroir* is the "somewhereness" of the grape, as wine legend Hugh Johnson phrased it. From start to finish in the grape's life, the entire process and its unique circumstances are thought to be reflected in the resulting wine.

Similarly, each speaker has their own *terroir*: we are the product of our journey. As speakers, our ongoing path of self-discovery can be broken down into our own distinctive history, based on the climate in which we grew, how we were handled and what decisions we made in our maturation process. Unmatched like a fingerprint to any others in the business, our unique *terroir* encompasses our outlook, personality, life experience, character, niche, and lessons learned (oh, yes—and all of those workshops and seminars!).

Age has its Rewards

In the human world, aging has gotten a bad rap. When it comes to youth, there are strong associations with attractiveness, energy, a blank canvas brimming with potential. But what is more valuable in the long run—mere potential or the fulfillment of that potential?

Let us take our cue from the wine world here and remind ourselves that most of the world's legendary wines are only considered such in their mature form. A robust Barolo may be undrinkable if sipped before its time; the tannins would feel like teabags in your mouth and you would wonder about all the hype. But after the prescribed years of development, this wine earns its title as the Italian King of Wines.

Sure, there are some delicious wines that are meant to be sipped while young; these offer simple, refreshing satisfaction and light-heartedness to their fruit. It is the more mature wine that commands respect, where we carefully ponder each sip and look for the subtleties in its message. As long as we gain valuable complexity in our maturation process, we are well on our way to becoming complex and full of inimitable character.

Bottling our Best

Wine is a living, breathing blend of organic ingredients; the same bottle of wine will never be exactly the same if opened at any two points in time. So when is the ideal time to experience each wine? When will you uncork your true message?

As we continue learning, growing, and evolving, we are never the same person more than once at each point in our lives. Think about the books you've written, the speeches you've given, the jokes you felt were best for your audience. Have these changed over time? Would you write the same memoir at any two points in your life?

Even as we may outgrow some earlier marks of ourselves, we can take comfort knowing that we were always ourselves. And, like wine classics such as Bordeaux and Cote-Rotie, often what we thought was pretty decent was only the beginning. The best is yet to come.

~ WHAT IS YOUR EXCUSE? ~

by Esther Jacobs

WHAT IS YOUR EXCUSE?

"I DON'T HAVE TIME OR MONEY..."

"I'VE GOT RESPONSIBILITIES..."

"THIS IS NOT THE RIGHT MOMENT..."

MANY PEOPLE HAVE EXCUSES AS TO WHY THEY ARE NOT FOLLOWING THEIR DREAMS. I SAY: "WINNERS MAKE GOALS, LOSERS MAKE EXCUSES!" Follow these steps to stop giving excuses and start following your dreams.

1. Know What You Want and Communicate It

If YOU don't know what you want, how are others going to know? So talk about it and you'll be amazed at the suggestions and help that will come your way. In the Netherlands, I knew a guy who was going to quit his job to sail around the world. When his employer, a large telecom company, found out, they refused to let him go and even offered to sponsor him for a year!

If you don't know exactly what you want, that's okay. Sometimes you have a vague inkling, or you just know what you DON'T want. Ask yourself the following questions:

- What would you do if you only had a limited time left to live?
- What if you won the lottery?
- What have you always wanted to see or learn?
- What location, activity or kind of people makes you happy?

2. Face Your Worst Fear

What is the worst thing that could happen? And is that really so bad? Once you cross your own boundaries, you'll never be afraid again.

During my travels, I often get challenged. Two years ago in Madagascar, I discovered that it was not possible to use my ATM or credit cards, so I was almost penniless. I had to travel south, but I had no money for a flight. A nightmare scenario! But then, some fishermen offered to take me along in their sailing boat, warning me that it could be more than one week's travel, depending on the wind. It was a great experience. All day I sat in their tiny boat made of a hollowed tree trunk. At one point, my iPod was empty and all my to-do lists were made. Because I had nothing to think about, I reached an ultimate peace in my head.

My participation on the Survivor television series was really about facing my worst fears. I was used to eating every two hours, was a vegetarian and not a group person at all. Being on Survivor with no food, having to catch, kill, and eat my own fish and live with other candidates, I had to cross many boundaries. But I learned a lot, and it brought me new adventures.

3. Start NOW!

Don't wait for the ideal moment, when all circumstances are going to be perfect. That moment will never come, and your dream will never be realized. Take the first step NOW, and the next step will materialize. Any problems can and will be solved along the way.

I sometimes use my Coins for Care project to illustrate this. In 2002, the Euro was going to replace the national currencies of 12 European countries. I came up with the following idea: What if I collected all obsolete foreign coins for charity? It sounded like a simple plan. But without money, resources, a network or relevant experience, it was bound to become complicated—especially for a 28-year-old girl. I'm just triggered when people say something is impossible. Even in the most desperate situations, I see opportunities. I started this project without having a clue where it would lead. In the end, it led to 25 million dollars!

4. Work with What You Have

Again, Coins for Care is a great example of how to achieve more with fewer resources.

Coins for Care was a great idea, but because I had no office, money, contacts, and reputation, nobody believed that my plan was feasible. But precisely because I had to start from scratch, I was very resourceful. It may sound weird, but it really helps to start a project with NO budget. If you do have money available, you'll be thinking about what you can do with that amount. Having no resources, you'll have to think creatively, out-of-the-box. For example, when we needed 4,000 collection boxes to put in supermarkets and banks, we used transformed sewer pipes. We got sponsors to help with nearly everything. That worked because it was a charity project. But you'd be amazed how much you can get for free or very little if you just ask. Use the Internet to get in touch with people offering services and products. Be very specific about what you need and what you can offer in return.

5. Take Little Steps

How do you eat an elephant? Bite by bite!

I don't advocate that everyone should quit their jobs and live like me, but I do want to show that within your own context, you can always change things. For example, you could choose to spend your next holiday differently. Why not take the kids camping in South Africa? Thanks to the exchange rate, this trip could still be within your budget.

I would encourage people to look at their options instead of limitations. Could you live in a smaller house so you have to work less? If you are not completely happy with your life, there are always possibilities to do things differently. It often helps to think in small steps. For example, if you have the dream of ever going to live in Mexico, you can start taking Spanish lessons. If you take the first step, then the next one often becomes clear.

6. Don't Be Afraid to Fail

In our society, we learn from childhood to opt for security, not to risk taking a different path or to go for what we really want. We think we are safe because we save for our children's studies, or we buy insurance against all kinds of things, but security is an illusion of the eyes; life is about taking risks. The only way to learn is by doing, even if that means failing many times. That's what happened to me, and I learned a lot! Think of it this way: wouldn't it be a shame if at the end of your life you were thinking: "I wish I had done this or that"? Wouldn't that feel more like failing?

~ RUNNING IN A POSITIVE DIRECTION ~

by Karl Gruber

HAVING BEEN A RUNNER FOR MANY YEARS ALREADY, I WAS PRACTICING MY DAILY LIFESTYLE OF GOING ON MY MORNING RUN. This particular 7-mile run took place on a frigid, but clear and sunny, February morning, and took me through the gorgeous but hilly countryside in Hocking County in Southeastern, Ohio. I loved this course, which involved a combination of winding asphalt country roads, and a series of rough dirt and gravel back roads. It gave me an awesome challenge, and a great workout to start my day off on the right foot before I went to work.

With my frosty breath visible before me as I charged up another hill, an idea came to me that would literally change my life in the long run: an idea that would hopefully make the world a better, healthier place. I would run 52 marathons in 52 weeks to raise money and awareness for leukemia research! Now anybody who runs on a regular basis would generally consider this idea not only foolhardy, but also crazy and impossible. But the more I thought about this idea, the more it fired me up to accomplish it. Later on, in the midst of my year of marathoning, a good friend confided to me that he thought I had a lot of chutzpah! My response was simply that ignorance is bliss!

❄

So, after quitting my job of 16 years as a disc jockey at WHOK-FM in Lancaster, Ohio, and renting out the beautiful home in which I lived in gorgeous rural Hocking County, Ohio, I went on to successfully complete the "impossible" by running 52 marathons in 52 weeks from May 5, 1996 through April 27, 1997. I called it my Super Run for the Cure, as I used all 52 of my marathons to raise money and awareness for leukemia research. To accomplish this, I did radio, television and newspaper interviews in each city I visited. I sincerely believed (and do believe) that one person can truly make the world a better place through their individual effort, no matter how big or small.

I had a gradual transition in my character and beliefs in the years prior to this incredible adventure of running marathons for a whole year for charity. Over a number of years, I went from the carefree, partying, hippie-type to understanding that there was and is a deeper meaning to life. I became a disciple of the philosophy of positive thinking. Great inspirational icons such as Dr. Norman Vincent Peale, Napoleon Hill, Dr. Robert Schuller, Dr. Wayne Dyer, Zig Ziglar, and many others led me down a new path of belief, faith, light, and truth with their astounding wisdom, love, and knowledge. My nose was always in a positive thinking book. Every time I drove my car, my ears were tuned to inspiring audio books from these same amazing, inspiring, and positive leaders.

Slowly, I started to believe a little more in myself and my ability to contribute good things to the world. I remember the final turning point was a quote from Dr. Robert Schuller that kept looping over and over in my head: "If it's going to be, it's up to me!" I certainly can tell you that my year of running the 52 marathons was anything but easy, and it came at a great personal price to me, but I would do it all over again at the same price.

❄

You must believe you can and will accomplish your greatest dreams and goals! Never give up! If you fall down on your quest, get up, brush yourself off and press on. You can be certain you will succeed if you hold this attitude steadfastly. To me, the worst fate any man or woman can meet is getting to the end of their life having to say "I would've, I could've, and I should've…"

My personal credo is this: Ordinary people can accomplish extraordinary things!

~ EVERYONE IS A NATURAL SINGER ~

by Claude Stein

EVERY HUMAN BEING IS BORN WITH THE CAPACITY TO SING IN A WAY THAT ALIGNS HIS/HER INNER AND OUTER MESSAGES AND FREES THE SOUL. Yet most of us don't take advantage of the instrument with which we are born. Some of us believe we are "tone-deaf," which ends up being a self-fulfilling prophesy. Some of us insist we just aren't good enough to even try, and we lack the nerve, patience and faith to simply practice. Most of us are terrified at the thought of being in the moment, revealing our real voice in front of others.

This, however, is the place from which we can grow the most. As we energize and give voice to unspoken words and feelings within us, we can elevate and integrate the many aspects of ourselves while improving our tone and rhythm at the very same time.

Because singing on key is an autonomic process that requires trust and being "in the moment," we can overcome the debilitations of fear-based thinking and paralyzing self-consciousness. We can develop enormous creativity, musicianship and the ability to inspire others with who we really are. Songs can be used to integrate and dignify our light and our dark sides, our joy and our blues. When we sing our inner truths, we are emotional, vulnerable and powerful. And when our messages are energized in song, it creates a more beautiful sound. And therein lies the magic.

Expressive arts are deeply influential when we are authentically and passionately ourselves. As we embrace our humanness and sing despite our imperfections and fears, we can hit the notes better and bring greater change to the world.

When I give singing workshops, failure is off the table. The results are often breathtaking, and build a remarkable sense of community and common purpose. The breakthroughs go far beyond singing. The inability to speak up fully and "sing out" is deeply linked to some of our most challenging core issues. We triumph as our true essence, charisma and presence emerge. We become more articulate, authentic and spontaneous. The more comfortable we are at being more ourselves, the richer the content and the better the sound.

Your voice—the instrument with which you were born—connects your psyche, your spirit, your heart, and your body. It's your right, your treasure and a direct access point to the beauty of your soul.

— THE NEXT HUNDRED YARDS: —
FEELING FAILURE, FIGHTING BACK

by Dorothy Erlanger

ONE SUNDAY, READING THE LOCAL PAPER, AN ITEM JUST JUMPED OUT AT ME. There was a picture of a big guy, around my age, starting on a training program for a mini-triathlon for the 50s crowd. I was intrigued.

I had just come through a couple of tough years health-wise, and even though I should have been thrilled to come through relatively unscathed, I was very down and I had lots of anxiety. I should have been accelerating in my business, but I was dragging myself through projects. I truly did not understand this at all.

Reading on, I suddenly found myself thinking, "Maybe this is what I need to do." I wanted to declare "I'm back" by doing something completely new and different, and I thought this could be it. I looked more closely: 300-yard swim—I could do that, even though I might have to stop and rest along the way. 12-mile bike—Hmmm, I owned a bike I had in college. Maybe I could build up to that distance. Three-mile run—No way! Well, let's think about that. Perhaps I can work up to walking that distance.

Let's be clear (reality check time) I was never an athlete. I didn't even participate in sports in high school beyond required gym classes. College? At the University of Chicago, there is a famous quote from former president Robert Hutchins, who said, "Whenever I get the urge to exercise, I lie down until it passes away."

After college, I had always been a classic three-weeks-in-January exercise club person. I had great, short-lived intentions. Top that with having recently gone through several months of medical treatments, and I was in pretty poor shape. But the event caught my imagination. So, I signed up and went to the first meeting of the training group. I felt immediately reassured—there were no jocks, no six-pack types, and everyone there was as clueless as I was about triathlon.

I won't bore you with the "starting at zero" training sequence; just one example—a swim workout a few weeks after we started was six lengths of the pool (150 yards total), and I stopped to rest after every two lengths. And that was progress! I had started out resting after each length.

If you look back to my reasons for signing up, the choice was all about me. The surprise for me was the amazing community, support and group enthusiasm that I found. What a joy that was. None of us were there to "beat" someone. All of us were there to accomplish something new and challenging; something that we never would have imagined being able to do.

Six months later, and there we are, starting off down a lane in the pool, timing device on ankle, bike set up in the transition area (did not even know what that was before the training), off and running, so to speak. By then, I was feeling okay on the swim, great on the bike, and even running part of the 5K rather than walking. What a feeling of accomplishment. "You are a triathlete," they said to us as we crossed the finish line. Hard to believe, but true. Oh, and I even came in second in my age group (split into 5 year increments). Wow!

Satisfied? No. When is the next event? Uh oh, I was hooked.

✳

Fast forward to fall 2008 at Lake Mead in Nevada, just outside of Las Vegas... I had qualified for the Halfmax National Championships, but now that I had arrived, I was ready to quit and go home! I had traveled there by myself. My triathlon buddies were back in Richmond. So were my husband and my coach. The race? 1.2-mile swim, 56-mile bike and 13.1-mile run. Had I done that distance before? Yes, several times. So, why the fear?

As one should do, I arrived a couple of days before the race. I located where the swim would end and drove out and back, 50 miles of the bike course. As I drove up one steep mountain section and down the other side, my stomach sank and then balled up into a knot of fear approaching terror. The mountain climbs were brutal, and I have always been weak on hills of any sort. On top of that, I had taken a minor fall (scrapes only) a few weeks earlier on a hilly ride near home, and was still a bit nervous about speed. As I got back to the lakefront, I decided I was overmatched, that the race was simply unsafe for me and that I would just do the swim part, maybe a little part of the bike and then stop. With shaking hands and feeling almost sick to my stomach, I called my coach to tell him about my decision.

"Michael, I can't do this race. Have you looked at the bike course on this race? It's impossible!"

"Dorothy, of course I know the course; I looked at it months ago, before I set up your training program. You are trained for this, you can do it. Think back to all of the hill work you've done." His message to me was essentially: "I'm your coach, that's my job, trust your training."

"Michael, the hills in Richmond are *not* the mountains outside of Las Vegas. I just drove 50 miles of the course and the climbs are brutal. Also, I'm really afraid of building high speed coming off of them."

"Dorothy, you have to realize that when you drive a car, the hills look like a constant up with no variations. When you're out there on your bike, you'll find that there are flatter sections where you can do some recovery even in the midst of a seeming straight up. And if you are really concerned about the downhill speed, brake it back just a bit to what you are okay with."

"Well, maybe." He's sort of getting through to me and my stomach is calming down a little. "But this is constant, nearly the entire distance."

"Dorothy, you cannot think of the entire course, not even the entire next climb. You have to laser-focus on just the next hundred yards in front of you. What does it look like? Does the hill let up a bit at any point? What's your strategy for just those next hundred yards? Take that into the race and focus on it at every stage. It's natural to jump ahead, but you have to fight it. I even find that I will start thinking about transition before finishing the bike, and it always messes up the last part of my biking. Don't do that."

I'm finally really listening and buying in.

"Okay, Michael, I'll give it a go. No promises on finishing, but I'll use 'the next hundred yards' as my mantra."

Early morning, I set up, do the swim and start off on the bike. At every point, I'm focused on "the next hundred yards." Could I climb those mountains? Yes—trust your coach and your training.

Oh, there is a "rest of the story" on this, too. Remember that I said the bike part of the race was 56 miles? And remember that when I called my coach to tell him I wasn't doing the race I had driven 50 miles, back to the lakefront? What I had not realized was the last 6 miles of the bike were all up, climbing continuously, getting steeper as you went along. But by then I was so thoroughly into my next hundred yards, strategy, execution, next hundred yards that I didn't even doubt I could do it. As I came over the final 9% grade and into the bike/run transition area, I knew I had won. I hadn't even done the run portion yet, but it did not matter. I had taken on something that seemed impossible, something at which I believed I would fail, and I had beaten it.

✳

Where is there a challenge that seems impossible? Something you can't even imagine reaching the end of?

Try to take just the first hundred yards, set a strategy for that, and just go for it. It worked for me!

~ MOTIVATIONAL MAYHEM ~

by Beth Terry

"YOU CAN'T ALWAYS GET WHAT YOU WANT..." Of course that's the title of the Rolling Stones' megahit from their 1969 album Let it Bleed. But it's also Mick Jagger and Keith Richards' most intelligent lyrical work. I think its high time "motivational" speakers begin telling the truth.

So many of us trot up onto the stage and say things they heard another speaker say, who got it from another speaker, who read it in a book somewhere and misquoted it. The real question is: are those speakers living what they preach?

The chorus of the Rolling Stones' song begins..."*You can't always get what you want...*"

If I hear any more speakers say, "You can be *anything* you want!" I swear I will run up to the stage, grab the mic out of their hands and send them to their room!

No.

You.

Can't.

If that were true, and if the "law of attraction" were always true, all of us would be twenty pounds lighter and careening around in hot cars while flashing our loot from the lottery. Some people in the '70s discovered it ain't true. Of course, they were on acid when they discovered humans can't fly without an airplane, or at least a parachute. But they wanted to fly..." I can be anything, do anything I want! *Whheeeee!*"

Splat.

Not only is "You can be *anything* you want!" a foolish thing for motivational speakers to say, it's also irresponsible. For a time, the audience is pumped. The energy alone from some speakers could make the phonebook interesting.

But two short days later, those once-rapt listeners feel down, dejected and depressed. "If I can be anything I want and I'm living this miserable life, it *must all be my fault!*"

Sure, there is what I call the Consequence Rule: "All your choices *do* have consequences." If you choose to spend your life on remote control patrol and the cushions have imprints of your cheeks from doing too much couch potato time... yeah, you caused that weight gain and sad social life.

But this latest economic collapse is a beacon in the wilderness proclaiming "We have *no* control over events out there." All of the magical-thinking maestros want us to believe that *somehow* our *Collective Unconscious Brain* was bored and decided to shake things up..."*Hey*, let's have a complete meltdown and then see who floats to the top!" (And you *know* what floats to the top... it's not just crème and it's usually dead.)

✳

Believing we have more control over life than we do is a wonderful fantasy that keeps us out of the funny farm. Sometimes hope and faith is all we have to hold onto. That's okay. Hold onto them until you can figure out a solution.

Stuff just happens. Oh well. It's our job to figure out how we will respond. It's our job to come up with a solution that works for us. We simply *must* stop believing (and stop saying) that if we wish really really really hard, and say it "70 times infinity," that only good things will happen to us. It is simply *not true!* Affirmations created by someone else don't always work.

The chorus of the Stones' song continues... *"But if you try sometimes..."*

That's not to say we can't affect our future. Like I said, "Choices have consequences." If I step in front of a speeding bus, I will probably die. Or I will have a protracted and painful sabbatical in a hospital on the east side. So I don't step in front of buses. I don't smoke— that one has pretty well been proven to do dastardly things to lungs. And I need my lungs. I try to make good choices. I don't always do a great job of that.

What we *should* be saying, if we are driven to saying anything at all, is, "You have a reasonably good chance of getting where you want to go, provided you are willing to do the work, take the risks and make good choices for yourself." We should also add, "And it might not work. It might not be your time, your turn or good for you. So get over it and move on."

✳

The chorus of the Stones' song turns the corner... *"you might find..."*

As speakers, friends, family members, or even counselors, we must dig a little deeper into the psyche of those whom we want to impact. This economic malaise has challenged people's ideas about themselves. At their core, our audiences are shaken, discouraged, dumbfounded and distressed. Boomers especially, who have been drinking this "you can be anything" Kool-Aid for far too many years, stare in dumb silence at the economic chaos of their lives. We just expected things would keep getting better. We expected that the past predicted the future. We were wrong.

People everywhere are legitimately suffering. Blaming them for "not wanting it badly enough" or "not attracting the right things" doesn't help. It harms.

None of us had the crystal ball to see the full impact of this meltdown. And even if we did, it's done. Getting on stage or sitting with people and telling them to be *HAPPY HAPPY HAPPY!* is just stupid. At this point, cause is immaterial. Solution is paramount. Part of that solution is to help people move forward, get over the regret and resentment, and start to rebuild.

✱

The chorus of the Stones' song resolves..."*you'll get what you need.*"

If we in the helping and healing professions are serious about moving this country forward one audience at a time, we need to be real. Cut the trite and cliché phrases out of all talks. Provide solid and practical ideas that will encourage forward movement. Provide processes to help people get up every morning and keep on keepin' on. Be *in* the trenches with them. Be on their side.

Knock off the *Motivational Mayhem* that doesn't work and provide *Emotional Encouragement* that does. We are messing around with people's heads and we need to be responsible. Riddly Walker said, "Don't walk in my head with your dirty feet." Let's be sure we are authentic and grounded when we counsel others about their lives.

"*...you'll get what you need.*"

I do believe in Hope and Faith. I know these philosophies have helped me through many a dark moment in my life. And I believe we impact our lives with our thoughts as well as our actions.

I know that all our thoughts are affirmations. If we affirm disaster, somehow we'll find it. But that doesn't mean we caused it—whether it's an Indian Ocean tsunami or an economic hurricane. There are forces greater than us. Acknowledging that and setting aside the magical thinking will help us find solid ground to build a healthier future.

CHAPTER 11:

Bouncing Back

"THE TEST OF SUCCESS IS NOT WHAT YOU DO WHEN YOU ARE ON TOP. SUCCESS IS HOW HIGH YOU BOUNCE WHEN YOU HIT BOTTOM."

— *George S. Patton*

At times, the delusion may seem that it would be easier to give up; however, regardless of the intensity of the challenge, the pain or disappointment, even the smallest glimmer of hope is the fuel that makes the difference.

For each of us, the journey of life includes surprise detours, twists, turns and sometimes painful bumps and deep, dark caverns. No one is immune. Everyone faces disappointments, failures, setbacks, broken hearts and other challenges. Many are simply frustrating, some are painful and others seem to rob the joy from life.

Rising as a phoenix from a painful experience, starts with this first step: Even before you are able to believe it, declare each day anew with the following affirmation: "I deserve and welcome today to be the best day of my life so far."

From this new starting point, be mindful of inspiration, guidance and answers that will become part of your map as you continue to journey forward.

— *Sumner Davenport,*
author of "Rubber Butt"

⁓ WHAT WOULD STOP YOU? ⁓

by Sally Franz

WHAT WOULD STOP YOU FROM ACHIEVING YOUR GOALS? Financial ruin, losing your home, the death of your mother, a diagnosis of cancer, a close friend dying or your spouse being unfaithful? How would you proceed facing all of these at the same time? And what if while all of this was happening, you were trying to recover from an illness that paralyzed you from the waist down?

What skills do you need to overcome what life throws at you? What skills can you give your children and grandchildren so they can make it past the roadblocks life can hand out?

These are questions I never really thought much about until all of the above happened to me.

✳

Everywhere you look, there are superstar experts telling you how to do this and that, promising you will have ultimate success, wealth and happiness. But they don't know you. They don't know what you're up against. I listen to some of those motivational speakers and I just want to scream, "Get real!" So here's a secret confession.

Once upon a time I was one of those superstars. I traveled all over the world teaching the top 10 percent of business professionals in companies like SONY, Intel, Texaco-Chevron and Yahoo! I showed them how to power-out *big* results. I was sharp, I was effective, I was funny and cute to boot.

You may have seen me on the Today Show, CNBC, or perhaps you caught me on Lifetime. Maybe you saw me doing stand-up comedy in places such as Caroline's or Stand-up NY. Yup, my career was flying. I was a much sought-after speaker, trainer and comedian.

✳

I became paralyzed from the waist down in less than half an hour in a freak auto-immune occurrence. (You know the kind of occurrence when the doctors say things such as, "very rare," "read about this once," and "don't know much about this one.")

Week after week, lying on my back, waiting for the nurse to come put me in a wheelchair, I had a lot of time on my hands. I would count all the ceiling tiles twice and sing every camp song I ever knew. Gradually, I started taking stock of what I had left. My grandfather used to say that when you need to make a decision in life, take out a piece of paper and draw a vertical line down the middle. On the left side you list the pros, and on the right side you list the cons. I started making a mental list.

I kept this list going for the next few years. The pros side was not only lacking, it was dwindling. As I mentioned above, I lost my job, income, marriage, my mother, a good friend, and I had a bout with cancer. Did I mention losing a big book deal, $80,000 in investments, and oh, yeah, I permanently lost my good health? I cannot run, ski, rollerblade or drive my fancy sports car (okay, sounds like Richie Rich complaining, but I loved that car!). Add to that I am in *real* pain 24 hours a day, seven days a week, 365 days a year. This necessitates copious amounts of medicines, kind of putting the kibosh on that memory course I'd paid for.

And on and on goes the list of cons. So much for "positive thinking," "plan your work and work your plan," and "think and grow rich." Some days I'm lucky to "think" how to make coffee and remember to drink it. Where does that leave me? Where does that leave anyone up to their eyeballs in roadblocks and a list of cons longer than the post office's most-wanted list?

On the pros side of the ledger, I had these three items left, the three skills that saved my life: 1. Sarcasm, 2. Curiosity, 3. Faith.

❋

Sarcasm always came naturally to me. I learned it at home. We grew up in New Jersey watching Red Skelton, Uncle Milty, and Rocky and His Friends. Irony, satire, banter and cynicism all allow you to speak the truth of your pain and be clever at the same time. From a young age I connected to this form of humor.

When I grew up, curiosity came largely as a result of our freedom. We didn't have play dates. We had the woods, the stream and the fields. After school, we just went outdoors and found adventure. We found arrowheads, we chased snakes and we dammed up the stream. We made tree forts and snowball forts, and ducked behind bushes away from car headlights. We built models and asked for chemistry sets. At home, we were problem solvers, as my dear sainted mother used to say, "Don't ask me—figure it out yourself."

And faith was something all around me. My great aunts loved me, my grandma loved me, and they believed in a loving God. I knew, regardless of my worthiness as a child, which I was pretty sure was nil in the scheme of world greatness, God loved me with the passion of a mother bear protecting her young.

So, there you have it, three life saving skills. Faith is trusting that which you cannot see. Curiosity is wondering about all the things you do see. And sarcasm is laughing about everything in between.

❋

When I lay in the hospital bed with the doctors scratching their heads perplexedly all around me, I realized that my life as I had known it was to be no more. Then suddenly, it occurred to me that the hand of God was on me, and life was about to get a whole lot more interesting. And with my strong sarcasm, curiosity, and faith, I moved forward.

— RUBBER BUTT™: —
BOUNCING BACK WHEN YOU HAVE BEEN KNOCKED DOWN OR LOST YOUR FOOTING DUE TO A LIFE EVENT, CHANGE OR CHALLENGE

by Sumner Davenport

RESEARCH CONDUCTED BY NEUROSCIENTISTS AT NASA CONFIRMED THAT IT TAKES THE BRAIN 28 DAYS TO TRULY ACCEPT A CHANGE, AND THESE RESEARCH RESULTS SUPPORT THE THEORY THAT WE HAVE HEARD FOR MANY YEARS: THAT IT TAKES THREE WEEKS TO CHANGE OR REALLY FORM A HABIT.

Additional NASA research also indicated that it is essential that the 28 days be consecutive without any breaks. When a day was missed, all progress is lost and the day count must start again at day one.

The movies and television shows you watch have influence over your emotional state. If what you are feeling is stressed and anxious, and you watch a movie that is violent, or the depressing segments of the news, you are reducing your ability to bounce back from whatever is occurring in your life. Alternatively, watch a short inspirational movie or comedy. Fifteen minutes of inspiration, or something that motivates you to laugh, makes everything much easier afterwards.

There are many things in life that we cannot prevent and others that we will never be able to control. However, we can control our reactions to what happens in our lives, and whether we choose to land with a *splat* or choose to bounce back.

✱

It can happen to anyone—expected or unexpected challenges occur in our lives, including challenges that involve finances, relationships, our career and our health. In addition, often we get more than one of these challenges at a time. Sometimes we see the challenge coming and feel helpless to stop it. Other times, it shows up as a complete surprise that we feel unprepared to handle.

Like many people, I have experienced several challenges and painful bumps in my journey: from financial ruin, betrayal, relationships and loss, to health and even rape. Regardless of how many people may be going through what you're experiencing, being told that is usually not a comfort. Your situation is unique—because you are unique. Even so, sometimes we can all benefit from the tools used by someone else. The tools I have found most helpful include the following.

1. Let yourself feel the grief.

When you lose a job, a marriage, a friend, a goal, or money, you should go ahead and grieve your loss. Of course you will be sad, and you will experience pain, but if you allow yourself to grieve, you will find that you bounce back much more easily after your loss.

2. Select your support group carefully.

As Mark Twain wrote, "Keep away from people who try to belittle your ambitions. Small people always do that, but the really great people make you feel that you too can become great."

You may feel like you want to be left alone and therefore try to isolate yourself. To bounce back from your challenge, it helps to have good supportive people around you. We commonly reach out to family and friends for support, and attempt to communicate our concerns and needs. Unfortunately, sometimes they may see us how we used to be, or how they want us to be (according to their standards), making it difficult to receive impartial support.

Nothing is more destructive than to hear someone tell you, "I knew he/she was a jerk," or, "If you had done (something) different," or, "I told you so," or, "This is for your own good."

Run—don't walk—away from these people. If it is difficult to avoid these people (like family), then be willing to recognize when you are getting the support you need and when you need to control what you share.

Find at least *one* person who you know you can trust; who you, and your secrets if you need to share, are perfectly safe with. The role of this person is to *listen*, so you can vent and be heard. This person is not there to tell you how to fix anything (unless you ask), not to judge you, not to throw your own words back at you and *not* to join in on the negative. Just vent, get if off your chest. Once you have vented your frustration, anger or whatever else you are feeling, you may then have a more clear space to see or hear a solution and be ready to take action for what's next.

3. Focus on where you want to be.

Years ago, a lesson I learned while having fun made a difference in how I deal with bumps I now encounter in life. While ice-skating with a friend, he did his best to teach me how to glide gracefully across the ice, to no avail. I crashed on the ice more times than I successfully skated.

Then I observed something he did: he started to stumble but instead, he seemed to immediately bounce back up, as if he had rubber on his butt. It was as if the fall never happened. He explained that when he sensed that he was heading for a fall, he would accept it and then focus on the solution—the rise again. He wouldn't place his focus on the stumble or the fall or the splat, or even on how he would get back up; he simply saw himself up and going forward.

Conversely, when facing a stumble or challenge in our lives, many of us consistently obsess with "Oh no, it's gonna happen," "It's happening," "It happened" or "How did I get here?" Then, while still thinking about falling down, we struggle to get up or move through whatever the challenge may be.

Instead of placing your complete focus on what is hurting or challenging you today, focus on your rubber butt and how you are going to bounce up and how high. My wish for you is to discover how bounce-able your butt really is.

— JUST JUMP: —
THE PROACTIVE APPROACH TO SELF-MASTERY

by Cynthia Ryk

DO YOU REMEMBER SITTING AROUND A CAMPFIRE, HEARING THE ROARING, CRACKLING FIRE AND INHALING THE WOODY SMELL AS WELL AS THE CRISP, CHARCOALED MARSHMALLOWS... ALL THE WHILE LETTING YOUR IMAGINATION RUN WILD? I remember one night my imagination took off as a friend asked me, "Pretend you're surrounded by a pack of hungry wolves. What would you do?"

I started seeing it: the fierce piercing eyes staring through me; the slow, silent, determined walk of each wolf; their tongues hanging out in anticipation of dinner. As I imagined them tearing my flesh apart piece-by-piece, my palms began to sweat, my heart raced, my chest tightened. What would I do? Fight? Run? Scream? I turned to my friend with wide-eyed terror and squealed, "Wow, I don't know what I would do! What would you do?" My life now depended on her answer. Without a concern in her bones, she replied, "I'd stop pretending."

That simple yet profound answer has always stuck with me. But as I grew older, the stakes seemed to get higher and the fears became more real: the fear of running out of money, or choosing the wrong partner, or not being healthy. These fears are real! To just stop pretending is not so easy. How often do we cower to fear instead of confronting it for what it's worth?

✳

A few years ago, I took what I thought would be a leisurely hike with my son and a trail guide. Within 15 minutes, the path led to a fork in the road. We could choose the short route or the long route. The short route meant jumping off a ledge; it meant jumping off what looked like a cliff into a small pool of water.

Next thing I knew, my son and the trail guide were jumping off, looking for me to follow. The decision had been made *for* me. What they didn't know was that I was *terrified* of heights.

There I was, 20 feet above, looking down at my son in this very small space. "C'mon on— you can do it, Mom. It's fun, just jump!" Franklin was laughing and splashing.

Has anyone ever said to you, "Just do it," while you are gripped with *fear*? The trail guide was kind enough to meet me at the top, to show me that it was safe and to guide me through; so I did it. I jumped! And as I landed safely in the water, my son was grinning from ear-to-ear...

Well, it could have gone that way, anyway...

There I stood, stuck, paralyzed from the waist down, and in that moment, all I was thinking was, "What's so good about taking risks anyways?"

"Come on, Mom, you can do it. It's fun, just jump," Franklin yelled up to me again.

Okay, one, two, three.

Not a limb moved. All of a sudden, I felt dizzy, nauseated and short of breath. That's when the "what ifs" moved in. I was imagining the worst: What if I hit my head and went unconscious? What if I were to get trapped under a rock? What if I needed an ambulance— we're out in the middle of nowhere!

✳

The beauty in *fear* is that it's a call to action. It's asking you to look at what story you have created and why. Sure, it keeps us alert to possible trouble but... most often, FEAR simply stands for "False Evidence Appearing Real." We make the mistake of seeing the symptoms of fear as truth and get stuck in our imagination—the howling of the wolves gets louder and louder. The key to remember is that we cannot hope to eliminate fear; we can only manage it. Fear is the undercurrent that either controls us unconsciously in our everyday decisions or gives birth to new levels of self-mastery. So, what can we do to stop pretending and create a more empowering life story?

I went through a process while I was on that ledge, one that I've since distilled down to four steps that work for me with any challenge I face.

F: Feel the fear.

On that ledge my entire body shut down, and I felt the adrenaline pumping through my heart. Emotionally, I felt stupid and embarrassed, so much so that I started to back down. I told my son, "Go ahead; I'll take the other route and meet you on the other side." But then I saw the disappointment in my son's eyes and the pout on his lips, and I remembered my vow to show him that adults take risks sometimes. So, I began to do what I now call the second step.

E: Explore the truth behind the fear.

What is the belief, assumption or story you hang onto that may no longer be true?

Memories of my childhood came flooding in. My father was a physician, and caution was a major theme of my childhood. There were many times I was warned not to take a risk for fear of injury. I really feared injury; so staying away from physical risk taking was easy! I had convinced myself that physical activities weren't very much fun, but I realized that maybe that was not true. The trail guide and my son were having a blast. Because I had now explored and challenged the truth behind my story, it was totally in my control to take the next step, the hardest one.

A: Act.

I had to take action and challenge the story I was so fiercely hanging onto. I told the trail guide, "I'm gonna do this!" So he began coaching me through the steps. I took slow, steady breaths to manage the adrenaline. He asked that I *picture* myself jumping with success. I obliged; doing it over and over again, ad nauseam, until I heard Franklin's somewhat impatient voice cry again, "C'mon, Mom, jump! You can do it; I'm right here for you." My heart started beating louder because all of a sudden, the joy of seeing my son be proud of me taking a risk was now a little, tiny bit greater than the fear of injury. I was still scared, but I was ready to stop pretending. The next thing I remember was the rush of water and bubbles, the cold silence, my son's hand touching my shoulder as I rose above the water, above my fear! Ahhh, there is nothing greater than challenging your fears: you un-cage yourself to experience the last step.

R: Reclaim your courage.

There can be no courage unless there is fear. Courage is the *mastery* of fear—not the *absence* of fear. They are the two sides of one coin: self-mastery and fear. That night around the campfire, we were asked to share what we would remember most, and when it was my son's turn, he proudly stated, "I'll never forget the courage my mom had today."

— THE VOLCANO CALLED ANGER —

by Dr. Rev. Carolyn Porter

A VOLCANO OFTEN SIMMERS FOR MONTHS, YEARS OR EVEN DECADES. The simmering continues until it reaches the boiling stage as the magma beneath the surface churns over and over. Then one day, with little warning, it erupts and spews its deadly contents over everything in its path, pouring out devastation to the innocent below with its searing rage until it reaches its ending. And so it is in the life of a volcano.

Sadly, this same scenario presents itself in the lives of many on this Earth. Someone says or does something that upsets or hurts you. Their perception may not see the situation the same way as you do, but because the issue isn't aired and discussed, it remains buried within you. This angry or hurtful situation continues to fester, simmering until it reaches the boiling stage. Then it erupts in some form as it spews its contents over all that is in its path, destroying much along the way.

Have you noticed that each time you recount a story that upset you; you actually activate the pain into a deeper and stronger level? By the time you've told the story three times, you've increased your anger and stress, and made the entire situation at least ten times stronger than the original episode!

Think of two people who were close friends all through their college years. One day, they had a significant difference of opinion, and as a result, they quit speaking to each other and went about their lives separately. Twenty-three years went by and they never communicated with each other, even though they had once been inseparable friends. One day, they met unexpectedly. They began talking and catching up on their lives. They actually started to laugh and wondered how they could have let something so silly get in the way of their friendship with the result that they didn't speak for 23 years. They had missed so much during those years that they could never get back.

✳

Forgiveness does not mean, "What you did is okay to me." It simply means, "I am no longer willing to carry around the pain in response to your actions." You can still love someone even if you disagree. In fact, real unconditional love allows each of you to feel and believe what you want without changing the love. This is powerful and an incredible place in which to live!

Life is so very short, even if you live to be 100. People who live in fear are miserable even if they don't admit it. Harboring anger, guilt, shame, hurt or letting pride grab you, really only affects you. And someday, somewhere, when you may least expect it, it will erupt and spew its contents, destroying all in its path. Is this what you want for your life?

Take a minute right now and think about a person with whom you've had an issue. Perhaps you haven't spoken in years just as the two college friends hadn't. Isn't it time for you to take the first step of releasing the hurt and forgiving that person?

Don't let pride get in the way of repairing whatever you perceive is a grievance. Think about the happiness, peacefulness and above all, the love it can bring to you if you let go of the fear and allow in the love. The cost of hanging onto old wounds is way too high—the price of broken relationships can never be measured.

Instead, choose to live in freedom and love.

— MOVE OUT OF THE PAST —
AND INTO SUCCESS WITH RESPECT

by Donna Theresa Haddad

"YOU ARE UNIQUE, AND IF THAT IS NOT FULFILLED
THEN SOMETHING HAS BEEN LOST."

- Martha Graham

ALTHOUGH WE MAY NOT WANT TO LIVE IN THE PAST, THE PAST LIVES IN US. Beginning early in life, we all have countless experiences that wound or tear open our hearts, leaving their imprint on our subconscious mind and bodies. Loss of confidence, loss of respect for our talents and abilities, loss of trust in ourselves or in others, are only a few of the by-products of these past experiences.

When faced with challenges or difficult times, our past disappointments, perceived failures and insecurities can bring fears, doubts and frustrations roaring to the surface. These confuse and complicate our present situation. This is the time we must reawaken trust in our world and ourselves, rediscovering belief in our ability to succeed, and reconnecting to our purpose. In order to do these things, we must remember our Divine nature and our inherent worth, and then move forward with RESPECT.

Resilience is not easy, especially when it seems disappointments and difficulties are unending. It is important at these times to remember that change and challenges are part of the essential nature of life; they are not meant to harm or destroy you. Focus your time and energy on moving forward with the deep conviction that nothing and no one can knock you down and keep you down.

Enthusiasm is essential to success because it is the internal candle that only you can light, and only you control how brightly it burns. When you begin to doubt yourself, you must look inside your heart to see your candle. If it is flickering rather than burning brightly, you should fuel the flame with your passion, and a deeply held belief in yourself and your goal.

Self is the most important factor in achieving your goals and desires. You are the person with whom you have the most intimate relationship. If you do not know, trust, accept and believe in yourself, you will find yourself in a "funhouse of the mind." You'll look into distorted mirrors and believe that the distorted images and surroundings you see reflected back to you are your reality.

Purpose represents your desired outcome. Maintaining motivation is much easier when you have a strong personal incentive to achieve what you desire. Does the purpose improve your life or the lives of others? Do you have a talent or gift to share with the world? What you believe to be your purpose at one point in your life may change at a different point, and that doesn't matter. What is important is to think and act in a purposeful manner regardless of what you are doing at any one point in your life.

Extraordinary is who and what you really are. You may have a job you consider ordinary, you may think you look ordinary, you may see your daily activities as ordinary, but in reality, there is nothing ordinary about you. Each person has the ability to do something no one else can do in exactly the same way. Each person can care for or take care of someone or something in a way no one else can. Each person can feel love and express love in a way no one else can. Each of us is a special and unique creation who is in the world for a reason. Don't just "hang in there" or just try to "get by." Focus your thoughts and energy on being the extraordinary person you really are.

Commitment has been hard for me in the past because I was a world-class procrastinator. Nothing will ever get done if you keep putting off what needs to be done to achieve your goal. Take a moment to think about why you keep putting things off. Are you afraid of failure or rejection, knowing that if you don't try, you won't have to worry about being rejected or failing? Are you afraid of success because you have had a "poor" mentality for so long you wouldn't know what to do with success? Or maybe you don't feel worthy of succeeding? You have a choice of how you will "see" and respond to your past. Fear and doubt drain your energy, wound your spirit, tear at your heart and have no place in the life of someone who believes in themselves—someone who knows success is right around the corner.

Trust is faith in yourself, your goal and your God.

~ But Why Do You Continue? ~

by Kara L.C. Jones

FOR OVER 11 YEARS NOW MY PARTNER HAWK AND I HAVE BEEN OFFERING WORKSHOPS AND PRESENTATIONS ON THE TOPIC OF GRIEF AND CREATIVITY. We began our work after the stillbirth of our son Dakota. At first the process was mostly about finding our own way through the chaos of grief. But as we continued to share our experiments, we began learning how to mentor attendees as they found ways to move from the moment of trauma into learning how to live again. Through the years, our speaking experiences have been personal, meaningful, and vital to the transformation of our grief.

But recently I was asked why we continue to do this work. Wasn't it difficult to keep telling our story? Wasn't it like continuously tearing open a wound? Why would we want to keep connecting with people who are grieving? When would enough be enough, and we'd "get over" our experience?

In that moment, I was taken back to the very first public event I did after our son died, in the fall of 1999.

✳

In the previous months, I had mustered up the courage to submit some of my grief writings to a Northwest publication called Poets West. They had accepted several of my pieces, and then invited me to participate in a public reading at the Frye Art Museum.

When we arrived, I got a bit nervous seeing the theater stage and all the seats filling up with audience members. When I got up on stage, the nerves eased a bit when I realized the stage lights were so bright that I would not be able to make out a single face as I spoke and read. After a couple other presenters, it was my turn.

I approached the microphone and began sharing our story. The tears came quickly. After all, it had only been six months or so since our son's death. But I pushed on and presented through the tears. The editors and organizers had seen something in the work, so I figured it must be worth sharing in whatever way I could manage.

At the end of the event, the lights came up in the theater. The audience began filing out, and I made my way off the stage, down to meet with Hawk. As I approached him, a woman came toward us from a few rows back. She came to us and placed one hand on my arm, and the other hand on Hawk's arm. She had tears in her eyes.

While I don't recall her exact words, the conversation started as she told us something like, "I'm in my eighties now. Fifty years ago, I had a baby who died the same way your son died, and I was never allowed to see him. I was never allowed to name him. I have never talked with anyone about him. Thank you for telling your story."

In that moment, I became an advocate. The reality of being a childless parent struck me hard as I stood there with this fellow bereaved mother. How many others were silenced? How many others had become invisible because we were supposed to "get over it" or follow the "five stages of grief" and then be done with it? How many mothers lived a lifetime without ever sharing the name of the child who died? Whatever their numbers, in that moment, I took on my role as a public speaker and knew that I would speak out, not only sharing my story, but also the stories of all others who have been silenced.

✳

To this day, Hawk and I continue to explore the topic of grief and creativity with as many groups of students, families and caregivers as we possibly can. Sometimes, prior to participating in one of our events, people will say things like, "Oh, I'm not very creative," or "I'm no artist," or "We don't use art therapy in our practice."

I'm quick to answer that while art-making is one of the creative tools I personally use in my own process, the creativity we are talking about has a much broader definition. After all, it takes a lot of creativity to figure out why you should get out of bed the day after your child dies!

Why do we continue to present and tell our story all these years later? Because it is the way we advocate for anyone who has been silenced and closeted in grief, whatever the circumstances of their loss.

Sharing our story is only part of each event. The more important part of every interaction is offering attendees creative tools to explore their own stories, find their own voices and learn to make creative choices every single day. I continue to do this work because I will never forget the woman who was silenced and alone with her grief for 50 years!

～ FRUSTRATING THE FRUSTRATION ～ AND GOING ON STAYCATION

by Lena M. Fields-Arnold

❦

IN THE PAST SEVERAL YEARS I HAVE BEEN FRUSTRATED BY RELATIVES WHO ONLY CALL WHEN THEY NEED SOMETHING, OR WHO WANT MONEY. They are never available for me when I need them, yet their wants have consistently hindered my efforts to move forward in my life.

It took a major life-changing event to force me to personally embark upon a voyage of emancipation from them. That is when I entered into the *Season of Me!* From the moment I first entered this season, my life would be about me! What I want, where I am going and what legacy I want to leave my children. As I made this change, I warned everyone that if they wanted something from me, they had better be willing to think about giving me something of value back in return. I had simply given too much too many times.

✳

Though I attempted to stay away from these draining people, I saw them slowly creeping back into my life, and I almost let them. It started with a seemingly simple request: a relative suggested that her daughter stay the summer to "help you with the kids."

Anytime I tried to say, "No" to her babysitting requests, my family always had a way of making me feel guilty and I would cave in. She got two summers of free babysitting, and I got another headache.

Last year, she didn't call me for a month. When she finally did, she stated that both her daughter and another cousin's daughter were coming to my house for two weeks. It made sense, right? Because, as she put it, "You are at home all day, and they can play with your daughter." Never mind the fact that I have other kids, a husband and a stay-at-home job— these two decided for me how two weeks of my life would be!

"I will be on staycation all summer." I told her. "You guys are on your own!" So then, both the above-mentioned women were frustrated by me. Both sarcastically remarked that they hoped I'd enjoy my staycation!

"I will," I proudly proclaimed, thinking to myself, "I'm staying away from *your* wants, *your* drama and your *constant* woe-is-me whining about your self-imposed crap!

✳

I now encourage others to enter into their Season of Me and to take a staycation. We all have ordained missions to accomplish, and you cannot accomplish your mission by allowing frustrations to get the best of you. Turn the tables on the people frustrating you by cutting them off! Become unavailable. They may even have the nerve to ask you what you are doing that is so important (as one of mine did.) Guess what, you don't have to answer them! You are not accountable to them for your time. You are only accountable to your mission.

So let me give you some concrete steps on how to go about a staycation:

1. Decide to do it.

2. Make a list of the people in your life, and put two columns by their names. In the first column, write the word assets; in the second, write the word liabilities. In the "Assets" column, write down all the ways that each person enhances your life and supports you in the accomplishment of your goals. In the "Liabilities" column, write down all the ways each person hinders you and keeps you from your goals. If the "Liabilities" column is greater than the "Assets" column, commit to never allowing their desires, wants and needs to outweigh your own.

3. Become unavailable. Stop answering the phone when that person calls. Don't answer voicemail messages. Only call them back when and if you are strong enough to resist their negative pull against you.

4. Be okay with saying "No!" Yes, they are going to get mad at you. But you have to decide that it's okay if they do. Guess what, their anger only serves to prove your point.

5. Move on to a new set of people! Actively seek out friendships with people who are assets. People like you, who don't mind giving to people who want to give something back.

I found my new set of people through a colleague who was forming a circle of women. All of the women desired to love unconditionally, accept without adversity, give with generosity, and provide care compassionately.

All of the women in the group spent a year together attending monthly workshops, holding one other accountable for reaching personal goals, supporting each other through tough times and hanging out. When the year was over, we had made a solid group of friends whose only objective was to help one another achieve our personal and professional goals.

My fervent prayer is that you will accomplish every dream and desire that the Master has etched on your heart. Seek wisdom, and journey towards your dream with positive people who will affirm you, support you, and lift you up.

It all starts with two simple sentences: "This is the Season of Me," and, "Sorry, I'm on staycation."

— YOU-TURN: —
CHANGING DIRECTION IN MID-LIFE

by Dr. Nancy B. Irwin

WE START SCHOOL AT AGE SIX, GRADUATE HIGH SCHOOL AT 18, FINISH COLLEGE BY 22 AND RETIRE AT 65. BUT THE NUMBERS DON'T STOP EVEN THERE. Who says we have to stop growing, changing and evolving as we continue to grow up? Not me. And not the millions who, as they reach what I call "middle-escence," stand at the crossroads of their past and future, and decide to take an alternate route.

As a young person, you might have agreed to follow in your father's footsteps and become a doctor, or had dreams of being a writer until an English teacher scoffed at your talents. And now here you are, eager for new challenges or revisiting old ones, yet you find yourself stalled with excuses.

"Can't teach old dog new tricks."

"I'm too old to start over."

"It's too late."

"Oh, I could never do that."

"I've been doing this for so long, why quit now?"

Whatever set you on your original path, now you're looking for a new direction and new meaning. You're not alone. You're one of the 84 million people born in the United States between 1946 and 1964 who have now reached middle age, and who are on a quest to find a new way of life. By our very existence, we changed the economy, music, medicine, fashion, technology—you name it, we did it. So don't stop now! The only limits are the ones we place on ourselves.

Instead of plunging headfirst into a midlife crisis, believe instead in the transformative powers of middle age. This is the time to turn it all around, to please yourself, to make your own choices and to create what you want. All you need is a "you-turn," a complete reversal in opinion, action or policy. When you embrace a you-turn in your life, you set in motion a self-fulfilling prophecy of empowerment and possibilities.

✳

My life journey took me on many detours until I made my own you-turn. Originally from Atlanta, Georgia, I trained as a young woman to be an opera singer. My passion for performing led me to New York City, where I soon changed direction and began a career as a stand-up comic.

I worked gigs all over the country and internationally. I moved to Los Angeles in 1994, when I heard Hollywood needed more blondes. While I was doing fairly well as staff emcee at the Melrose Improv, comics only work about 30 minutes a day, so I had a lot of time on my hands. I began volunteering in the community, a move that would induce my biggest life-change to date.

While working for Children of the Night, a shelter for sexually abused children, I experienced an epiphany—I wanted to spend my life educating, counseling, and advocating for kids like this. Not only did this experience wake up the healer in me, but it allowed me to begin healing the wounds from my own childhood sexual abuse at the hands of a clergyman. I decided to pursue a doctorate in psychology, specializing in the prevention and healing of child sexual abuse.

Today, in addition to my thriving private therapy practice in Los Angeles, I'm a busy public speaker for Children of the Night, as well as for other advocate groups like Planned Parenthood and the Rape, Abuse, and Incest National Network (RAINN).

I once thought my entire first and second careers were a misstep, or that I was just idling, wasting time. But my 10 years in opera and nine in comedy were not mistakes; after all, if I hadn't been a bored comedian, I may never have sought out volunteer work and had the healer in me awakened. Mistakes get a bad rap, though they can often serve as stepping-stones towards success. If it weren't for that "mistake," I'd never be where I am now.

— Lasting Legacy —

by Mellanie True Hills

WHEN YOU'VE BEEN TO DEATH'S DOOR, LIFE TRULY BECOMES PRECIOUS. You cherish simple things, such as sapphire skies with wispy clouds and fragrant flowers. You live every day as if it is your last.

At age 51, my life changed dramatically as I experienced symptoms of a heart attack. Women rarely get the crushing chest pains that men do, and instead are more likely to experience shortness of breath, indigestion, nausea, fatigue, or pain in the left arm, shoulder, jaw, or elsewhere in the left side of the body. I had shortness of breath and pain in my left shoulder, and was treated for a heart attack.

I was lucky that I recognized my symptoms in time, and thus didn't have a heart attack, though I was probably only minutes away from one. What I did have was a 95% blockage in a major coronary artery, and almost died on the operating table—but I got a second chance.

Many women aren't as lucky since women's symptoms can be subtle and easily missed. You may not think of women as having heart attacks, but surprisingly we lose more women than men. Heart disease is a woman's #1 risk—not breast cancer—but the great news is that we now understand much more about women's heart disease.

Take Care of You

My doctors were stunned since I didn't have the usual heart disease risk factors—no smoking, diabetes, high cholesterol or high blood pressure. We thought there might be family history, but my doctors have discounted that, too. I was simply overweight and overstressed, like many of us. At the time, stress wasn't considered a risk factor, but we now know that it is.

Women tend to care for everyone else first and take on everyone else's stress. We must put ourselves and our health first. It's not selfish; it's unselfish because it means we'll be here to take care of those we love.

Here's my simple five-step plan for living to 100. Yes, even heart disease survivors can aspire to that. This plan can work for you, too.

1. Control your stress. Start here, because hyper-busy lifestyles put you at risk, but once you control your stress hormones, these other steps are easy.

2. Get enough sleep and relaxation. If you get at least 7-8 hours of restorative sleep each night, nap when you need one and take vacations, you'll protect your health.

3. Eat right. Eat fruits, vegetables and grains, and have good fats in moderation while avoiding or minimizing bad fats. This helped me lose 85 pounds. If necessary, lose weight.

4. Exercise every day. Take that 30-60 minute walk each day to strengthen your heart. Get weight-bearing exercise at least twice a week to keep your muscles strong.

5. Take proactive control of your health. Educate yourself on health and partner with your health care provider. Know your risk factors and control them.

One more thing—if you smoke, stopping will add years to your life.

It's never too late to make changes to optimize your health. As Albert Einstein said, "The clever person solves a problem; the wise person avoids it. " Do these things for 21 days and you'll have healthy habits to ensure a long, vital life.

What will you do with the rest of your life?

Getting a second chance makes you ponder your mortality, which may lead to changes as you seek answers and new meaning from life. It meant starting over for me.

First, changing jobs. I left my corporate road-warrior job where I made a difference for companies, so that I could start making a difference for people. I now use my second chance for speaking and writing to spread the word about how to avoid heart disease and stroke by living a healthy life.

Second, changing pace. We moved to the country, slowed down and simplified to enjoy every precious day. We now enjoy nature, wide-open spaces and beautiful views.

✳

One day, a woman named Mary was in my audience. She recognized herself in my story, and her doctor found that she had heart disease. Mary told me that she now has a second chance at life.

By reading this, you have a second chance, too. I hope you will use your second chance to ponder the questions that I pondered, questions that could change your life. Please take time to go into the silence of your mind—tune out distractions and sit quietly—and ponder them.

- What have I always dreamed but haven't yet done? What's stopping me? How can I do it?

- Am I making a difference in the world?

- What do I want to accomplish by the time my days are through? Do I have a written plan to get there?

- Am I taking care of my health? Do I have a written plan for it?

- Am I putting myself first? If I don't, who will? Will I be there to care for those whom I love and to see my grandchildren or great-grandchildren?

- Do I have the resources to carry out my dreams? How can I handle the unexpected—medical bills, job change or even disability?

- Just in case, are my affairs in order?

- Have I told those whom I love today that I love them?

Getting a Third Chance

Seven months after my initial heart problem, I learned that heart disease is forever—once you have it, you're at risk for more heart problems. This time, I had blood clots and a near-stroke due to an irregular heartbeat called atrial fibrillation.

Living with atrial fibrillation is like living in hell. And since the blood-thinner medication I was taking to prevent strokes didn't work properly for me for genetic reasons, I was literally a stroke waiting to happen. Fortunately, I discovered this and had a new surgery. It stopped my atrial fibrillation and I've been afib-free ever since. I got my life back.

As I pondered what this third chance at life meant, I realized that I got rid of my afib, but many others were still living with this disruptive and debilitating disease. Someone needed to help them and it might as well be me. So I started a non-profit patient advocacy organization and web resource, StopAfib.org, for individuals and families living with atrial fibrillation. I now criss-cross the country speaking about not only heart disease and strokes, but also atrial fibrillation.

✳

It's through this journey that I have found my life's work. I had been preparing my whole life for this—from giving my first speech at the age of 4, to leading the creation of one of the first corporate websites, consulting on web strategies and writing books—I just didn't know it.

By speaking out to help wipe out heart disease and stroke, and hopefully save other families from these killers, I can make a difference.

By raising awareness of atrial fibrillation so that those with it get diagnosed and treated before they have a stroke, or two, I can make a difference.

By educating those with it in how to live with and control it, I can make a difference.

By giving a voice to a community that didn't have one, I can make a difference.

By creating and participating in coalitions that push for education and policy changes around the globe to ensure treatment for those with it, I can make a difference.

Each of us can make a difference in our own way. What difference will you make? What will be your lasting legacy?

CHAPTER 12:

Change

"PEOPLE WILL KEEP DOING WHAT THEY'RE DOING UNTIL THEY
GET TIRED OF IT. THEN THEY WILL DO SOMETHING ELSE."

Snakes can teach us a lot about change.

When a snake sheds its skin, it does so in one continuous piece. It starts by brushing against something hard to cause a rip in the skin. Then it slowly works on the rip until it shed the skin completely. During this process the snake moves about its world with raw, new skin at the top and then dragging the old skin behind until the transformation is complete. It does this several time a year.

When we experience change, we usually are bumping up against something we resist. It can be raw and uncomfortable. We're not quite in our "new skin" yet and are still dragging parts of the past behind us that no longer serve us.

This is just another cycle of life. The snake doesn't resist the change; it just works with it until it's complete.

How different would our lives be if we took a similar approach?

— *Marty Stanley,*
author of "Lady Gaga and the New Normal"

‒ GIVING WHEN IT HURTS ‒

by Valda Boyd Ford

❧

"YOU ARE JUST STUPID!"

His words hurt that time as they had hurt every other time he said them.

"How many times will you let people take advantage of you? Isn't it enough that you give so much time to your job? Do you think you have to give your money too?"

"No, I did not have to give her the money. And, I really don't think that giving her a little money makes me stupid. She just needed a little help and it didn't hurt me."

"Well, you may think that it did not hurt you but when you let people use you, you end up looking like a fool."

The "discussion" had gone on for more than ten minutes and my head was beginning to throb. How could a simple gesture turn into so much of a debate?

"I wish I had not told you," I said.

His cold look and slow shake of his head said more than words. His look was one of pity, saying again, without words, "You are too stupid to even know when you are being used."

At the end of a very long day, another fourteen hours of an official twelve-hour shift, I was too tired to try to make my case. But when I sank down into the chair, savoring being off my feet for the first time since early morning, I could not help but be reminded of the events of the day.

✳

Adele Caudill was a thin, meek woman who looked and acted much older than her 27 years. While she was always scrupulously clean from the neck down she always appeared to be in need of a shampoo. Her dark blonde, stick straight hair had no style, always appeared greasy and hung about her shoulders as limp and lifeless as a wet dishrag. Her teeth were not the American ideal of big white Chiclets. She would have benefitted from braces during her formative years. Her shoulders were in a constant state of hunching, giving her the appearance of someone who had no belief in her worth.

She was but one of a legion of parents, guardians, grandparents and foster parents responsible for the children I cared for at the pediatric hospital in middle Tennessee. It was a good hospital but, not unlike most the staffing, left a lot to be desired. With so many of the parents generally in absentia, Adele was a welcome sight—always in her daughter's room and always doing all she could for her tiny beautiful daughter. I could see Adele as a child by looking at Frankie—a sweeter, cheerier version of the shell her mother had become.

I understood why my husband was suspicious of Adele's request for financial assistance because I had talked about the terrible life I imagined she lived. On more than one occasion, we had found empty liquor bottles between the crib mattress and the springs of Frankie's bed when we changed the sheets. The first time we said nothing to the nursing supervisor, but we counseled Adele.

"I never drink, ma'am," she said while casting her already tear-filled eyes to the floor. "I don't know how that bottle got there."

I did not believe her, but my patient load of twelve juveniles, ranging from 8 days to 18 years of age, did not allow much time for speculation or judgment. When an empty beer bottle was found under the mattress not quite a week later, she was desperate to make me believe that she was not at fault.

"How can you possibly expect me to believe that? You are here with Frankie every minute that I am here! Who else would put an empty bottle in a baby's crib?"

"It was Frankie, ma'am. I am ashamed to say it, but it had to be Frankie."

Right. The baby put the bottle in her bed, I thought, but said nothing.

"No, ma'am. It's Big Frankie I'm talking about. Her daddy."

It made sense now. "Big Frankie," as he was called, was not known for his warmth or paternalistic virtues. He was a bit frightening and the kind of person you would not want to see if alone in an alley. I had practically forgotten about him because his visits were rare and always occurred after the end of my shift. I had the misfortune of working late one Saturday and had seen him threatening Adele with just a look. Even Baby Frankie was quieter when he was around, as if the four-year-old would know not to provoke this unkind man.

And then today, when Baby Frankie's doctors told Adele that she could take the baby home, Adele looked anything but relieved. She just stood there looking crestfallen as I gave her the discharge instructions for her daughter.

I continued to make rounds, rushing to try to get all the medications given, all the dressings changed, all the intravenous lines re-taped so small hands could not remove the fragile catheters, and find time to give a bit of love and laughter to the motherless children on the ward.

Though I was preoccupied with my chores, I felt, rather than saw, someone nearby. There was Adele, literally wringing her hands, looking more cowed than usual and with an expression that could not mask that what she was about to say would not come easily." I am really sorry to trouble you, ma'am, but I cannot take my daughter home. Is there some way you could let her stay here for five more days?"

"No, Adele. We cannot keep her here any longer. She is well enough to go home. As long as you give her the antibiotics on schedule for the next five days, she will be fine. I would have thought that after four weeks here you would be ready to go home."

"Yes, ma'am. I am ready to go but I cannot give Little Frankie the medicine you told me about. There is just not enough money for the medicine, ma'am, and you just told me that if I don't give it to her she will be sick and back in here again. So, could you just keep her here those five more days, ma'am. Then she'll be fine and I can take her home."

I stopped what I was doing for a moment, locked the medication cart, and walked to a quiet alcove with Adele. She was silently crying as she walked. She seemed so small and so very sad. I talked with her about possible ways to solve her problem but none of them were reasonable in her situation. I even checked with the pharmacy to find out the cost of the medication and if the hospital ever gave grants or waived the fees in special circumstances.

"Here, Adele. Here is ten dollars. Five dollars for the medicine and five dollars for milk for the baby until the first of the month."

I could not tell if she was happy or shocked or suspicious as a flurry of emotions seemed to cross her face.

"I don't know what to say, ma'am. I don't know how I will pay you back but I will. I will pay you back, I promise," she said as I looked at her with barely concealed doubt and with a reassurance that it did not matter if she repaid the debt.

"Consider it a gift to little Frankie."

✳

When I relayed the entire story to my husband late that evening, he was incensed and the debate began. Was I stupid? Possibly. Did I regret what I did? Not really, until now, when I was told over and over again that I was a fool, gullible and willing to fall for any sob story.

The year passed and I never heard from Adele. When the letter finally came, it was a bit of a curiosity. The small envelope was addressed in childlike, loopy-lettered script. The return address was somewhere in Appalachia. The card was handmade from the type of construction paper that preschoolers learn to cut and paste. Outside the card read "Thank you" in big, block letters. Inside was a child's drawing of a little girl and a mother standing on a hill with a gigantic smiling sun and a house with smoke curls from the chimney. As I looked at the card and tried to imagine what it was for, I noticed a small piece of paper still in the envelope. When I opened the paper, I started to cry. The note read:

Dear Nurse Valda, Little Frankie made this card for you. She remembers you and she still sings the song you taught her. She is a very healthy and strong six-year-old and she is learning to do things at school. I always remember your kindness and your gift made all the difference in the world. Little Frankie has been well since we left the hospital. I finally had the courage to leave Big Frankie back in Tennessee and I have come back home to stay with my folks. Thank you for saving my daughter and saving me.

I sat there for a long time reading and re-reading her note, allowing myself to remember the last time I saw Adele and little Frankie. Little did Adele know that the repayment of the very small and inconsequential amount of money did more than simply repay a debt. Her gesture helped me start my own journey to stay strong in myself and in my convictions. I knew that from that day forward, I would not feel stupid for doing something for another person. Adele had, in fact, saved my life.

— SAVING JOY, ADOPTING JOY, IN TOUGH TIMES —

by Colleen Kettenhofen

"WHEN YOU COME TO THE EDGE OF ALL THE LIGHT YOU KNOW,
AND ARE ABOUT TO STEP OFF INTO THE DARKNESS OF THE UNKNOWN,
FAITH IS KNOWING ONE OF TWO THINGS WILL HAPPEN: THERE WILL BE
SOMETHING SOLID TO STAND ON, OR YOU WILL BE TAUGHT HOW TO FLY."

- Patrick Overton

IN LATE OCTOBER 2002, MY HUSBAND AND I HAD LEFT ORANGE COUNTY, CALIFORNIA, AND WERE LIVING IN A BEAUTIFUL SUBURB OF ATLANTA, GEORGIA KNOWN AS PEACHTREE CITY. It's a favorite with pilots because it's close to Hartsfield-Jackson airport, and the city was fashioned after Hilton Head, South Carolina, with gorgeous green trees, golf courses and golf cart paths everywhere. The fall air was crisp and the leaves were turning bright shades of yellow, crimson, and orange. I loved the change of seasons and felt the sense of a fresh start.

We'd been contemplating adopting a rescue dog, yet it didn't seem right with our travel schedules. My husband at the time was an airline pilot, and I was an international motivational speaker.

I had lost my unborn daughter Caroline exactly one year before, after complications with my pregnancy, and only a few weeks afterwards, my 18-year-old cat "Baby" had also passed away. Still reeling from the previous year's losses, I wandered into an animal shelter having convinced myself I would "just look."

In the shelter was a calm, sweet-faced puppy, eight or nine weeks old, who caught my attention. It was instant chemistry—like when I was single and used to look at a ruggedly handsome man across the room! With this puppy, sensing our mutual chemistry and trust, I did what you're never supposed to do: I put my hand into her cage to pet her. While looking up at me with her big brown eyes, she licked my hand over and over. This innocent puppy was also highly intelligent and obviously knew how to sell herself! After many minutes, I pulled away and forced myself to walk towards the door. Already in love with her, I turned around, and there she was… still looking at me with those eyes!

A new puppy sounded wonderful, except that it didn't seem to fit into the lifestyle of an airline pilot and an international speaker. And my husband kept telling me how much attention puppies require. I'd never had one before so I had no idea. Still, my gut feeling was that it was fate that we were supposed to have her. I couldn't stop thinking about her. There was a constant nagging feeling that I couldn't forsake. I resolved to go back to the Peachtree Animal Shelter in the next few days to visit.

✳

Early in the morning a few days later, while at a garage sale, two smiling women, a mother and daughter, walked up to me holding a puppy. As I looked more closely I thought, "No, it can't be!"

I realized this was the exact same puppy. The one I'd been thinking of adopting! The women placed her in my arms before I knew what was happening and said, "Would you like to adopt her? She's from the Peachtree City pound. We can't have any more pets. We already have five dogs, but she only had two hours to live, so we got her out. And we've named her Joy because she's already brought such joy to our lives." Two hours to live. I was stunned. I had no idea Joy's time could've been cut so short!

She fit perfectly in my arms as she gazed up at me with those puppy-dog eyes. There was an inexplicable connection and incredible bond. I wanted to talk to my husband first, even though I had a feeling he'd say, "yes" this time! They'd even offered to pet-sit her for free. They were the kindest, sweetest people and seemed to come out of nowhere.

Later that day, lunching with a friend who was listening to my story, she said, "My gosh, Colleen, it's fate! You're supposed to have that puppy! Let's go see her tonight." My husband was flying, so my friend and I drove to their home on the outskirts. As we pulled into the driveway, my friend shrieked, "Oh Colleen, its fate, its fate!" I had *no* idea what she was talking about. She pointed to the car in front of us in the driveway, and in huge capital letters was a bumper sticker that simply read, "FATE." How many more "signs" did I need? The family explained to us that night that their son had died unexpectedly a year earlier, that this was his car, his bumper sticker, and that he'd always believed in fate.

✳

After playing with this happy puppy named Joy, I went home empty-handed that night. I needed to read some inspirational literature and really think this over. I take adopting a pet so seriously. It's a lifetime commitment. And I wanted to make sure this puppy would be with us forever. As I pulled out this little book with its daily word message, I gasped. In big letters, the word of the day was JOY. It was fate!

I don't recall reading any inspirational literature that morning. But since then, I've found that spending time in solitude each morning clears my mind and allows greater access to insight. My intuition becomes stronger. Silence is refreshment for my soul. And when your mind, body and spirit are renewed, you're better equipped to make decisions and assist others. The other we were going to assist was this adorable rescue puppy.

The next day, my husband and I brought our bundle of Joy home. On the anniversary of Caroline's death, October 30th, 2002, there I was with Joy sitting in my lap riding in the car. I don't think dogs are supposed to ride there, but it was the *only* place she would sit. She refused to be anywhere but my lap.

Little did I know how dramatically life would change after adopting this adorable rescue dog. Joy has been a priceless gift.

Shortly after adopting Joy, I was in a souvenir shop. There were some souvenirs with different names ranging from A to Z hanging on a display rack. The sign said that on the back of each name was the meaning of that particular name. Curious to find out the meaning of "Caroline," I anxiously turned over the souvenir. It said, "Song of JOY."

Immediately I felt a sense of surprise, awe and wonder wash over me as if this was no coincidence. More like a miracle! Joy was meant for me. Her arriving in my life at a precise moment was no accident. It's as if Joy is an angel who came down from heaven and descended on earth disguised as a dog. I don't know how it all works. But I do know there have been many coincidences, supernatural synchronicities and miracles since Joy came along.

✳

I've learned to look for the light in every dark situation. In school, we're given the lesson first, then the test. In life, we're given the test first, the lesson later.

Turning obstacles into opportunities and conquering your past can be the passageway to your purpose. It's one of the secrets to adopting Joy.

THERE IS NO PSYCHIATRIST IN THE WORLD
LIKE A PUPPY LICKING YOUR FACE.

- Ben Williams

◦ The Power of Thought ◦

by Sister Bhavna Bhen

৯৯

Have you ever made New Year's Resolutions with such zeal and enthusiasm on the 31st of December, only to break each one by January 7th (or sooner)? Why is this? I know many souls who upon being asked, "What is your resolution this year?" reply glibly, "The same one I made last year!"

Hopelessly and with expectance we watch each resolve fade and break away, such that by this point, most of us barely hold on to the possibility of effecting change in our lives at all. Often we believe we are incapable of keeping a promise; we have broken so many in the past. Perhaps we wish to lose weight; or stop smoking; or be kinder and less reactive to things beyond our control, including other people, circumstances or events; thereby building a stress-free life complete with happiness, peace and improved health.

Whatever the change in behavior I wish to see in my life, I must first begin to realize that thoughts are like seeds. Whatever my thoughts, so will be my attitude and behavior. So the emphasis needs to shift not so much on the behavior, as the thinking that creates it.

Where does your experience of happiness or sorrow take place? In your mind. The person or event to which I have assigned "blame" for my experience of sorrow or stress is not in my mind. I control my own thinking.

Do you not think your own thoughts? Yes, there are many things out there who will try to influence the way I feel, but I decide how I think and how I feel. I choose what things I will let in and what things I will leave out. We are careful not to ingest poisonous food for the body, and yet often we allow the mind to "eat" whatever poisonous thoughts are offered to us. If you keep a diet of "junk" food or spoiled and rotten foods, you will get an upset stomach, and your physical health will deteriorate. In the same way, if you permit yourself to think negative, sad or worrisome thoughts, you can expect to have an upset mind, to suffer the illness of sorrow, peacelessness, and stress. Your mental heath will begin to deteriorate as well.

If, on the other hand, you imbibe only those thoughts that will feed your mind in a healthy way, you will begin to have control of your mind to such an extent that you are free from the common stresses and sorrows of this life. You begin to enjoy a life of constant happiness, peace and well-being.

When I am not in the practice of checking the quality of my thoughts throughout the day, my mind will begin to race and I will react sensitively to little things. I become vulnerable to the opinions of others as well as my own limited way of understanding.

✳

You are what you think. Love, peace, wisdom, happiness… the more you think of these things, the more you will become them.

When you build a house, every brick counts. When you build character, every thought counts.

Whatever you wish to achieve, nothing happens until you first think about it. Thought precedes everything, so make your thoughts strong and happy, and so will be your experience.

A very wise friend, Dadi Janki, once said: "When you talk to yourself in your mind, which self do you address, and how do you speak to yourself?" Usually, most do not speak to their divinity, but to the most superficial aspects of their every day personality. Often it's a stream of fears, complaints and a mindless repetition of old things. If we talked that way to others, we would have to apologize.

Learning to talk properly to the self is a spiritual endeavor. Thoughts from the past and worries about the future do no make good conversation. Instead, learn to talk to your mind as if it were a child. Talk to it with love. If you just force a child to sit down, he won't. A good mother knows how to prompt a child into doing what she wants. Be a good mother to your mind. Teach it good, positive thoughts so that when you tell it to sit quietly, it will.

✳

Would you like to get rid of two-thirds of your sorrow right now? It's very easy. So easy, you'll wonder why you didn't think of it years ago. Here's what you do: Don't think of the past or future.

You have enough to deal with in the present, don't you? The past is finished, and there's nothing I can do about it. I have no connection with it. No matter how much I cry or complain, not a single moment of the past can be changed. Once the photo has been taken, there's nothing I can change in it. I can complain that I wish I had worn a different color lipstick or that my hair was different, but no matter how I complain, that picture has already been shot! I can learn for the future picture that blue lipstick really doesn't look very good on me… but I can do nothing about that picture.

The future is equally elusive. When does the future come? Tomorrow? When tomorrow comes, that's today! I have nothing but now… right this moment. Thinking of the past or the future falls into the category of what we call "waste thoughts." No benefit can come from this way of thinking. But as we have experienced for ourselves, what can and does come from this way of thinking is sorrow, stress and anxiety. I need to be aware of how much damage is being caused by negative thoughts. Negative, wasteful thinking over a long period of time will drag me down so low that I, out of self-preservation, begin to call it *up!*

I must first change myself, and then I can change the world. If I want to see peace in the world, for example, I must be that peace. What is the world made up of after all? People! Not governments, communities or organizations, but people, and people are made up of their thinking! I wish to see peace between countries that don't speak the same language, have different features and customs, and yet I can't make peace in my own country because there isn't even peace in a state, or peace in one city, or even in one neighborhood, or even in my own family, my own household. Because there isn't even peace within my own self!

So the first thing I must do is change my attitude and behavior. Then, as I change, it will have an impact, and will be an inspiration for others to change as well.

— LADY GAGA AND THE NEW NORMAL —

by Marty Stanley

BOTH LADY GAGA AND THE NEW NORMAL ARE CHANGING OUR CONVERSATIONS TO REFLECT THE NEW WORLD CHALLENGES AND OPPORTUNITIES.

To understand exactly what the New Normal is, let's take a look at the past.

When I left the corporate world in 1999 and started speaking publicly about accountability and integrity, not many people were interested. Accountability wasn't sexy or the next big idea. After all, we'd had continuous improvement: TQM, process re-engineering, Seven Habits, Six Sigma, Five Whatever... Unfortunately, most of those processes ended up in three-ringed binders that were put on the shelf until the next new process came along. I still have boxes of binders from 1988.

Here are just a few of the things we have seen in the past ten years, when there has been no accountability or integrity:

- The dot-com bust, 9/11, Enron, Katrina, FEMA.
- Scandals everywhere: politics, religion, sports.
- Bernie Madoff, bailouts and industries collapsing.
- Product recalls, contaminated foods, greed, waste, and excess.

In the past, many organizations touted their vision, mission and core values. But for many, their operating policies and practices weren't aligned. When there is no accountability or integrity in the structures to support those ideals, things run amok!

Despite cultures that espouse open communication or leading by example, we've seen blatant examples of information being withheld, falsified and denied. We've seen the result of management by fear and intimidation, which prevents people from truly "doing the right thing." And lest we forget, the "leadership invincibility" factor—which is simply, "I'm just so (*fill in the blank...*) I won't get caught."

To succeed in the future, true leaders will assure alignment of the vision, mission and core values. If employees are the *greatest assets*, then hiring, compensation and benefit practices will reflect those values. An organization that wants to *delight* the customers or says it *values* its clients will have operating policies and practices that make it easy to work with them. Callers won't get stuck in a telephone maze where they can't talk to a real person. Billing practices will be easy to understand and there will be transparency and open disclosure.

The people who will succeed in the New Normal will really be leading by example and communicating in a way that translates the organizational values into operational practices. There will be clear demonstrations of the values in the most mundane ways. It's in everyday conversations and everyday ways of doing business. They won't be carrying around silly wallet-sized copies of the core values to flash at innocent bystanders to prove they *get it*.

So what about Lady Gaga? While she may not look *normal*, she is changing her industry and transforming how recording companies make money. Ever since music could be downloaded from the Internet, record labels have been going broke. But with the *360 deal*, the record label promotes Lady Gaga upfront, and gets paid on the back-end based on revenue from her tours and merchandise, rather than record sales. Brilliant. And everybody wins, including the consumer.

Lady Gaga is also changing what it means to be a product spokesperson. MAC Cosmetics launched a campaign for AIDS awareness for women through which a percentage of each sale went to the cause. On Good Morning America, looking like the Statue of Liberty, Lady Gaga declined to comment on her celebrity status and meeting the Queen of England by saying, "I'm here to talk about MAC Cosmetics and what they are doing to increase AIDS awareness for women. I'm blessed with this responsibility and it's an important issue. That's what I'm here to talk about."

As people drank their morning coffee, they were captivated by the conversation of a 23-year-old woman wearing a crown on her head, while she proceeded to talk about safe sex for women at any age.

Not only is she a smart businesswoman, Lady Gaga *gets it*. And people are listening.

✳

To succeed in the future, it will not be "business as usual." It's not about process improvement. It's not about incremental improvements. It's about transformational change. It's about taking a close look at what's really working and what's not. No sacred cows.

While there are a lot of critics and cynics about how things aren't working in many organizations, make no mistake, it takes courage to change. It takes courage to speak up and acknowledge that it's time for change. And it takes commitment and stamina to break out of the mold, to create a new vision and stick with it.

As Albert Einstein said, "The significant problems we have cannot be solved at the same level of thinking with which we created them." The New Normal leaders understand that new thinking is needed. They are creating new visions for the future and new conversations to support that future. The New Normal culture will include accountability and integrity.

This approach can be applied to creating a new vision for failing school systems, a new vision for transforming how homeless people are served, how performing arts can be revived and even how families operate.

It's not hard and it's not complicated. But it does require courage and commitment and willingness to change.

CONVERSATIONS CHANGE THE WAY YOU SEE
THE WORLD AND EVEN CHANGE THE WORLD.

- Theodore Zeldin

The dialogue and new conversations begin with you and me.

So I ask you this: What's your vision for your organization's future? Do you have the courage to take the first step to change and be ready for the New Normal?

— FutureThink for the New Normal —
Speaking Is Not a Business Strategy

by Edie Raether

Change has changed. The velocity of change has changed. We all know the speaking industry has changed, but have you? Having been a professional speaker for over 40 years, I have witnessed many changes and experienced many transitions, while some topics simply cycle, such as motivation, which may be in high demand at times, but then may be perceived as fluff with no real value. The questions is, are you changing to be current or are you in a perpetual niche switch?

Some speakers prefer to have one strong keynote to present thousands of times, while others have developed an extensive menu of topics and services for a specific client base to reduce marketing expenses. There are actually four choices to make regarding your focus, depth and breadth as a professional speaker:

1. How do you define your expertise? While a specific focus may limit your client base, it does allow you to go deep within a defined industry where you and your services become woven into the fabric of the industry, and you become the provider of choice.

2. While your topic and expertise may be focused, your speaking may have a broad audience appeal, such as many motivational keynotes, or a topic such as stress management, which has value for everyone.

3. A third consideration is to offer a wide breadth of services, such as keynotes, training, and follow-up coaching with a depth of focus in a very specific industry, such as technology or financial institutions.

4. The last option is to be a speaker, trainer and coach where your expertise is as a process facilitator rather than in a specific topic or industry. *You* are the brand. For example, Oprah is her own brand.

The important thing is that you choose a path and remain true to it, changing only to meet the needs of a changing marketplace. You must stand for something. As a speaker, trainer, coach, or consultant, who are you? Who do people think you are? If the two are not in sync, review your marketing plan and do some serious revisions. Your talent and expertise must become a clear, concise brand identity such as that created by Tony Robbins or Zig Ziglar. What playing field will you claim (or create) as your own? Why fight the crowds and the competition?

While you certainly may have more than one area of expertise, remember that a confused mind says "no." Unfortunately, people prefer to pigeon-hole, and if you present yourself as an expert in every area that you can make a buck, you have defined yourself as a jack of all trades and master of none. Meeting planners prefer to hire the "master" and will always pay more for it. It is why you pay more for an electrician or plumber than a handyman who may be able to do both jobs quite well.

It is important that you keep your expertise in various areas separate, such as having different marketing materials and separate websites for each area of proficiency. For example, while I will continue to maintain my branding on Breakthrough Thinking for Mastering Change and do motivational keynotes, and seminars in sales, leadership and change management, I have recently developed a children's character building program for which I am the CEO (chief enlightenment officer). While I do have experience and credibility in both areas, an executive at IBM seeking a speaker for her management group would not be looking for a kids' coach!

✳

The issue is that the fine art of speaking is no longer what will financially sustain you in the speaking industry, and like financial investing, new marketing approaches and strategies are crucial to maintaining your presence on the platform. You must continually reset, refocus and reinvent yourself to meet the challenges of the new business environment.

While excellence as an orator will always be essential for inspiration and impact, current content, information and solutions meet the needs of today's marketplace. You must be relevant and credible: an expert who engages but is also accessible, accountable and action-oriented. You must more than inspire—you must transform.

— STRESS AND HAPPINESS —

by Elizabeth Manuel

CAN YOU BE HAPPY AND STRESSED AT THE SAME TIME? Yes and no. You can have a general feeling of happiness, but if you are clearly under stress, you cannot fool your body for long. While under stress, your heart rate increases, and your blood pressure will likely rise as well. During this time, the stress hormones cortisol and adrenalin flow through you to ensure that you feel even more wired and ready to react or respond. When afraid or under stress, you are likely to have worried thoughts; physical sensations like a faster heart rate, sweating and increased breathing; and behaviors like trying to escape the situation that made you afraid in the first place!

The amygdala (Greek for "almond," which is its shape) is the part of the brain that reacts most strongly when you're confronted with fear and stress. Under stress, the amygdala orders the release of neurotransmitters, which can cause increased doubt, fear and anxiety. In the "fight or flight" response, a quick message is sent to the amygdala, releasing more adrenalin than you probably need for your situation. This may show up in stress symptoms such as increased blood pressure, increased breathing and heart rate, reduced digestive function, and dilated pupils.

❋

Problems arise when your daily stressors trigger your stress response. This means that you are constantly on alert, and too much stress for too long can result in an imbalance. There are few situations in modern life (unless you have just come face-to-face with a hungry bear in the mountains) where such a response is optimal. Taking a final exam requires sitting in a chair, not running away from an enemy. The focus on survival that stress and hormone release causes generally results in poor decision making and concentration—the very things that help you to be successful at work, sports and in your personal relationships.

In the short term, it is important to manage the "fight or flight" response. A step to take in coping with stress is to identify and then take action to reduce your stressors. If you are constantly overscheduled and being run ragged, you must do one of two things: either change your mental response to your busyness by reminding yourself that you are choosing to and looking forward to participating in these commitments, or release some of the commitments and choose to honor your life.

I suggest you implement some relaxation techniques, such as deep breathing, meditation and/or clinical hypnotherapy, to reduce the stress in your body. In the long term, stress management helps to reduce fatigue and burnout, and promote wellness, health and happiness.

⁓ AMAZING ⁓

by Jennifer Powers

ॐ

OK, here's the thing… You are amazing!

When was the last time you heard that?

If it's been more than a day, it's been too long.

You know why we don't hear that enough? Because we believe that statements like this are meant to come from SOMEONE ELSE.

And there, my dear friend, is the problem.

Let me lay it out for you.

There is no one on this earth that is a bigger authority on you than YOU.

YOU. WONDERFUL YOU.

No one knows your **truth.**

No one knows your capacity, potential and drive.

No one knows your talents, passion, love or delicious qualities better than YOU.

This is true for all of us. Yet we wait, hope, beg and plead for others to see the amazingness that lies within us. In other words, we give others the power to dictate and determine our worth. We give others the power to make us feel confident (or not). We give others our power by waiting for them to tell us that we are good enough. And guess what? They don't take our power... we GIVE IT TO THEM.

Sometimes for years...

Well, if you are doing this now, rest assured, you are normal.

But who wants to be normal?

Normal ≠ Good

Just because something is normal, doesn't necessarily mean it's good.

And you so deserve to be good. Better than good, actually.

So, take a look at your life.

All of it.

Who are you waiting for validation from?

Who are you relinquishing your power to?

When will you be ready to stop?

How does NOW grab you?

Do yourself a favor.

Stop relying on everyone else to make you feel amazing,

powerful or worthy.

There is no way you're going to win

at this game called life

by relying on your herd of scapegoats.

You deserve better than that. The only person

who has the power to determine your amazingness is YOU.

After all, this is *your* life.

No one but *you* is responsible for your confidence.

No one but *you* is responsible for making you realize how fabulous you are.

No one but *you* is responsible for the way you feel about yourself.

No one but *you* is responsible for validating who you are, how you act and what you think.

You're the boss, applesauce.

Own it.

OK. Now that we know the problem, let's look at the solution.

This is easy. Super simple. So simple, in fact, that you may be tempted to discount it. Don't do that.

Trust me.

Do this and you will begin to eliminate your scapegoats, recapture your power and realize that you really don't need ANYONE else's help in making you feel ANYTHING.

Now, at this point I could very easily just tell you how awesome you are and hope that some of it sinks in and that the feeling you get lasts more than six and a half minutes. But that would clearly defeat the point I am trying to make. Plus, I love you too much to keep you in that vicious cycle of dependence on others.

So that means you're going to have to work for this one. You ready?

Let's do this.

SAY THE FOLLOWING... OUT LOUD.

(Note: Out loud does not mean in your head. It means moving your lips and vocalizing syllables. The vibration of the words you are about to say is what gives them power. So if you don't say it out loud, you'll be cheating yourself of the full effect... but, like always, it's your choice.)

OK, here we go.

In actuality, I am freakin amazing. I have confidence in who I am, what I do, say and think. I am the only person who has the power to assess my amazingness. I decide how I feel about myself.

And this feels so good.

I am amazing because I say I am. I am amazing. The way I am right now is perfect. The way I am makes me ME. I am enough. I am enough because I say I am enough. No one, no thing, no event could ever take that truth away. This is my truth.

I am amazing.

Ahhhhh!

Good.

Now go back and say it again (out loud, of course).

And this time FEEL the words and own them as truth.

Your truth.

Your new truth.

Resonate with the statements by

paying closer attention to their meaning.

Feel how your heart literally fills up as you say

these words and mean them.

Let your body become erect with confidence in these statements.

Let your voice accentuate the words that are most important to you.

In other words,

don't just say them… feel them.

(Note: Again, you don't have to do this next step, but it is sooooo powerful when you do. Like always, it's your choice.)

.

.

.

Nice job, oh powerful one.

Now, saying this out loud twice is a good start,

but clearly not enough to make it stick.

So, I challenge you to say this any time

you find yourself waiting for validation.

Anytime you are disappointed that someone

failed to recognize you,

compliment you or appreciate you.

Anytime you feel like you are not all that.

Anytime you need it to be reminded of your

absolute awesomeness.

This is your challenge.

This is your job.

Are you up for it?

I know you are.

Because you're freakin amaaaaaaazing.

~ BREAKING THROUGH UNCERTAINTY: ~
WELCOMING ADVERSITY

by Jim McCormick

❧

"THE GREATER DRAGON IS

NOT THE EXTERNAL THREAT...

OR ANOTHER CHALLENGE.

THE REAL DRAGON IS THE

SELF-DOUBT WE CARRY

WITHIN US."

It was mid-morning on a warm and pleasant Saturday. I was in the midst of my first skydive of the day. It was my 2,123rd jump since having taken up the sport fifteen years ago. After about one minute of freefall and at 5,000 feet above the ground, I parted ways with my fellow jumpers to get far enough away from them to open my parachute safely. I initiated opening around 3,000 feet above the earth.

My parachute opened with some twists in the lines between the parachute and me. This is not that uncommon. What was different this time was that I was not able to clear the twists.

The twists in the lines caused my parachute to take on an asymmetrical shape. Receiving asymmetrical inputs, the canopy did what it is designed to do and initiated a turn—that's how it is steered. The problem occurred when the turn quickly became a rapid, diving-downward spiral that was spinning me a full 360 degrees about once every second. This was a problem. I looked up to assess my canopy and saw something I don't often see—the horizon clearly visible *above* the trailing edge of my canopy. This meant my canopy and I were now on roughly the same horizontal plane. In that I could see the horizon behind it, I was actually above my parachute, and it was leading our fast-spinning parade rapidly towards Mother Earth.

My first need was to acknowledge that I was not going to be able to solve this problem. This is not as easy as it seems. Having successfully completed hundreds of jumps without having to resort to my second parachute, it was hard for me to believe I had really encountered a problem I could not solve. I had a natural inclination to assume I could fix this problem as I had all those in the past.

Sound familiar? It's always easy to lapse into denial when confronted with a problem. Until we acknowledge the problem and our possible inability to solve it—or to use the methods we have used in the past—we don't have a chance of making things better. Fortunately, the urgency of this situation caused my hard-headed nature to yield much quicker than usual. That decision probably took a second or two.

✳

The next step, having accepted the need to follow a different course than in the past, was to determine the course. Fortunately, fifteen years of training and practice before every day of jumping took hold. I looked straight down at the two handles on either side of my chest—one to release me from my malfunctioning canopy and one for deploying my reserve parachute—and realized I needed to quickly get them in my hands. I could not help but notice when I made eye contact with them, as had been ingrained in me during my First Jump Course way back in 1988, that by now the rapid spins had turned me back to Earth, and there beyond my toes was once again the horizon. This was bad!

Time was of the essence at this point not only because I was now rapidly progressing toward the horse pasture below me, but also because the centrifugal force I was starting to experience would soon make it impossible to get my hands to those two handles. With my hands now securely on the handles, I was confronted with a bothersome question: Now, which one goes first? The wrong order could cause my reserve parachute to deploy into my spinning main parachute that would result in an incurable entanglement.

Fortunately, ingrained training once again took over and I pulled them in the right order. First the handle on the right side, which released me from my spinning main parachute, followed by the handle on the left side to deploy my reserve parachute. This brought on a wonderful experience. My malfunctioning black, teal and magenta canopy was replaced with a bright, yellow, never-before-used reserve parachute. What a lovely sight! And all this by 1,700 feet—plenty of time to spare.

✳

Many years ago, I read a book about the challenges and responsibilities of Secret Service agents. One of the sad aspects of that profession is that agents who never have the chance to validate their years of training by responding to a threat sometimes struggle severely in retirement. They are faced with not knowing with certainty how they would respond when faced with the paramount challenge their career can deliver. For this reason, agents who have faced such a challenge successfully are admired within the culture of the Service.

That Saturday morning, I had the privilege of facing a similar, life-threatening and, I now realize, life-defining challenge. I faced what Secret Service agents call "the dragon."

For all of us, the greater dragon is not the external threat, whether it is an assassin's bullet, the unforgiving and fast-approaching earth, or another challenge. The real dragon is the self-doubt we carry within us. For those few splendid moments after landing safely, I was able to put my foot firmly on the neck of the dragon… and it felt great.

Keep this in mind the next time you are confronted with adversity. On the far side of the experiences the adversity presents, there could be a valuable gift—a renewed confidence and certainty.

— Changing Our Perspective —

by Thomas Blackwell

I grew up in a small town. Sometimes in small towns, there can be certain perspectives that are deeply embedded in its people. One of those perspectives was about a young man about age 20, named Mike. Our parents always told us to stay away from Mike because, "You never know what he might do."

Mike was not your typical 20-year-old. He looked normal: he was tall and well built, but he was mentally challenged. Most of the time, he could be found on his bike cruising around town. Everyone knew Mike, and that he didn't have a mother. His dad didn't seem to care much about anything except his next drink of liquor.

I was six years old when my perspective on Mike changed.

My two older brothers and I had been playing in an irrigation channel that had a very strong current. It ran about 150 yards in length, and then it went underground. There were two ladders at each end of the channel. We thought it would be fun to climb down the ladder on one end, let the water take us down, then grab onto the ladder at the other end. The current was extremely powerful, and standing up was impossible for us. And if you happened to miss the ladder at the other end, the result would most likely be death. Other than that, it looked like a good time.

My oldest brother was the first to give it a shot; he successfully grabbed the ladder at the end of the channel before it went underground. Next it was Garrett's turn; he was just two years older than I was. There he went, racing down the vicious channel, but when he got to the other ladder, he lost his grip and fell back in the current. My heart sank and I screamed in terror as we were about to witness our brother being carried away into an irretrievable abyss of irrigation water. There was nothing we could do. We knew we would be easily swept away as well if we tried to save him.

✳

It was one of those times you hope and pray that God intervenes and sends a guardian angel. Well, I will never forget that God did send an angel that day.

In the blink of an eye, Mike was all of a sudden there at the end of the channel. With no hesitation, he got off his bike, jumped down into the irrigation channel, stood up in the ferocious water, caught my brother before he was swept underground, and put him back on dry land. Then, Mike just got on his bike and rode away as if nothing had happened.

My oldest brother and I just stood there, in awe of what had taken place. We then realized we couldn't find Garrett, whom Mike had just rescued, anywhere. Then we heard, "*Psst, hey guys,*" coming from the cotton field across the street. We quickly found out that the situation had been more precarious than we had expected, and the current had been so strong that it had pulled my brother's shorts right off of him, and he was now hiding naked in the cotton field.

I distinctly remember that the thought of having to tell mom we were playing in a dangerous irrigation channel, and that her son was now naked as a result, seemed more serious than telling her he'd almost drowned. That's the perspective of a six-year-old for you. Of course, my oldest brother devised a plan with two options: 1) I would give Garrett my shorts and then ride home in my undies, or 2) I would ride home and get some particulars for him while he hid in the cotton field. I chose option two, having previously experienced option one. Either way, mom was destined to find out, and… she did.

After that near-death experience, whenever we boys left the house to play, my mom would say, "Make sure and take Mike with you!" She obviously gained a new perspective about Mike, as did many people in that small town. Almost overnight, our new friend, who was previously considered a dangerous nuisance, was now accepted and respected.

I hope we will base our perspective of people, or whatever the situation may be, on our personal experience, and that we don't simply succumb to what everyone else ignorantly believes. You never know when someone's life might be saved as a result of it.

ABOUT THE CONTRIBUTORS

DAVID C. ALLEN, MA is a keynote speaker, author, executive coach and has been a successful entrepreneur for more than twenty years. His is a dynamic blend of education and experience paired with perspectives from coaching on the athletic fields and leading in the boardrooms. Today, he speaks to and works with corporations, organizations, CEOs, small business owners and individuals, providing foundations to excel in the face of challenge and change. **www.trunorthadvisors.com**

KRISTIN ARNOLD, MBA, CPF, CMC, CSP is one of North America's most accomplished professional meeting facilitators. A consummate author, speaker and trainer, she is on a crusade to make all events in the workplace more engaging, interactive and collaborative. One of the first women to graduate from the US United States Coast Guard Academy and the only woman stationed onboard a Coast Guard buoy tender, Kristin learned firsthand how to build high-performance teams, engage others in the workplace and get the job done. **www.boringtobravo.com**

LENA ARNOLD is the author of For This Child We Prayed: Living with the Secret Shame of Infertility; Strong Black Coffee: Poetry and Prose to Enlighten, Encourage and Entertain Americans of African Descent; and In the Absence of My Father. Her books are available on Amazon.com and Barnes & Noble. **www.strongblackcoffee.info**

NANCY BAUSER, ACSW, BCETS, BCDT survived a head-on collision that resulted in a severe brainstem injury in 1971. She decided to continue her education and received a bachelor's degree from the University of Michigan in 1973 and a master's degree in social work from the University of Wisconsin-Madison in 1976. After graduation, she achieved admission to the Academy of Certified Social Workers. From the years 2002 until 2004, Ms. Bauser obtained recognition from The American Academy of Experts in Traumatic Stress. She is a board certified expert in traumatic stress and holds a board certification in disability trauma. **www.survivoracceptance.com**

PATTI BECKHAM is the senior vice president of public relations and communications for Ag Workers Mutual Auto Insurance Company, formed in the historic city of Fort Worth, Texas in 1948. Retired from Lone Star Land Bank, an association of the Tenth Farm Credit District Bank of Texas, she joined Ag Workers as director and senior vice president. From the city street to the country roads in Texas, Ms. Beckham enjoys the countryside of Texas, touching the deep roots of American people's dreams. She is the author of The Orla Flash, which is available from Amazon.com

GILAT BEN-DOR, MBA, CSW is known as The MBA Sommelier™—a speaker, author and wine expert who speaks about passionate living and success, often using wine as a metaphor. Combining her background in business, training and a fierce passion for wine, Gilat is also the founder of Renaissance Wine Academy™, a wine education company. **www.gilatben-dor.com**

SISTER BHAVNA BHEN has studied metaphysics since 1970 and has been a teacher with the Brahma Kumaris World Spiritual University since 1994. Yearly, she travels to India for advanced training. She speaks nationally as well as internationally. Sister Bhavna has released two guided-meditation CDs: Garden of Angels and The Body Is Doing What It Has To, And I Am Doing What I Have To. Her practical and down-to-earth approach to deep matters, coupled with her sense of humor, help to make her a most enjoyable and enlightening speaker, teacher and author. **www.thetransformationstation.us**

NGAHIHI O TE RA BIDOIS, international leadership speaker and author in the business, education and cultural sectors, has been described as inspirational, awesome, one of the most powerful experiences of my life and highly memorable. He has developed many leaders' personal and professional leadership and speaks on ancient wisdom from his indigenous New Zealand Maori culture as modern solutions for you. Ngahi has spoken at Google in New York, HR conferences throughout Asia and international education conferences and believes the most important resource many organizations have is their people. Let him help you develop your most important resource! **www.ngahibidois.com**

THOMAS BLACKWELL is a speaker, corporate trainer and author of Watch Your Language and Everything Always Works Out for Our Good. He has inspired thousands over the last ten years in the business. Thomas attended Northern Arizona University as a Division 1 tennis player and also earned a scholarship in vocal music. He is married to his high school sweetheart, Kimberly, and together they have four gorgeous daughters. **www.thomasblackwellspeak.com**

MARIDEL BOWES, MA has one passion greater than her love of writing and speaking: using those abilities to evoke women's soulfulness, sassiness and spirit on life's evolving journey. She is a therapist, professional astrologer and workshop facilitator. Maridel is the author of Who Are You Calling Grandma? True Confessions of a Baby Boomer's Passage. **www.evolvingjourney.com**

VALDA BOYD FORD, MPH, MS, RN grew up in the segregated South. She ignored the advice of guidance counselors who told her to forget about college and went on to obtain masters degrees in nursing and public health. Over the past thirty years she has worked in more than two dozen countries with refugees of war and natural disaster, helped developed long-term programs to improve health, and has been a successful entrepreneur in the United States and the Caribbean. She has one son, Alphonso, and is "Auntie" to many actual and adopted family members around the world. **www.centerforhumandiversity.org**

TERRY BROCK, MBA is an international marketing coach and professional speaker who has helped businesses generate profitable results since 1983 in more than 25 countries. He is also a columnist for business journals around the United States, writing about technology, marketing and the Internet. He served for six years on the Board of Directors of the National Speakers Association. **www.terrybrock.com**

DEBORAH (DONALDSON) CHAMBERLAIN, MA has a master's degree in mass communications from the University of Wisconsin-Milwaukee and has taught classes on mass media, advertising and consumer behavior. She is the owner of Donaldson Media & Marketing Services, LLC.

Deborah has been a Community Columnist and blogger for the Milwaukee Journal Sentinel, and is a contributor to several other publications. Deborah recently published her memoir Orange Picnic. **E-mail: orangepicnic@gmail.com**

PAIGE LANIER CHARGOIS, DM in has engaged in ministering to, motivating, encouraging, and inspiring people for the past 30-plus years – verbally and in print. She is a published author as a result of that work and the work of racial reconciliation locally, nationally, and internationally. She is passionate about the work of forgiveness and hospitality with which many folks struggle much of their lives. She is the author of Certain Women Called By Christ, available from **www.newhopepublishers.com**

LAUREL CLARK, DMIN, DD is the President of the School of Metaphysics and Dean of Intuitive Research at the College of Metaphysics. She has been teaching metaphysics since 1979. Laurel is an intuitive counselor and interfaith minister with the Interfaith Church of Metaphysics. She frequently speaks to business and professional groups, offers guest sermons, and speaks at international conferences on subjects like communication, visualization, dreams, meditation and intuitive development. She is an author of several books, including The Law of Attraction and Other Secrets of Visualization; Dharma: Finding Your Soul's Purpose; Concentration; Karmic Healing; and Interpreting Dreams for Self Discovery. **www.som.org**

LARS CLAUSEN, MDIV holds the Guinness World Record for the longest unicycle ride—a tour through all 50 United States. Along with his degree in engineering and in ministry, he also has received national awards for his two books, One Wheel—Many Spokes (www.onewheel.org) and Straight Into Gay America **(www.straightintogayamerica.com)**. Presently, Lars spends his days consulting with authors **(www.americanauthor.com)** and in the evenings, he can be found watching his kids at their sporting events.

MATTHEW COSSOLOTTO, creator of Make a Promise Day and author of The Power of Making a Promise, is a former aide to the Speaker of the House of United States Representatives, a CEO-level speechwriter, and a communications executive at MCI Communications, GTE and Pepsi-Cola International. His other books include The Real F Word: The 7 FAILURE Traps of Highly Disempowered People and All the World's a Podium. **www.makeapromisenetwork.com**

BILL CROW has played with the big bands of Claude Thornhill, Gerry Mulligan and Benny Goodman, and many small jazz groups including the Stan Getz Quintet, the Terry Gibbs Quartet, the Marian McPartland Trio, the Gerry Mulligan Sextet and Quartet, the Marty Napoleon Trio, the Gene DiNovi Trio, the Al Cohn and Zoot Sims Quintet, and the Bob Brookmeyer and Clark Terry Quintet, all during his long career as a string bassist. Crow has also doubled on bass and tuba for many Broadway shows, including "The King and I" and "42nd Street." He is currently an active freelancer in the jazz field, and appears regularly in New York with various jazz groups. He is also the author of two books on jazz, Jazz Anecdotes and From Birdland to Broadway, both published by Oxford University Press. **www.billcrowbass.com**

ROSEANNE D'AUSILIO, PHD, an industrial psychologist, consultant, master trainer, bestselling author, customer service expert and president of Human Technologies Global, provides needs analyses;

instructional design; customized, live customer service skills trainings; and executive/leadership coaching. Rosanne has authored six books, including Wake Up Your Call Center: Humanize Your Interaction Hub, Customer Service and the Human Experience, How to Kick Your Customer Service Up a Notch: 101 Insider Tips, Volumes I and II. **www.humantechtips.com**

SUMNER M. DAVENPORT is a professional speaker and coach, teaching clients how to live the life of greater success. She calls herself a Bounce-Back Expert because of her personal experiences with financial ruin, bankruptcy, betrayal, abuse, rape, divorce, health challenges and more. She has co-authored several books and is actively involved with several charitable organizations. **www.sumnerdavenport.com**

REVEREND MERILYN DAVIS, preacher and inspirational speaker, calls herself Kingdom Woman, and delivers keynotes with humor, power, passion and fire, and is much sought after for ministries, conferences and retreats. She is the author of A Clarion-Call to MEN, [and WOMEN, too!]. **www.kingdomwomanministriesinternational.org**

PATRICK DONADIO, MBA, CSP, MCC is a certified speaking professional and master certified coach. Since 1986, he has helped leaders and their organizations improve the way they communicate with staff, customers and the general public with his presentations and one-on-one business communication coaching. From the boardroom to the frontlines, he teaches people to increase profits, improve presentation and verbal communications, enhance their credibility, deepen relationships and boost performance—in less time. **www.patrickdonadio.com**

SANDY DUMONT's passion is to transform clients as she first did for herself at age seventeen. Sandy's lifelong love of art, color and psychology has honed her skills and made her a leader and pioneer in the world of color and image. Sandy lived in Brussels for 23 years, thanks to her Belgian Air Force pilot husband, Stefaan, whom she met while he was stationed in the United States. **www.theimagearchitect.com**

ALICIA DUNAMS is a top-selling author, speaker, and promotional expert. She provides her audiences with strategic tools and techniques to become sought-after experts in their industries. Her strategies help her audiences publish books, increase their revenue streams, promote their businesses, market their messages and build their brands. She is the creator of The 17-Day Book Challenge. **www.aliciadunams.com**

SALLY FRANZ is an award-winning, bestselling, humor writer who knows how to deliver a punch line. She has been an international motivational speaker to Fortune 500 Companies such as Intel, SONY, Yahoo! and Texaco-Chevron. Sally has appeared three times on NBC's Today Show, and is a former stand-up comic in clubs such as Stand-up NY and Caroline's. Ms. Franz is also a grandmother of two, a jewelry designer, and she holds a patent on a device that comforts headache pain. **www.sallyfranz.com**

MONICA GARAYCOECHEA, MD started her professional life as a medical doctor working in her home country of Spain, and left her career of 14 years in a traditional medical practice to search and explore many avenues of personal growth and spiritual realization. In 1994, she moved to the United States, and now works and lives with her partner in Florida, traveling to Europe to visit her son and family while offering her Feminine Coaching and Creative Questions workshops. **www.creativequestions.com**

WENDY GILLETT is a pioneer in the competitive and ever-changing hospitality industry. Owner and president of Caliluna Consulting, she offers a distinctive system for evaluating and documenting a company's current level of customer service. A long-time columnist for the industry-leading magazine Restaurant Startup and Growth, as well as Travelhost magazine, she offers ideas on changing your way of thinking in order to better your business. Wendy's true passion, however, is as a motivational speaker. **www.extraordinarycustomerservice.com**

JEFFREY GITTERMAN is an award-winning financial advisor and the CEO of Gitterman & Associates Wealth Management (www.gawumllc.com) and Beyond Success Consulting, a firm that brings more holistic values to the world of business and finance. His first book, Beyond Success: Redefining the Meaning of Prosperity, was recently published by AMACOM. Jeff has been featured in the past in several print, television and radio programs, including Money, Financial Advisor and New Jersey Business Journal, and on CNN and News 12 New Jersey. In 2004, he was honored by Fortune Small Business as "One of Our Nation's Best Bosses." **www.beyondsuccessconsulting.com**

JAMIE GOUGH is the owner and operator of Simple Site Guru website design. She is a graduate of the University of California, Berkeley, and lives in Northern California with her husband. When they aren't traveling together, Jamie can be found in her home office, busily designing yet another fun web project. **www.simplesiteguru.com**

JOHN GRAHAM, president of the Giraffe Project, has lived a life of high adventure. He shipped out on a freighter at sixteen, made the first ascent of Mount McKinley's North Wall at twenty, and hitchhiked around the world at twenty-two. A Foreign Service officer for fifteen years, he was in the middle of the revolution in Libya and the war in Vietnam. In 1980, a near-death experience on a burning cruise ship pushed him to a deeper sense of purpose. Since then, John has used his vision and experience to help thousands of people find the meaning of their lives through service. **www.giraffe.org**

KARL GRUBER lives and works in Columbus, Ohio, and has done freelance writing for Central Ohio publications for the last 25 years. From 1996 to 1997, he successfully ran 52 marathons in 52 weeks, all for leukemia research. In 2007, Gruber published a book, Running for Their Lives about his year of marathoning for charity. He continues to run on a daily basis for his health and sanity. **www.3pti.com**

CYNTHIA GUSTAVSON, MSW, ACSW, LCSW is the author of six poetry collections and six poetry workbooks for therapists. Her poetry won the New Millennium Writings Award in 2002 and was a finalist for the Rita Dove Poetry Award from the Salem College Center for Women Writers in 2004. Her children's book Ballad of the Rag Man (2009) won an Indie Excellence Award for children's fiction. She works as a writer, teacher and psychotherapist in Tulsa, Oklahoma, where she lives with her husband of 41 years. **www.cynthiagustavson.com**

DONNA THERESA HADDAD Donna Theresa Haddad is a certified clinical hypnotherapist, holistic behavioral therapist, author, inspirational speaker, and a Grief Recovery* Specialist. She has spent the last 13 years helping clients move beyond grief, depression, anxiety, lack of confidence, and into creating greater success in their lives. Her first book, Looking At The World Through A Fractured Lens was published following her brother's suicide. Her second book, Yes, You Can Have Success, Love, and Abundance is a little book of hope and inspiration. **www.donnathaddad.com**

LETA HAMILTON is the mother to three young boys, and the author of The Way of the Toddler. In addition to workshops and speaking engagements, she hosts a radio show on the I'm Thankful™ Network called "The Way of the Toddler Hour," interviewing spiritually compelling guests who are redefining what it means to be a successful parent raising successful children. **www.thewayofthetoddler.com**

MIKE HANDCOCK is the chairman of Rock Your Life, a global company committed to creating the number one team of transformational leaders on the planet, an international bestselling author with ten books, a speaker who has worked in over 30 countries, a philanthropist who is on the board of three foundations in New Zealand, India and Australia, and who was mentioned by President Clinton for his work. He produced and directed the inspirational feature film "Dreamcatchers," released in 2010, now being shown in over 15 countries. **www.rockyourlife.net**

LEWIS HARRISON speaks and writes on a diverse range of specialized topics including stress management, leadership, peak performance, motivation, wellness, and using Barter-based business systems to create wealth. He is the former chairperson of the Wellness Professional Experts Group (PEG) of The National Speakers Association and is presently the president of the NSA-Tri-State Speakers Association and the International Association of Healing Professionals. **www.lewisharrisoninspires.com**

BETH HENRY, MS is a speaker, consultant, wife, mom, nurse and survivor of 9/11. She graduated from the University of Buffalo with a master's degree in psychiatric mental health and is board certified in professional development. Beth is a co-founder and immediate past president of the first virtual international chapter of the National Speakers Association (www.nynsa.org). Recruitment, retention, rewards and succession planning are the main focal points of her speaking career. **www.generationworks.com**

DAN HOLDRIDGE, because he accompanied his friend on a cigarette break, was spared on the September 11th, 2001 attack on the Pentagon. Everyone on the other side of the wall next to Dan was killed, while Dan and his colleague survived. Feeling handpicked by God to live, Dan has a personal mission to honor the 184 heroes who died that day at the Pentagon. A corporate president, CEO and National Speakers Association member, Dan's message of the Purpose Conduit™ challenges audiences to understand the value of life through gratitude, respect, appreciation of others and hope for a better world. **www.purposeconduit.com**

DONNY INGRAM is a motivational speaker and president of Ingram Management Group. He has worked in sales and marketing, as well as training and development for both government and corporate America. Donny is responsible for the development of Recognizing Your Potential, a corporate training program that focuses on human design, communication and attitude. Donny's experiences from living, traveling and working in the Middle East have enlightened and entertained audiences around the world. He has a goal of helping people to recognize their true potential and maximize their efforts in order to live life to its fullest. **www.donnyingram.com**

NANCY IRWIN, PHD is in private practice in Los Angeles, co-leads group therapy sessions for sex offenders, and is also a speaker for Children of the Night, the Rape, Abuse and Incest National Network, and Planned Parenthood. She has been quoted in Cosmopolitan, Redbook, Women's World, and others, and has appeared on numerous radio and television shows, including CNBC, The Rachel Maddow Show, The Greg Behrendt Show, Mitch Albom's show, and more. Dr. Irwin is a member of the American Academy of Experts in Traumatic Stress, the Southern California Society of Clinical Hypnosis, and sits on the Education Committee of the California Coalition on Sexual Offending. She is also author of You-Turn: Changing Direction in Midlife. **www.drnancyirwin.com**

ESTHER JACOBS is a motivational speaker and author of the book What is your excuse? Her motto is: "If you do what you always did, you will get what you always got." She organizes workshops on "Out-of-the-box thinking," in which she demonstrates how to achieve more with fewer resources. She studied business and anthropology, traveled to more than a hundred countries and speaks more than seven languages. She works a few months a year and lives in Curacao, Miami and Amsterdam. **www.estherjacobs.info**

TED JANUSZ, MBA is a professional speaker, author and marketing consultant who has been invited to appear on "Geraldo at Large" on the FOX News Network to share his business insights. Janusz has conducted nearly 400 full-day seminars in 48 of the 50 United States, in Puerto Rico and across Canada. He is also a runner who has covered over 30,000 miles. **www.januspresentations.com**

KARA L.C. JONES is a Different Kind of Parent since the death of her son, Dakota. Though he died, the love, time, energy and money she would have given him is not gone. She has channeled these things into a life's work with her partner, Hawk, whereby they publish grief support books, articles and artworks through their independent imprint, Kota Press. In grief and creativity presentations, Kara and Hawk explore what they call KOTA (Knowing Ourselves Thru Art). **www.motherhenna.com**

ALLI JOSEPH is founder and president of Seventh Generation Stories, to which she brings her 16-year background as a television and print reporter, producer, writer and published author. Ms. Joseph, a member of the Shinnecock Indian Nation in New York, developed her journalism, branding and marketing skills working for large media companies like NBC, Grey Advertising Worldwide, Newscorp, Viacom, and America Online. Ms. Joseph sits on the board of the Radio and Television Digital News Association, and is a member of the Producer's Guild of America and the Author's Guild. She is currently codirector of New U: News Entrepreneurs Working Through UNITY, a funded training program for entrepreneurial minority journalists. **www.7GenStories.com**

J. ADAY KENNEDY, the differently-abled writer, is a ventilator-dependent quadriplegic making her dreams come true a story at a time. As a speaker, Aday entertains, instructs, motivates and inspires audiences of all ages. By focusing on what she can do instead of what she can't do, Aday embraces setting and achieving her goals. She surrounds herself with family and friends and positivity in Texas. **www.jadaykennedy.com**

COLLEEN KETTENHOFEN is a dynamic international speaker and author who has presented in 48 states and six countries for top associations and corporations since 1995. Her areas of expertise are overcoming adversity/change management, leadership and difficult people. She was honored as the number one sales producer in the history of the company both in the United States and Canada for a major Fortune 500 publishing firm out of 180 representatives. She also draws on her background as a former advertising executive and manager. **www.colleenspeaks.com**

SCOTT KLOSOSKY currently engages clients on a broad array of advisory tasks that include IT department restructuring, software implementation and design, and technology utilization within organizations. In addition, he speaks professionally on subjects such as technology and leadership, and currently serves as an advisory board member for Critical Technologies, a company for which he served as CEO from 2001 until 2004. Scott is a protégé of former President Richard M. Nixon's chief of staff, H.R. Haldeman, and the two collaborated on The Haldeman Diaries, a New York Times bestselling book. **www.klososky.com**

ROY LANTZ (a.k.a. Ebenezer Scrooge) is a huge fan of Dickens' A Christmas Carol, with well over 200 different editions in his personal collection, including one from 1844. Roy recently released his own version of A Christmas Carol, an audiobook in which he brings to life 24 characters from Dickens' immortal tale. **www.achristmascarolreading.com**

DON LUBOV teaches his Six-Step Path to Enlightenment at two colleges and in one community. The Path has proven itself to be successful and prompt. Life's purpose is a spiritual one—conscious union with your creator while still being in your physical body. Don's Six-Step Path reveals how to use your daily life to transcend suffering and have a spiritual awakening. You learn to live in the moment: 100-percent involved and 0-percent attached. You morph from being a fear-based, separate individual to a love-based part of the whole... from being part of the problem to part of the solution. **www.donlubov.com**

BARRY MAHER has been featured on the "Today Show," the NBC "Nightly News" or CNBC, and he's frequently featured in publications like USA Today, The New York Times, The Wall Street Journal and Business Week. A highly motivational keynote speaker and workshop leader, Barry has a client list that ranges from innumerable small business and trade associations to AT&T, ABC, Blue Cross, Hewlett-Packard, Johnson & Johnson, McDonald's, Verizon and Wells Fargo. **www.barrymaher.com**

ELIZABETH MANUEL has over a decade of specialized experience in increasing clients' happiness and self-esteem. She is a speaker, coach, and the author of two books and six audio CDs. Her message has reached thousands of people through memorable presentations and one-to-one coaching. Elizabeth offers insightful ideas and principles that can re-shape visions of what is possible. After spending time with Elizabeth, amazing things happen. **www.elizabethmanuel.com**

RICHARD MARKER is an internationally known expert on philanthropy, serving as Senior Fellow at NYU's Center for Philanthropy and as co-principal of Marker Goldsmith Philanthropy Advisors. Since 1968, he has been a professor, a university chaplain, a private sector consultant and international non-profit executive. He has spoken in 32 countries on 5 continents, and in over 40 of the United States. His book Saying Yes Wisely is used in universities, by other consultants in the field, and anyone who gives money to charity. **www.wisephilanthropy.com**

PAUL LEE MARR is a facilitator, speaker, motivator, coach, author and songwriter with over

25 years experience. Paul has facilitated large and small group settings, hundreds of Internet and satellite broadcasts, panel discussions and interview-style formats. He has trained over 140,000 students and has over 450 published articles. His clients include: Delta Airlines, AT&T and Ford Motor Company. He is currently writing a new book and completing a six-song CD. **www.linkedin.com/in/plmproductions**

ANDY MASTERS, MA is an author, speaker and humorist who presents entertaining "business humor with a purpose" programs on sales, service and work-life balance, providing the ultimate "learn through laughter" experience. Andy has earned four degrees and written four books—including the acclaimed Kiss Your Customer: 77 Reasons Why Sales & Service Are Just Like Dating & Relationships. **www.andy-masters.com**

JIM MCCORMICK, MBA is an expert in performance improvement through intelligent risk-taking and creating a culture of innovation, and the author of The Power of Risk. He is a former corporate chief operating officer, holds five skydiving world records and was a member of a successful North Pole skydiving expedition. **www.takerisks.com**

KARL MECKLENBURG rose from a college walk-on and twelfth-round draft choice to an NFL career that included three Super Bowl and six Pro Bowl appearances. The former Broncos captain was arguably the most versatile player in the NFL, playing all seven defensive front positions often in the course of a single game. Karl is an author and motivational speaker inspiring long-term positive change in teams and individuals. He approaches his speaking career with the same intelligence, passion and intensity that punctuated his great football career. **www.karlmecklenburg.com**

JOHN MELUSO, CSP is an internationally acclaimed motivational speaker and is the author of three books: eye TALK™: Bridging from Communication to Connection, Becoming Your Greatest, and The Next Step for Positive Living, co-authored with Joseph Bernard, PhD. Achieve personal, professional, financial and relationship success beyond your wildest dreams! **www.meluso.com**

KRIS MILLER, LSA, CEPS, LDA, calls herself the Senior Life Coach, and is based in Hemet, California where she has practiced for more than 20 years as a Certified Senior Advisor and Estate Planning Specialist. Her award-winning music is available on iTunes and most other online outlets. **www.krismillerspeaker.com**

JOHN B. MOLIDOR, PhD is a professor and assistant dean at the Michigan State University College of Human Medicine and serves as the CEO and president of his medical school's clinical campus in Flint. Prior to that, he served as dean of admissions, student affairs and educational programs for the medical school. He has a long-standing interest in how individuals select and recruit candidates by employing an interview process that uses sound decision making principles and effective communication styles. His work and research have been presented throughout the United States to universities, organizations and professional groups.

ANAKHANDA SHAKA MUSHABA, martial artist, metaphysician and minister is the author of Mind over Illusion. He has developed his own unique system of teachings called the Mushaba Esoteric Movements of Life and Sound. This technique enhances mental health by facilitating harmony and balance of the body and mind, creating a mental state similar to that of deep meditation. A member of the World Martial Arts Hall of Fame, Mushaba was also featured in the documentary film Warrior Within, alongside actor and martial arts expert Bruce Lee, designed his martial arts system using a combination of movement and breathing techniques that use the energies of Mother Nature and the universe to the body's advantage. **www.mushabacenter.com**

BARBARA MUSSER, MBA is a transformation junkie. She has experienced many wake-up calls and has used them as a springboard for her own transformation. Kind and compassionate, Barbara combines a long-standing spiritual practice with practical common sense and business experience in service of her passion to help others realize their own magnificence. She lives in Northern California with her teenage daughter and two cats, Fred and Ginger. **www.barbaramusser.com**

ANDY NEILLIE, PhD, CSP, in addition to his leadership speaking and writing, is a senior training consultant with Richardson where he has served since the late 1990s. Richardson is a leading international sales training and consulting firm working with Fortune 500 and Global 1000 businesses. At Richardson, Andy has worked with multi-national corporations such as Cisco Systems, CNA, Pfizer, PG&E, PwC, Shell Oil and Sports Illustrated. Andy earned his doctorate in 2003, and his dissertation studies enabled him to read deeply and interview key leaders on the importance of personal trust and leadership effectiveness. **www.deepintheheart.org**

GARY O'SULLIVAN, from entering the world of direct sales at the age of 18 to becoming a senior vice president of sales and marketing for a national company, understands the challenges and triumphs of the entrepreneur and the free enterprise process. He conducts seminars and workshops across the country, and is a featured keynote speaker. He and his family currently reside just outside Orlando, Florida. **www.garyosullivan.com**

KATHY PERRY, MBA is an author, speaker and social media marketing specialist who inspires and motivates people to live an empowered life. Formerly an executive in corporate American, she is now the creator of the nationally recognized Hub Socializer System and the founder of iwomanlife. com. Kathy was named 2010-2011 NAPW Professional Woman of the Year, is a University of Tampa MBA Leadership Coach and is an Omega with Best Buy-Wolf. **www.kathyperry.com**

JUDI PIANI, CGA has raised four children and helped to raise 22 more foster children. She assists teams and families in understanding and cultivating productive dynamics. She is a coach and advisor in both the corporate and private sectors. Judi is a featured speaker and teacher for the Association of Graphoanalysts, and also speaks before elite CEO groups. **www.TraitSecrets.com**

REVEREND CAROLYN PORTER, DDIV is a spiritual life and health coach, speaker, trainer for speaking, coaching and angel practitioner, angel channel, author of multiple books, audios and e-books, and owner of Where Miracles Happen Healing Center in Woodstock, Georgia. Carolyn has dedicated her life to helping individuals step into their own power and accept their brilliance so they can create the life they truly want and deserve. **www.drcarolynporter.com**

TOM POTISK, DC, known as "the down-to-Earth doctor," is a holistic family practitioner, author and speaker. He empowers people to make wiser health care decisions, and empowers doctors with more joyful practices. He helps us to see health and wellness in a new light. Dr. Potisk is the author of Whole Health Healing for a general audience, and Reclaim the Joy of Practice for physicians. **www.thedowntoearthdoctor.com**

JENNIFER POWERS, MA coaches, speaks and writes from a place of honesty, service and pure giddiness. She is a believer in the human spirit and her mission is to help others find their truth, whatever that may look like. And whether she has met you yet or not, she is your biggest fan. Oh, and when she does meet you... expect a hug. Jennifer's book Oh, Shift! is available in bookstores nationwide. **www.jenniferpowers.com**

CRAIG PRICE has helped some of the most effective and diverse corporate leaders around the country, from multibillion-dollar manufacturers to top universities, find the path to success through his work as a speaker, author and entertainer. An award-winning stand-up comedian, experienced actor and certified instructor, Craig has a background in customer service, information technology and safety. Craig uses his sharp wit, intelligence and straight talk to deliver entertaining, yet informative programs that allow people to believe in themselves under any circumstances. **www.speakercraigprice.com**

DAINA PUODZIUNAS (pronounced Dinah) is 57 years young and has been passionately working in the field of women's self-empowerment her entire life. She lives and offers women's retreats on 40 acres on Enchanted Lake by Grand Rapids, Michigan in an energy efficient home she designed and helped build. She raised her two daughters as a single parent and healed herself in nature there. Nature is her muse, church, friend and healer. Daina is a grandmother of five and a fun loving, free spirit at heart. **www.awakenedpotentials.com**

SHARON QUINN is a dynamic lecturer and teacher. She hosts "The Edge of TRUTH," an Internet radio show she co-hosts with Will Gable. She is also an educational strategist, Essene minister, Montessori teacher/trainer, vibrational healing facilitator and cofounder of an innovative educational non-profit. **www.selfgnosis.org**

PAUL O. RADDE, PhD is a practicing psychologist, author and professional speaker on personal and professional transformation. Paul founded The Thrival Institute, headquartered in Longmont, Colorado. He is an avid racquetball player, skier, hiker, camper and biker. His transformational interests include three paradigm shifts from survival mentality to thrival mentality and life style; top-down "power over" politics to side-by-side "power with" relating; and the transition from a shame-based damnation mentality to an acceptance-based "heaven on earth" mentality. **www.thrival.com**

EDIE RAETHER, MS, CSP is an international speaker, trainer, coach and author whose six books have been translated into numerous languages. She has also co-authored eleven anthologies and is an expert resource for hundreds of publications such as The Wall Street Journal, USA Today and Reuters. An expert in behavioral psychology and change, Edie has also been a college professor and a television talk show host with ABC. **www.edieraether.com**

CLARENCE REYNOLDS, MS went to work for the cable-shopping giant QVC after graduating from university. Later, as the executive producer and host of "Black Entertainment Television (BET) Shop," he led the creation of the nation's first African American-themed shopping program on BET. Clarence earned a master's degree in counseling psychology from Troy University in 1997, and used that training to produce and host award-winning public affairs programs for PBS affiliates in Indianapolis and

Orlando. Clarence has also worked as chief correspondent on "Antiques Roadshow FYI," a spin-off of the popular PBS series, and helped to launch the morning show on the Indianapolis FOX affiliate, WXIN.

SHARI RIGHTMER was trained in the medical field and landed a job working with world renowned doctors in Beverly Hills. She crossed paths with the rich and famous every day, and she married a rock star. After his tragic death, she found herself in a homeless shelter, sleeping in Bunk #11. She is now a speaker, author and advocate for the homeless. **www.sharirightmer.com**

TERI ROSE is an author, speaker, coach and trainer. The experience of dying during a car wreck in the '70s caused her to realize that little of what she experienced "on the other side" was anything like what she had been taught and feared. She awoke in the hospital day's later thinking only about what she had been shown and the indescribable love she had felt. Her quest began to turn her new insight into practical application and take charge of her life. **www.peaceofsuccess.com**

CYNTHIA RYK, MEd is a speaker, career counselor and seminar leader. With a master's degree in career development and counseling, she is well-versed in assisting people in stirring up their divine gifts that are waiting to be expressed. Cynthia draws on her wisdom from both her professional background of more than fifteen years of assisting laid-off employees or those going through personal transition as well as her own extensive personal development experiences. **www.cynthiaryk.com**

ADENA SAMPSON is a life coach, motivational speaker, singer-songwriter and author. She is a graduate of the Berklee College of Music. She is also a certified facilitator and graduate of The Soul Center for Spiritual Healing. Currently, Adena facilitates spiritual retreats for women with The Peaceful Woman Corporation on Maui, and is in the process of writing a book and getting her PhD from the University of Metaphysical Science. **www.outloudproductions.tv**

ARNOLD SANOW, MBA, CSP is a speaker, trainer, facilitator, coach and author of six books, including Get Along with Anyone, Anytime, Anywhere and Deliver Every Presentation with Power, Punch and Pizzazz. He has delivered over 2,500 presentations to companies, associations and governmental organizations focusing on improving oral, interpersonal and organizational communication. He recently was named as one of the five best "bang for the buck" speakers in the US by Successful Meetings Magazine. **www.arnoldsanow.com**

JOHN SCHAEFER and his team at Schaefer Recognition Group help companies realize and react to what he calls the employer/employee disconnect. He's sought out for his straight talk, loved for his humor and dedicated to helping people have more fun, be more productive and save their companies tons of money. He earned his industrial engineering degree from Arizona State University, first working for a 6,000-employee manufacturer, then a small family business. He is currently working on a second book, Get More Productivity for Less Money. **www.schaeferrecognitiongroup.com**

CHRISTINE SCHWAN, MS is an author, speaker and entrepreneur whose life mission has been to empower women and children around the world. As a master's level, certified speech language pathologist, she has specialized in helping others find their true voice and their passion. **www.secretsofempoweredwomen.com**

ROSALIND SEDACCA, CCT is a passionate writer, award-winning speaker and student of personal growth. She is recognized by many as the voice of Child-Centered Divorce and is founder of the

Child-Centered Divorce Network. She is also the author of How Do I Tell the Kids About the Divorce? based on her own experience with divorce as a parent. Rosalind also runs workshops on leading from the heart, as well as relationship and dating challenges for singles and couples. **www.childcentereddivorce.com**

ALBERTA H. SEQUEIRA is the author of Someone Stop This Merry-Go-Round: An Alcoholic Family in Crisis, and a public speaker on the effects of alcoholism on the whole family. Private engagements are offered to halfway homes and alcoholic rehabilitations. Ms. Sequeira also teaches a workshop entitled "Bring Your Manuscript to Publication." She lives in Rochester, Massachusetts with her husband, Al. **www.albertasequeira.com**

KATE SHERIDAN is an author, business consultant and international speaker. She is best known for her work in support-staff training. CEOs from the United States to Russia call upon Kate to motivate and focus their teams during times of transition and fast growth. Her results have made her a popular speaker for fundraising, corporate keynotes, woman's groups, churches and all branches of the United States Armed Forces. As an author, Kate writes inspirational and entertaining works for women. She resides in Atlanta with her children, Olivia and Liam. **www.katesheridan.net**

LINDA SHIELDS, MS, CCC-SLP is a speech pathologist, voice coach, keynote speaker, columnist, radio personality, and the award-winning author of The Voice That Means Business. She holds a Master of Science Degree in speech pathology and a Certificate of Clinical Competence from the American Speech and Hearing Association. Her client list includes top executives, and entertainment, media and professional presenters. **www.lindabshields.com**

PAULA SHOUP has 22 years of leadership experience in sourcing and manufacturing operations at Medtronic, Honeywell, United Technologies, and Motorola. While at Medtronic, she was Director of Strategic Sourcing, managed a $400 million budget and created the Supply Chain organization in Puerto Rico. Paula volunteers as the program co-chair of the National Speakers Association's Arizona chapter and as the vice president of Community Outreach for the International Coaching Federation's Phoenix chapter. She is also on the board of directors for the Alliance of Technology and Women in Phoenix. She is the owner of internalGPS, LLC. **www.myinternalgps.com**

MARTY STANLEY, the president of Dynamic Dialog, Inc., is an author, national speaker and facilitator who helps organizations create their New Normal. Her book and signature program, Get Out of B.E.D. (Blame, Excuses and Denial): Change Your Outlook—Alter Your Outcomes, provides the process for success. **www.alteringoutcomes.com**

CLAUDE STEIN is a multi-platinum award-winning voice coach whose Natural Singer Workshops have been presented at the Juilliard School, the NYU music therapy graduate program, the Rubin Academy in Jerusalem, the Omega Institute, the New York Open Center, the Actors Institute and Esalen Institute. He is on the faculty of the Massachusetts General Hospital Leadership Academy, the Center for Professional Excellence and is a main stage keynote speaker. **www.claudestein.com**

STEVEN STEINBERG, DDS is a dentist with Parkinson's disease who has spoken around the world as a dental expert and has been an inspirational motivational speaker for over 30 years. . As the Values Doctor he helps people overcome challenges and achieve happiness using the healing power of values. His upcoming book is titled Light, Love, Life, Shalom: Your Path to Happiness at Work and at Home. **www.valuesdoctor.com**

BRAD SZOLLOSE is a thought leader, author, entrepreneur, business coach and speaker specializing in transitioning leaders from Industrial Age methodologies to the management strategies and emerging markets of the Information Age. Brad is the author of Liquid Leadership: From Woodstock to Wikipedia, which is based on his experiences of applying a unique management style to a young, tech-savvy Generation… workforce during the dot-com boom. **www.bradszollose.com**

BETH TERRY, CSP is a communications and resilience expert. She works with corporations and associations to create better results and higher levels of productivity. She is also a speechwriter, author of the Cactus Wrangler and Face it Darlin' Blogs, and author of two books: Walking in a Crowd of Angels and 101 Ways to Make Your Life Easier. She has a third book on the way. **www.bethterry.com**

LAURENZO THOMAS, also known as "Mr. Electricity," is an inspirational speaker, public speaking trainer, and writer. He is the author of two upcoming books, including Life and Basketball. Laurenzo resides in Seattle, Washington in the great Pacific Northwest with his wife and two kids. **www.successinspeaking.com**

MELLANIE TRUE HILLS is a women's heart and health expert and CEO and founder of the American Foundation for Women's Health and StopAfib.org, a patient advocacy organization for those living with atrial fibrillation. She is the author of the multiple award-winning book, A Woman's Guide to Saving Her Own Life, and two intranet bestsellers. She was the Internet pioneer that led the creation of JCPenney.com, and an Internet executive and strategy consultant at Dell Computer and Cisco Systems. She has been featured by USA Weekend, More, Success, Better Homes & Gardens, Heart-Healthy Living, and many more. **www.mellaniehills.com**

VERSIE L. WALKER is from Chicago, raised by a teenaged mother who taught him the importance of hard work, integrity and family values. His childhood was fairly normal: he struggled with many of the same challenges that youths are facing today, including self-esteem, drugs and gangs. Through a series of unexpected events, he decided he wanted more from life. Versie lives in New York with his wife and kids, and is a public speaker and the author of the book Success: How I Ended Up Here. **www.versiewalker.com**

LESLIE BETH WISH, EdD, MSS is a nationally honored psychologist and licensed clinical social worker, recognized for her work with women's issues. The National Association of Social Workers named her as One of the Top Fifty. Dr. Wish is also an expert source for publications such as USA Today, Cosmopolitan, Self, Glamour and other media. **www.lovevictory.com**

LYNDA T. YOUNG, MRE, MEd is a speaker and award-winning author. One of her passions includes touching hurting families of children with chronic conditions through her writing and speaking. She and her husband, Dr. John Young, live in a suburb of Atlanta, Georgia, where he is in cancer research at Emory University. They have four children, eleven grandchildren, four great-grandchildren and lots of hands-on experience. **www.hopeforfamiliesonline.com**

ABOUT THE EDITORS

KENT GUSTAVSON, PHD is a professor of writing, language and leadership at Stony Brook University, where he is currently the faculty director of the undergraduate Leadership & Development and Community Service Living Learning Centers. He is the owner of independent publisher Blooming Twig Books, and he speaks around the world on both publishing and music. As the host of Sound Authors, he has interviewed hundreds of award-winning musicians and authors, and his music has been featured on National Public Radio's All Songs Considered. He is the author of the #1 Amazon.com bestselling biography of music legend Doc Watson, and has ghostwritten dozens of books. Dr. Gustavson has also released several audio recordings on his record label Ninety and Nine Records. He lives and works in Sound Beach, New York. **www.kentgustavson.com**

SALLY SHIELDS is an award-winning pianist, composer, speaker, author and radio personality. A frequent contributor to various magazines, Shields has been featured in Star Magazine, Obvious, My Day, Girlfriendz, For the Bride and many others. Endorsed by Dr. Laura Schlessinger and Martha Stewart, she has appeared on Fox & Friends, Rachel Ray, Tyra and the Daily Buzz with her #1 Amazon.com bestseller, The Daughter-in-Law Rules. A marketing coach at Outskirts Press, she has also penned Publicity Secrets Revealed: What Every PR Firm Doesn't Want you to Know and The Collaborator Rules: 101 Surefire Ways to Stay Friends with Your Co-Author! She lives in New York City with her husband and two children. **www.sallyshields.com**